THE WORKING
CLASS MAJORITY

THE WORKING CLASS MAJORITY

America's Best Kept Secret

Second Edition

Michael Zweig

ILR PRESS AN IMPRINT OF
CORNELL UNIVERSITY PRESS   ITHACA AND LONDON

The photograph on p. 142 © Robin Romano; reproduced with his permission. All other photographs © Jim West (jimwestphoto.com); reproduced with his permission.

First edition published 2000, second edition published 2012 by Cornell University Press.
Printed in the United States of America
First printing, Cornell Paperbacks, 2012

Library of Congress Cataloging-in-Publication Data

Zweig, Michael, 1942–
  The working class majority : America's best kept secret / Michael Zweig. — 2nd ed.
      p. cm.
  Includes bibliographical references and index.
    ISBN 978-0-8014-7733-1 (pbk. : alk. paper)
  1. Working class—United States.   2. Working class—Political activity—United States. 3. United States—Economic conditions—1981–2001. 4. United States—Economic conditions—2001–2009. 5. United States—Social conditions—1980–   I. Title.
    HD8066.Z84   2012
    305.5'620973—dc23   2011031081

Cornell University Press strives to use environmentally responsible suppliers and materials to the fullest extent possible in the publishing of its books. Such materials include vegetable-based, low-VOC inks and acid-free papers that are recycled, totally chlorine-free, or partly composed of nonwood fibers. For further information, visit our website at www.cornellpress.cornell.edu.

Paperback printing   10 9 8 7 6 5 4 3 2 1

Contents

Preface to the Second Edition

This second edition brings to the reader the latest data available in mid 2011, data that confirm the findings of the first edition. Some examples are new, while original examples that remain appropriate continue to be included. The structure of the book is unchanged, but individual chapters reflect new developments and findings.

Chapter 1 confirms the original finding that the working class is the majority in the United States. But while the overall percent of the labor force in the working class remained essentially unchanged (63 percent in 2010 compared with 62 percent in 1996), changes in details suggest two offsetting trends. The percent of the labor force engaged in traditional working class occupations has declined, particularly among clerical, precision production, and craft workers, as well as operators, fabricators, and laborers. At the same time, traditional middle class occupations among administrative, managerial, and professional titles increased their share of the workforce. Taken together, these trends would suggest that the working class is shrinking as increasing numbers of people have left working class jobs to come into positions of authority in the growing middle class. But that is not the case.

During this time period significant changes have come to the professions. As described more fully in chapter 1, traditional middle class professions like teaching and nursing have come under the discipline of corporate management in substantial numbers, resulting in a class shift *within* the professions. When we take into account the growing fraction of teachers, nurses, and other professionals who once had the autonomy and authority that made them part of the middle class, but who have since been subject more closely to the type of supervision characteristic of the skilled working class, the overall fraction of the labor force in the working class has remained virtually unchanged. The unchanged percent of people in the working class masks these two important developments: the disappearance of many traditional working class jobs and the simultaneous deterioration of the working lives of the professional middle class. Each of these contributes to the widespread sense of insecurity as the U.S. workforce moves further into the twenty-first century.

Several other new developments appear in subsequent chapters. While poverty has continued to inflict much suffering since the 1996 federal welfare reform legislation, and increased after the 2008 financial crisis, poor people have largely disappeared from mainstream political conversation. Chapter 4 examines the continuing burden of poverty, but looks at the ways many politicians, pundits, and media outlets have substituted immigrants for the poor as scapegoats for social ills, and as false targets for popular anger and frustration.

Chapter 6 newly introduces several social norms that flow from working class values, norms that provide concrete goals for specific policies that would advance the interests of working people. Chapter 7 now includes discussion of the global financial crisis in 2008–2010, new international government and economic relations, immigration to the United States, and the wars in Iraq and Afghanistan, all of which have occurred since the first edition appeared. In chapter 7, and in chapter 1, I consider the steady internationalization of class, whether among the capitalist class or the working class.

In chapters 6, 8, and 9, I look at changes that have taken place in the labor movement since the early days of John Sweeney's leadership of the AFL-CIO, when the first edition appeared. Chapter 9 now also presents a more detailed history of the rise of corporate power in response to labor's advances during the New Deal and 1940s and 1950s, especially following 1970.

Developments in the Internet have already made obsolete the listings in the original printed Appendix. In its place, you can find links to relevant organizations on the book's website, WorkingClassMajority.org, which also presents study guides for each chapter.

In preparing this second edition I have become sharply aware that almost everything it addresses is in the process of continuous development. Our economy and broader society are moving targets that cannot be properly described in a particular state over any length of time. While underlying class dynamics change only slowly, except in rare moments of radical social upheaval, the manifestations of these dynamics appear in new ways every year, if not almost every day. The rapidity with which circumstances change can make it more difficult to discern the more stable underlying class dynamics that largely drive events. Clarifying these underlying dynamics is the purpose of this book.

Updating and elaborating our understanding of this ever-changing presence of class must be a collective undertaking of continuous investigation, writing, and debate. As this book is used in classrooms, union halls, study groups, and community centers, I hope that students, working people, faculty researchers, and others involved in these issues will continue the work of updating and deepening our understanding of class based on the study of new data and examples. I hope their results will be presented and debated at Working Class Studies Association conferences and other gatherings of labor-oriented people, and published in popular venues and professional journals as working class studies becomes an accepted part of our public dialogue. Together we must come to better understandings of how class works to shape our life experiences, and how our knowledge of class can help us influence history to the advantage of working people.

Acknowledgments

In planning and writing this book I have benefited from the insight, experience, and challenging ideas of many people. For their interest and encouragement, and for their time taken for discussion, reading and commenting on various drafts of this second edition, looking up information, and helping me find my bearings in this material, I thank Joe Berry, Ron Blackwell, Jim Borbely, Ross Borden, Gene Bruskin, Jeff Crosby, Fernando Gapasin, Penny Lewis, Stephanie Luce, Maria Maisto, Jay D. Mazur, Jack Metzgar, Rachel Micah-Jones, Dennis O'Neil, Steven Pitts, Warren Sanderson, Heidi Shierholz, Craig Smith, Megan Smith, Ralph Tricoche, Luis Valenzuela, Victor Wallis, Kris Warner, Devon Whitham, and Anne Wiegard. Robert Sauté provided invaluable research and helped me think through some thorny questions. The State University of New York at Stony Brook granted me a year's sabbatical leave that made it possible to do this work. My thanks also to the staffs of Stony Brook Manhattan and the Joseph S. Murphy Institute for Worker Education and Labor Studies at the City University of New York for providing me with stimulating and productive work environments.

I continue to be grateful to all who helped create the first edition of this book: anonymous reviewers for Cornell University Press, Doug Andersen, Stanley Aronowitz, Ruth Ben Zvi, Mike Bianculli, Keith Cummings, Debra Dwyer, participants in the Economic Policy Institute Friday seminar, Frank Emspak, Bill Fletcher, Elaine Fuller, David Gold, Ted Goldfarb, Paul Groncki, Eduard Gros, Barbara Haber, Elaine Harger, Doug Henwood, Takashi Kamihigashi, Barrie Kelly, Eugene Kelly, Glen Koster, Marta Kusic, Judith Lang, Les Leopold, Jon Levine, Robert Lepley, librarians at the Tamiment Collection and Business and Social Science Reference Desk at Bobst Library of New York University, Theresa Li Cascia, Jay D. Mazur, Larry Mishel, Ruth Misheloff, Christopher Mittendorf, Stan Nadel, Jim O'Brien, Bertell Ollman, Dennis O'Neil, Greg Palast, Paddy Quick, Michael Reich, Jimmy Rich, Sumner Rosen, Elissa Sampson, Warren Sanderson, Elisabeth Sawyer, Danny Schechter, Bill Scheuerman, Michael Schwartz, Barbara Silverstone, Jane Slaughter, Roland Spant, Bill Tabb, Nick Unger, Dick Wheeler, and Gekee Wickham. Kathy Chamberlain offered wise counsel from the earliest days of this work to final editing of both editions. Fran Benson, my editor at Cornell University Press, believed in this project at an early stage. Without her support, you would not be reading this book.

In the late 1970s, I came to know Jimmy Scales, a young man who worked in the industrial world of northern New Jersey. He was a union activist with a clear understanding of the need to build a broad working class movement. When out of work he helped organize the unemployed and people on welfare. He got a warehouse job in New York City in 1980 and was a rising leader in District Council 65 as it was merging with the United Auto Workers. He had uncommon curiosity, insight, and humor, and we would talk at length about many of the ideas that have come to be included here. Jimmy died in 1981, still in his twenties. As I wrestled with writing this book, I sorely missed the chance to continue those talks. I dedicate this book to his memory and his work.

THE WORKING
CLASS MAJORITY

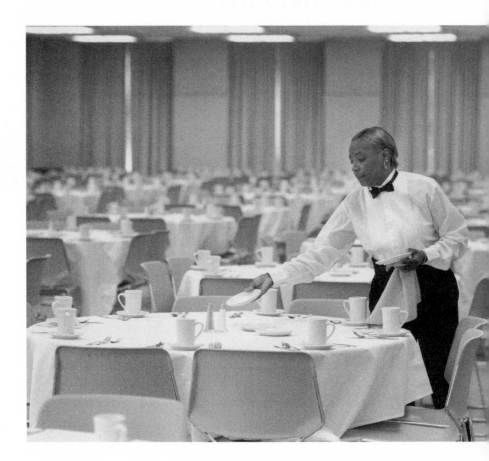

INTRODUCTION

Some years ago, a newspaper comic strip pictured a campus radical proclaiming his solidarity with the class struggle, only to be ridiculed by his professor, who dismissed him with a sharp retort: "The only classes in this country are in schools!" This remark pretty much sums up the conventional view of class in the United States: it doesn't exist.

This book challenges that view. It is about classes, but not the schoolroom kind. It is about social classes and class relations in the United States that not only continue to exist but, as readers will discover, exert tremendous influence over all of us.

When I talk about class, I am talking about power. Power at work, and power in the larger society. Economic power, and also political and cultural power. As I explore the class structure of the U.S. economy, I will be describing the contours of power that operate in every aspect of society, to the benefit of some, to the burden of others.

We all experience class, in different ways we are treated, in different lifestyles, in different parts of town. Some people are called "high class," others "low class," depending on their table manners, how loudly they talk in public places, or their choice of movies and magazines. One place where class is pretty sharply defined is in the sky. In the 1980s and 1990s, airlines rearranged their planes in ways that mirrored what was going on in the rest of society. The first-class section, serving a tiny minority of passengers, expanded. The seats became more comfortable, the food more sumptuous. Meanwhile, in the back of the plane, coach class got more crammed and even the peanuts disappeared.

Some aspects of class are more openly acknowledged than others. In this book, I explore aspects that are usually overlooked or denied, especially the way classes are structured by economic power. This book makes three basic points:

First, economic classes exist in U.S. society. I will describe who is in them and measure their sizes. It will become clear that the United States is not a mostly middle class society. We will see that the working class is the majority.

Second, class has a pervasive influence on the way we live, work, and think. Class is not just an abstract idea to score debating points. We will come to understand a wide range of important issues very differently when we look at them through the lens of class.

Third, class has great influence on politics—electoral politics and the more general contests of power that operate throughout society. This is true whether we recognize classes openly or not. By looking at issues through the lens of class, we can be clearer about what is at stake, and begin to see the potential for profound political realignments during the first quarter of the twenty-first century.

It is ironic that Americans pay much less attention to class than Europeans do, since American history is so full of violent armed conflict between workers and their employers. These conflicts are more widespread and more recent than anything in the history of European industrial relations. From the general strike of 1877 to Telluride and Bloody Harlan, from the GM workers' forty-four-day sit-down strike in Flint to more recent strikes by miners at Pittston's coal operations in southwest Virginia, by meatpackers in Minnesota, and by thousands of workers in the "war zone" of central Illinois, classes and open class struggle have been a persistent presence in U.S. history, up until the present day in Wisconsin and wherever public-sector workers are under attack.

Despite this history of intense class conflict, the most common myth about classes in the United States is that a vast middle class contains the overwhelming majority of our people. In this view, a small group of rich people lives at the top. Some are successful business leaders with names like Forbes, Rockefeller, Gates, Trump. Some are glamorous sports and entertainment stars, the Kobe Bryants and Lady Gagas of the world. As the saying goes, the very rich are different from you and me.

The dominant myth also recognizes a social fringe of poor people below the great middle class, sometimes called the "underclass." The poor are at the lower margins of society, pictured as different, lazy, damaged, scary enough so that we want to stay out of their neighborhoods. The poor are beneath the supposed vast middle class, who work hard and play by the rules, making a life through hard work and sacrifice.

The trouble with this story is that it hides an important reality. By looking only at income or lifestyle, we see the results of class, but not the origins of class. We see how we are different in our possessions, but not how we are related and connected, and made different, in the process of making what we possess.

Certainly a relatively few rich people do sit at the top of the income distribution, and a relatively small number of people are at the very bottom, with most people somewhere in between. But where to draw the lines—what is rich, what is poor, what is middle—is largely arbitrary. And just looking at a person's income doesn't tell us anything about how the person got the income, what role he or she plays in society, how he or she is connected to the power grid of class relations.

I define classes in large part based on the power and authority people have at work. The workplace engages people in more than their immediate work, by which they create goods and services. It also engages them in relationships with each other, relationships that are controlled by power. A relative handful of people have great power to organize and direct production, while a much larger number have almost no authority. In a capitalist society such as ours, the first group is the capitalist class, the second group is the working class.

The great majority of Americans form the working class. They are skilled and unskilled, in manufacturing and in services, men and women of all races, nationalities, religions. They drive trucks, write routine computer code, operate machinery, wait tables, sort and deliver the mail, work on assembly lines, stand all day as bank tellers, perform thousands of jobs in every sector of the economy. For all their differences, working class people share a common place in production, where they have relatively little control over the pace or content of their work, and aren't anybody's boss. They produce the wealth of nations, but receive from that wealth only what they can buy with the wages their employers pay them. When we add them all up, they account for over 60 percent of the labor force. They are the working class majority.

There is also a middle class, of course. It includes professional people, small business owners, and managers and supervisors who have authority over others at work. But the middle class is only a little more than half the size of the working class. Instead of seeing them as people with middling income, we will see them as people with middling authority. The middle class is caught between the working class and the capitalist class.

We can understand the economic, political, and cultural role of each class if we see it in terms of its relationships to the others, in the textures of social power, rather than simply as income category or lifestyle. This way—with power laid bare—the abstractions of class come to life.

Class is one of America's best-kept secrets. Any serious discussion has been banished from polite company. But classes exist anyway, and the force of events is bringing class back into focus. We will be looking at the circumstances that have hidden an awareness of class, and at those that are now giving new urgency to recognizing class once again. More and more, reality is poking through the myths and revealing the shape of class power. We will see how class is involved in the issues that have dominated economic and political life in the United States over the last forty years. For each, we will see that the issues have played out in a way that has strengthened the power of the capitalist class, degraded the life of the working class, and caught the middle class in the middle.

We will see that the dramatic increase in inequality is not just a case of the rich getting richer and the poor getting poorer, as the media often portray it. Our society's growing inequality of income and wealth is a reflection of the increased *power* of capitalists and the reduced *power* of workers. This basic change in circumstances forms the backdrop for much of the political debate of recent decades.

Class has its foundation in power relations at work, but it is more than that. Class also operates in the larger society: relative power on the economic side of things translates, not perfectly but to a considerable extent, into cultural and political power. These forms of power in turn reinforce, adjust, and help give meaning to classes. Our discussion of class will go beyond production, to search out its implications in the broader society as well.

Over the last four decades the working class has experienced lower real incomes, longer hours at work, fewer protections by unions or government regulations, and inferior schools. Politicians have responded by presenting targets for the anger and frustration of working people and much of the middle class. We have been told that poor people are the reason for hard times, ripping us off and draining us dry through welfare. We have been told that immigrants and workers in other countries are willing to work cheap to take our jobs away. We hear that taxes are the cause of our predicament, that teachers, firefighters, police, and other public sector workers are greedily gobbling up our resources, and even that government itself is the problem, not the solution. And on top of these policy angles, we have been preached a tale of moral decay, in which our problems stem from the decline of "family values." These targets have determined the main direction of public policy in recent decades. As we look at each in turn from the standpoint of class, we will see how each has intensified the attack on working people and strengthened the hand of the capitalist class. Far from solving the problems working people face, these policies have made working people worse off, and—by confusing the issues—helped to alienate the broad electorate from the political process.

The sooner we realize that classes exist and understand the power relations that are driving the economic and political changes swirling around us, the sooner we will be able to build a new politics that engages people by wrestling with reality. The potential power of an openly working class politics is one of the most exciting and difficult issues of the twenty-first century.

This book concludes with a discussion of the potential for working class power. We will consider the moral foundations of working class politics, which are in sharp contrast with the so-called "family values" agenda that has substituted lifestyle for economic justice as the subject matter of ethical debate. We will see how the raw individualism of the capitalist marketplace calls for a response based on very different values, values that are central to a working class politics: recognition of mutual responsibility, fairness, human dignity, and democracy, in place of self-interest run wild into greed. We will look at new attempts to develop working class power based on these values, in the union movement and in connection with other social movements.

Serious discussions of class are always controversial. Talk of the working class and the capitalists brings to mind the old days of factory life and Karl Marx. In this "postindustrial" service economy, steeped in mass consumerism, many people believe that the working class is surely a thing of the past and Marx irrelevant. In chapter 1 I will explain why class continues to be relevant even when some workers carry briefcases instead of lunchboxes. As for Karl Marx, anyone in the last 150 years who has thought seriously about class owes this pioneer of class analysis an enormous debt. Even the *Wall Street Journal* acknowledged his positive significance as one of "history's great thinkers" when it featured Marx in the first of a series of articles on "Thinkers Who Shaped the Century."[1]

My purpose, however, is not to discuss the pros and cons of Marx's analysis, but rather to examine America's experience in recent decades. My belief in the importance of class analysis rests on its power to make sense of the world, this world, now. An understanding of class can help us interpret what is happening in society, and what we might do to make things better for the great majority of people. I try to make the case to readers who may be skeptical, but who will approach the question with the world as their testing ground.

This book is an attempt to help reopen the discussion of class in America. In such a discussion, we will need to hear the voices of a great many people who do not often speak in public: working class people. I hope this book will stimulate a wide debate among workers, and also among academics, professional people, and all who are concerned about justice. I hope they will bring the experiences of different classes to bear, teach one another, and clarify the questions. The understanding of class that comes from this discussion can help us get to the bottom of what is ailing us and build the social movements needed to make life better for working people. Because class is a question of power, understanding class can add to the power of working people.

The working class began to experience a decline in its quality of life in the early 1970s. At that time, a book appeared with the same title as this book, *The Working Class Majority*.[2] In it, author Andrew Levison made a strong case for the existence of the working class and its political importance. But the book appeared at a time when interest in the working class was fading among traditional liberal allies. The working class was rapidly disappearing from public view. Unfortunately, Levison's book has long been out of print.

I hope that in this book, the one you are reading, the theme can be renewed in a social climate that will be more open to it. This book and Levison's have different structures and scopes, but the underlying points remain the same: the working class is the majority in the United States, and it is long past time that we all recognize that fact, explore its implications, and act accordingly.

1

THE CLASS STRUCTURE
OF THE UNITED STATES

What Are Classes?

I first learned about class growing up in Detroit and its suburbs. Long before I knew what classes were, I experienced them. Before I had the words and concepts, I saw for myself profound differences in different parts of town.

I went to grade school and junior high in Detroit with the children of autoworkers. For high school, my classmates were children of top auto executives in suburban Bloomfield Hills. My parents had found a house in one of the first subdivisions in the area, a corner of one of the finest public school districts in Michigan, where huge estates stood in sharp contrast to the housing I had known before. Other differences soon emerged. The auto plants closed on the first day of deer hunting season so thousands of workers could head into the woods of northern Michigan, but fathers in Bloomfield Hills took their kids hunting for moose in northern Canada or on safari to Africa. A high school boy I knew in Detroit who killed an old woman was put away, but a small group of my new classmates who beat a truck driver to death by the side of the road on a lark received barely two weeks' social probation at school. Whether we are aware of it or not, even when we don't have the words to explain it, the American experience is an experience of intense class difference.

A population as large and diverse as ours contains many divides. In recent decades, we have arrived at better understandings of race, ethnicity, gender, and sexual orientation, helping us to make progress toward overcoming discrimination. But as public awareness of these issues has developed, knowledge of class differences has all but disappeared.

It wasn't always so. At the end of the nineteenth and far into the twentieth century, newspapers were filled with stories of pitched class struggle. General strikes. The army called out to put down rebellious workers. Mass picketing and factory occupations in the course of union organizing drives. In cartoons, fat capitalist plutocrats with cigars in their mouths and dollar signs for eyes were denounced as enemies of ordinary people.

More recently, the general view has been that class, if it ever was important, is a thing of the past. No one argues that capitalism is a thing of the past, of course. Instead, we often hear that the relative decline of manufacturing and the tremendous growth of service industries have changed the basic facts of life in capitalist society. The relative decline of blue-collar factory employment and the rise of white-collar service jobs is supposed to show that the working class is history. The fact that we no longer see pitched battles between masses of workers and squads of armed goons hired by a company to kill union organizers is taken as proof that class struggle is over, that we've outgrown that sordid past. In short, the conventional wisdom is that postindustrial society is not industrial society.

True. But also not true. Life in the United States today is dramatically different from life thirty or sixty or a hundred years ago; many of the changes do correspond with changes in the economy. Yet much remains the same. A call-center worker today can tell you stories of speed-up and harassment by supervisors that equal anything reported by her grandfather who worked on the auto assembly line. And both are just as adamant about union representation. A temp services bookkeeper today is as subject to the whims of his employer as was the garment worker at the turn of the twentieth century. The political power of the economic elite today is at least as great as it was in the 1920s, and perhaps even greater since it is less effectively challenged by other class interests. And while service jobs have certainly grown as a share of the labor force, nearly two million more people were working to produce nonagricultural goods (in mining, manufacturing, and construction) in 1998 than in 1970, over twenty-five million people.[1] By 2007, before the effects of the 2008 financial crisis, goods-producing employment had fallen to just over twenty-two million people, but was still 16 percent of total employment in the United States.[2]

Despite all the changes in the economy, it remains as true today as it was forty and eighty years ago that the majority of Americans are working class people. To see this clearly, we first need to understand what classes make up modern capitalist society. The way to do that is to assess power.

Class is about the power some people have over the lives of others, and the powerlessness most people experience as a result. This way of approaching class is different from looking at income or status or lifestyle. When Americans do talk about class, these are the measures that usually come up, and for good reason. The working class does have different income, status, and lifestyles from those of the middle class and capitalist class. But if we leave the matter there, we miss the basic reason that classes exist in the first place.

Classes are groups of people connected to one another, and made different from one another, by the ways they interact when producing goods and services. This production process is based in the workplace, but extends into the political and cultural dynamics of society as well, where the rules and expectations that guide the economy are laid down, largely in accord with the needs of the economically powerful. Class is not a box that we fit into, or not, depending on our personal attributes. Classes are not isolated and self-contained. What class we are in depends upon the role we play, as it relates to what others do, in the complicated process in which goods and services are made. These roles carry with them different degrees of income and status, but their most fundamental feature is the different degrees of power each has. The heart of class is not about lifestyle. It is about economics.

Clearly it makes a difference whether you own the factory or are a hired hand. It makes a difference whether you are the CEO at the bank or the technician who repairs the ATMs. The chief difference is a difference of power: power to determine and control the processes that go on in the factory and the bank, and beyond that, power in the larger society, especially political power.

Power is complicated; it has many sources and is exercised in many ways. Some people have the power to determine which goods and services will be made, how, and by whom. Some set government policy and use the government to control others, through the police, through regulations, through the military. Others have cultural power to shape the ideas and values that tend to dominate our thinking. Elections involve still another type of power.

A person with power in one of these parts of life doesn't necessarily have power in another. But power isn't random. We can find patterns in the exercise of power, spillover from one area of society to another. Economic power and political power are related and reinforce one another. The power to affect our culture comes from control over economic and political resources, but influencing the culture tends to strengthen one's economic and political power as well.

Some power is obvious and some is invisible. The power that we can see we tend to identify with individuals. My supervisor has power. The president of the United States has power. A media critic for the *New York Times* and a program officer at the National Endowment for the Arts have power. I have power, and you do too, in the aspects of our lives that we can control or influence. Most of us are acutely aware of power in its visible, individual forms.

But other kinds of power are easy to miss. The power of inertia tends to perpetuate existing ways of doing things and existing relationships. We aren't necessarily aware, day to day, of the power that limits alternatives, the power of a kind of social automatic pilot, invisible as long as everyone goes along with the program. Invisible force fields of power are built into the structures that hold society together, giving it shape, setting the paths for our opportunity, and setting the limits as well. We tend to take these contours for granted, internalize them, and think of them as the natural order. But when some group of people seriously challenges this kind of power, in politics, in the culture, in assertions of new ways to organize the economy, what had been invisible roars into full view: the "powers that be" step out to demolish the threat.

Classes arise in these relationships of social power, visible and invisible. Class is first and foremost a product of power asserted in the production process. This means power over what goes on at work: who will do which tasks at what pace for what pay, and the power to decide what to produce, how to produce it, and where to sell it. But beyond that, production power involves setting the rules for how markets work and the laws governing property rights. Production power includes organizing an educational system that will generate a workforce with the skills and work habits required to keep production going. Production power extends into many aspects of our lives beyond the job.

We will see shortly that the majority of the population in the United States belongs to the working class. The working class does not exist in isolation, of course; it draws its existence from its relationship to other classes, other people also engaged in making and distributing goods and services. First and foremost among these other classes is the capitalist class, those who own and operate the major corporations. What is important about capitalists is not simply that they have the power to dispose of all that is made in their factories and offices. They have the power to control the work lives of their employees, most of whom are working class people. Their economic power finds its way into enormous influence in politics as well.

In a capitalist society, the "powers that be" are largely the capitalists, the corporate elite at the top of relatively large U.S. businesses. For the most part, capitalists set the terms of production, in all the senses just described, and more. They own or control the businesses so of course they have the power to make the rules. Owning or controlling the businesses, they have the money and social status and, with these, power to influence the political and cultural life of the country. Their influence tends to define everyone's opportunities and limits according to what will be good for capitalists, what will continue, broaden, and deepen their power. Sometimes this power is visible; when it is not, it just is, baked in the cake.

When I talk about the working class, on the other hand, I am talking about people who share a common situation in these social structures, one without much power. To be in the working class is to be in a place of relative vulnerability— on the job, in the market, in politics and culture.

On the job, most workers have little control over the pace and content of their work. They show up, a supervisor shows them the job, and they do it. The job may be skilled or unskilled, white-collar or blue-collar, in any one of thousands of occupations. Whatever the particulars, most jobs share a basic powerlessness in relation to the authority of the owner and the owner's representatives who are there to supervise and control the workforce.

Even when workers do have some influence at work, the basic power relations are unchanged because the capitalist retains the ultimate authority. At the Saturn plant in Spring Hill, Tennessee, General Motors and the United Auto Workers established a labor-management cooperation process that many observers have taken as a new kind of worker power. Before the first car was built in 1990, teams of workers and supervisors together designed the factory and the labor relations system. Workers helped make hiring decisions and were part of the product design teams. A union officer sat on the Saturn policy committee.

None of this, however, made the workers anything other than workers. They did not become capitalist executives. Whatever power they had came from two sources: 1) the power of their union to negotiate a contract that gave the workers power under the rules of cooperation, and 2) the agreement of the company, the boss, to allow the workers these powers.

In fact, tensions existed at Saturn between General Motors and the workforce, despite the forms of cooperation. In June 1998, when workers in Flint, Michigan, struck GM parts plants to limit outsourcing, the workers at Saturn almost joined in, because the same issues were at play there, despite cooperation.[3] The immediate problem was only one of many in a years-long pattern of conflicts of interest between the company and those who worked the line. Work teams and a respectful supervisor could offer some relief from the typical burdens of capitalist work rules (or teams could create a whole new set of problems). But these improvements hardly make workers into nonworkers. Nor did cooperation save the workers' jobs at the plant when General Motors top management decided to discontinue the Saturn brand and close the plant altogether in 2009, with an announcement that made no mention of their partner union nor production workers.[4]

The same conflicts continue even in companies where workers have employee stock ownership plans (ESOPs). In the first decade of the new century, about 11,500 businesses in the United States, with ten million employees, had ESOPs.[5] Stocks in such plans typically have various voting restrictions that make it impossible for workers to exercise control of the company. Instead, the plans are usually a form of pension program or sometimes a profit-sharing plan imposed in connection with wage concessions forced upon the workers.[6]

The employees at United Airlines, for example, were part owners of the company through an ESOP imposed when the company was in trouble in 1994. But that didn't turn the workers into capitalists, or even make them any less working class in the power they exerted. As evidence, in July 1998, nineteen thousand reservation takers, gate agents, and ticket sellers voted to join a union, the International Association of Machinists, when the company they "owned" continued to treat them as the workers they in fact continued to be.[7] When the company finally entered bankruptcy in 2002, the ESOP ended and workers gained no benefit in the reorganization from the ESOP's existence.

Occasionally workers really do own, operate, and control the company where they work. These worker cooperatives can offer some relief from the arrogance of power often found among managers in regular businesses. But worker cooperatives are typically small and have little market power. Workers in these co-ops exercise none of the broader social power that the middle and capitalist classes have. Overall they find themselves in the same social position as other workers.

Workers don't need to hold stock in the company they work for to have an interest in its economic health. Their jobs, pay, and working conditions are wrapped up with the health of the company. But just because workers want their employers to stay in business doesn't make the workers capitalists. After all, employers want workers to have affordable housing so the company won't have to pay high wages to support high rents. But we don't conclude from this shared interest that employers are workers.

Capitalists and workers are not the only classes in America. There is also a middle class, made up of professional people, supervisors and managers, and small business owners. We will see that it makes sense to put some people who are technically capitalists, those who own small businesses, into the middle class rather than the capitalist class, because of the very real differences in power that separate large and small business.

Throughout this book, we will look at many ways in which class power affects the lives of all people differently according to the class they are in. And we will see that although the working class is at an enormous disadvantage in the United States, it is not powerless.

To understand class, we need to measure it. This is hard to do, because class is not a simple category. But we can get close to the structure of classes by looking at the structure of occupations. The jobs we do give us a strong indication of the place we occupy, on the job and off, in the class structure. So before we examine the ways class works in the larger society, we will look at the work people do for a living.

Although I have measured class by looking at the labor force, people not in the labor force are also in classes. Nonworking spouses typically share the class position of their working mate. Children share the class position of their parents, and retired people typically retain the class standing they had in their working life. The relative sizes of different classes in the labor force closely reflect the class composition of society as a whole.

Before looking at the working class, let's look at the capitalists, the class with whom workers are most directly engaged.

The Capitalist Class

Capitalists and their top managers own and control businesses of all sizes. In a strict sense, *anyone* who makes a living by owning a business is a capitalist, even if she employs only a couple of people, or even if he is self-employed and has no one working for him. But it makes sense to distinguish between big and small capitalists, to recognize the difference in power they have over their workers, in the market, and in the political arena. Bill Gates and Donald Trump don't belong in the same class as the guy who has a small plumbing business and employs an occasional helper when work is steady. In 2006 (the latest year for which these data are available), twenty-six million businesses existed in the United States. Most were small, even tiny. Almost twenty-one million, 81 percent, involved the proprietor alone with no employees. Of the 4.9 million firms with employees in 2005, more than half employed just one to four people, accounting in total for just 5.2 percent of all employment that year. By contrast, just twenty-one thousand companies employed five hundred or more people each. These, 0.4 percent of all businesses in the country, employed 44 percent of all people working that year.[8] The Internal Revenue Service reports that in 2006, the latest data available, 58 percent of businesses had less than $25,000 in gross receipts, and all these very small businesses put together, 17.8 million of them, took in just 0.4 percent of all business revenue.[9]

The overwhelming majority of these small businesses are sole proprietorships, which the business owner does not incorporate. Any business profits are mixed in with the owner's other income and reported on his or her federal income tax form using Schedule C. Millions of these self-employed "small businesspeople" have working class jobs as their main source of support; their business activity is just another source of personal income, often much smaller than their job income. Sometimes a working class person will be forced to connect to an employer as an independent contractor, as when a hairdresser rents a chair in a salon whose owner has complete control over work hours and pay. For tax purposes, the "independent" hairdresser is a small business owner, but the reality is quite different.

On the other end of the scale are the incorporated businesses, or corporations. Even most of these are on the small side. Of the nearly 5.4 million corporations operating in 2006, only 19 percent, 1.1 million companies, had gross receipts above a million dollars. But the receipts going to this 19 percent added up to 96 percent of all corporate receipts that year.[10]

Clearly it is appropriate to make distinctions among capitalists, separating big business from small entrepreneurs. No clear, bright line separates the small business of the middle class entrepreneur and the big business of the capitalist class. A company employing fifteen people might be big in a town of five hundred residents; its owner might have a respected role in the local community and its political and social life. But in a larger city, such a business would disappear in the scheme of things, from the point of view of those who hold serious power. So there is no simple rule to differentiate big from small business. Any attempt has to take into account the overall social setting of the business. Still, the distinction is worth pursuing to get a clearer picture of the diverse interests of the "business community."

To begin, I call any business "small" if its owner works side by side with the employees and supervises them directly. This owner is in the middle class. The business becomes "big" and the owner a member of the capitalist class only when the owner no longer works directly with the workers, exercises control over the workforce through at least one layer of middle management, and becomes occupied full-time with running the business as a senior strategist and source of authority, largely removed from the production process itself. Again, there is no hard-and-fast rule to separate these types of businesses, but experience suggests that twenty employees is a reasonable cutoff, beyond which a small business becomes big.

By this measure, there were 639,000 big businesses in the United States in 2005, each employing twenty or more people. These were only 13 percent of all businesses that had any employees beyond the owner, but in 2006 they had 81 percent of all employees and accounted for 85 percent of the country's nongovernment payroll.[11] The boards of directors, principal owners, and top executives of these companies form the capitalist class. They are no more than 2 percent of the labor force. Most of these businesses are big fish in small ponds, holding sway in a local area but wielding little market or political power on a national or even regional scale.

To get a handle on the scope of big business and the capitalist class on a national scale, we can learn from how the business community itself approaches the question. One way is to look at the Small Business Administration, a part of the U.S. Department of Commerce that provides technical and financial assistance to small businesses. According to the rules of the SBA, established by Congress, any business with fewer than five hundred employees is a small business. This number indicates that the government views "big business" as a relatively tiny number of corporations. In 2005, by the standards of the SBA, there were only twenty-one thousand big businesses in the United States, 0.4 percent of all businesses with any employees, and 0.08 percent of all businesses in the country. Yet they employed over 44 percent of all business employees.[12] In 2006, this tiny percent of all businesses in the United States paid out 56 percent of the country's private payroll (not counting sole proprietorships).[13]

We can reasonably consider these twenty-one thousand big businesses to be the national economic elite. Their directors and senior officers exercise considerable power, not only within the companies they control but also in the larger society, which is affected by their decisions and opinions on strategies for investment, collective bargaining, and foreign affairs.

Even within this elite, power is concentrated in the very largest financial, manufacturing, service, and transportation companies. At the end of June 2010, there were 7,830 banks in the United States (not counting the separate branches many banks have): 6,676 commercial banks and 1,154 savings banks (not counting credit unions).[14] Banks are typically ranked in size by the amount of assets each controls. Thousands of banks are small businesses in small towns, important there but nowhere else. But the twenty-five largest commercial banks had assets ranging from $66.6 billion (Northern Trust) to $1.6 trillion (JPMorgan Chase). They were only 0.4 percent of all commercial banks, but this tiny fraction controlled 68 percent of all commercial bank assets in the country, $8.17 trillion. Even among these very richest and most powerful institutions, power is concentrated in the uppermost tier: the five biggest banks controlled 56 percent of the assets of the top twenty-five.[15]

Similar concentrations occur in farming. When we think of agriculture, most of us think of the family farm, the backbone of rural America. In 2007, of the 2.2 million farms operating in the United States, 28 percent were under fifty acres, but they accounted for just 1.8 percent of all farmland. By contrast, fewer than 4 percent of farms were larger than two thousand acres, but they covered 54 percent of the farmland in the United States.[16] In 2007, almost 60 percent of farms in the country sold crops worth less than $10,000 for the entire year, taking in a total of less than 1 percent of all farm sales. The biggest operations, with 2007 sales of a million dollars or more, were fewer than 3 percent of all farms, but they took in almost 60 percent of all farm revenue.[17]

These lopsided holdings are more than matched in manufacturing. In 2006, 286,000 firms were engaged in manufacturing in the United States. Almost three-quarters of these firms were small businesses employing fewer than twenty people; together they employed just under 9 percent of the manufacturing work force. At the other end of the scale, there were four thousand manufacturing companies that each employed more than five hundred workers. These big businesses were just 1.3 percent of the total, but they employed 55 percent of the manufacturing workforce.[18] Ninety-four percent of manufacturing corporations had under $10 million in assets in 2006, and together they took in only 7 percent of all corporate manufacturing revenue. But the 1,760 largest manufacturing corporations had assets in excess of $250 million apiece. They were only 0.6 percent of all manufacturing corporations, but they took in 81 percent of all manufacturing corporations' revenues, and 91 percent of the profit.[19]

These concentrations of power dominate industries we encounter in everyday life. The top three soft-drink makers, Coke, Pepsi, and Dr. Pepper/Snapple, have nearly 90 percent of their market.[20] At the close of the last century, the top five music album producers had 84 percent of their market. Ninety percent of the cigarettes sold in this country were made by three companies, while four companies dominated residential telephone service, and so on.[21]

Over time, corporate assets have become increasingly concentrated, a trend that continues. In banking, for example, while the number of commercial banks dropped from 12,500 at the end of 1990 to 7,100 in 2009, the share of bank assets controlled by the hundred largest banks increased from 50 percent to 82 percent. The share controlled by the ten biggest banks in the country almost tripled, going from 20 to 54 percent.[22] Concentration of banking assets among the largest banks increased still more after the 2008 financial crisis despite concerns that banks had already become "too big to fail" and threatened the stability of the entire economy.

Given the stark pattern of concentration of business assets in the relatively few largest corporations, it makes sense to consider big business as a distinct force in the economy, and to consider the people who run these big businesses as a distinct class with more economic and political power than others. The average board of directors of a big business operating on a national scale includes about fifteen people.[23] There are, then, a total of about 315,000 positions on the boards of directors of the twenty-one thousand national-scale big businesses in the United States. These are the senior corporate officers and the outside directors who represent major suppliers, customers, sources of credit, and other links to the rest of the corporate world.

Most directors sit only on one company's board, but some sit on the boards of two or five or even more corporations at the same time, forming intricate patterns of interlocking directorships among the major corporations. One detailed study of the directors of the eight hundred largest corporations in the United States found that 15 percent of directors sat on more than one company's board.[24] Taking these multiple director positions into account, we can identify 245,000 or so individuals who together constitute the governing boards of national-scale corporations. They are the "captains of industry" who dominate the U.S.

economy, the two-tenths of 1 percent of the private sector workforce who are the core of the capitalist class on a national scale.

The Ruling Class

From among these directors, the few tens of thousands who sit on two or more boards form a pattern of interlocking directorships among the major banks and nonfinancial corporations. This network, together with the top-level political and cultural leaders aligned with it, can fairly be called the ruling class.[25]

Classes are not simply the sum of many individuals who share certain characteristics or positions of relative economic power. The ruling class is bound together into a coherent social force by common networks and institutions that allow the ruling class to rule—to give strategic guidance to society. Think tanks, elite university research and policy centers, exclusive social and political organizations, media and cultural institutions, and the philanthropic foundations and wealthy individuals who finance these institutions, all interact to create an environment in which debates lead to policy formulation and political processes that broadly reflect the corporate interests at the center of the network.

Its members have substantial power but, like all classes, the ruling class is not a monolithic unit and it is not all-powerful. Both within the United States and internationally, its members have factional disputes among themselves, regional differences, and differences based on the interests of specific industries. The ruling class is limited by competition among corporations and by the organized power of other classes, but its members have enough similarity and coherence of interest and outlook to differentiate them from the rest of society. We can identify the ruling class as a small elite among the capitalists and their top allies in politics and culture. The entire U.S. ruling class could easily be seated in Yankee Stadium, which holds fifty-two thousand people.

How Classes Persist

Economic relationships are the foundation of classes. But class is not just an economic matter. While economic relationships may remain more or less stable over generations, the individuals who make up the different classes come and go, and must be continuously produced anew in every generation.

This means that classes are not just the sum of the people in them at a given time. Classes are produced whole over time, in a complicated set of processes involving almost all aspects of society: cultural representations and norms, so important in shaping our understandings of who we are and how we are related to others; education; religion; politics; academic research; and so on.[26]

Classes should be understood in part, then, as dynamic processes by which they reproduce over time. The capitalist class, for example, has created institutions vital to its reproduction as a class and the stability of its ruling class, including elite educational institutions, social clubs, and business, trade, and lobbying groups. Over time, these institutions shape young people and equip them with the knowledge, skills, and social networks essential for the continued existence of the capitalist class as a more-or-less coherent social force capable of giving strategic direction to business and the country as a whole. As blacks and women have entered into the capitalist and rulings classes, they have been absorbed into these networks, but with residual racist and sexist barriers. In response, they have developed their own institutions to acclimate and guide people into the higher reaches of economic, political, and cultural power.[27]

The working class is also reproduced across generations through the institutions and media representations that working people encounter, some of their own making, most not. The working class, like the capitalist and ruling classes, is not just a collection of individuals. It is a coherent social force, principally trained and brought together by educational and cultural institutions and their employers to produce goods and services. But, unlike the capitalist and ruling classes, the working class has no institutions designed to forge it into a social force ready to give strategic guidance to society.

The Middle Class

Understanding the structure and size of the capitalist class helps us to understand the middle class. The middle class is under constant discussion in American political life. As the working class has disappeared from polite conversation, the middle class has come to be accepted as the social position most Americans are in. Politicians appeal to the middle class. Tax cuts are designed for the middle class. Downsizing afflicts the middle class. Even union leaders almost always refer to their members as middle class.

Most people think of the middle class in terms of income and lifestyle. In short, the middle class has a middling income. Its members are not the rich, who are a fringe group of celebrities and business millionaires, nor are they the poor, the fringe at the bottom of society who are chronically unemployed, on welfare, outside the mainstream, the "underclass." The middle class are those people who, in Bill Clinton's phrase, "work hard and play by the rules," going to work every day just to get by. The common man, everywoman.

Just where to draw the line between the poor, the middle class, and the rich is arbitrary in this way of thinking. The middle class itself often gets divided into an "upper middle class," a "lower middle," and even a "middle middle." Rather than get sidetracked by the many possible income dividing lines that are used, we will get a better understanding of classes if we define them in a very different way.

Let's ask: What is the middle class in the middle of? If we answer this question in terms of power instead of income, we see that the middle class is in between the two great social forces in modern society, the working class and the capitalist class. These two classes are connected at work, in the production of goods and services. But they have sharply opposing interests, in production and in politics. The middle class is caught in the middle of these conflicting roles and interests. In the context of the sharp conflicts that arise between labor and capital, the middle class is caught in the crossfire. A look at the lives of small business owners, supervisors, and professional people will help make the point clear.

Small Business Owners

First, let's return to small business owners. They are caught between big businesses on the one hand, which impose intense restrictions on their ability to compete, grow, and make money, and workers on the other, who press for wages, working conditions, and social policies that are often beyond the capacity of a small business to finance.

As is typical of the middle class in general, small business owners share common ground with big business in the defense of property interests and hostility to organized labor, but they also have common ground with workers in their desire to find relief from the discipline of the marketplace dominated by big business. Small entrepreneurs are not in the working class, even though they work hard and many have themselves been in the working class in the past, especially in the building trades. Entrepreneurs have more independence than workers—that's the whole point of being your own boss. And to their workers they are the boss.

One example of the complexity of relations among working, capitalist, and middle classes comes from the world of the family farm. Back in the 1970s, small farms in southern Michigan and northern Ohio were growing tomatoes destined for sale to the Campbell Soup Corporation. These farmers employed farm laborers, mostly Mexicans and Mexican Americans. The farmworkers, under the leadership of Baldemar Velazquez and the Farm Labor Organizing Committee (FLOC), began to organize themselves into a union and sought higher wages and better working conditions in the fields, demanding, for example, access to clean drinking water and toilet facilities.

The small farmers said they couldn't afford the workers' demands, and pointed to the terms of the contracts they had signed with Campbell that set low prices for the produce. The workers' demands threatened them with ruin, they said. The workers were unmoved.

But after the impasse continued, FLOC changed its approach. Instead of going toe to toe with the small farmers who employed them, the farmworkers went to Campbell and demanded a better deal for the small farmers. FLOC went to the farmers, too, and ultimately won them over to go together to challenge Campbell, and to share with the workers the better terms that, working together, they were able to extract from Campbell, the big business that had been limiting them all. In 1985, after a long and bitter fight, Campbell finally was forced to improve the terms of their purchases from the small farmers, who in turn improved the wages and working conditions of the farmworkers.

It was no love fest on the part of the farmers in Ohio. Many had hated the union and its organizers for years. It was only after they began bargaining contracts and found out that they did in fact have more in common with the workers than the corporate processors that they warmed up to FLOC. As one FLOC staff member put it in 1999, "This isn't true of them all, but these days some of our biggest boosters are those same farmers who used to run Baldemar off their farms." These small farmers' interests were best served by siding with their own workers, developing a common strategy against a common enemy, and making concessions and accommodations to the workers along the way.

Not every small business is caught so directly and obviously between labor and big business. But in the larger play of forces in society, that's where they are. Many small businesses share with working people a common vulnerability to market forces dominated by large corporations. Small business owners have no health insurance except what they provide for themselves, as is true for millions of workers. Small businesses and workers alike have difficulty getting credit, and both groups are vulnerable to the disruption caused when a big corporation decides to move out of a community.

Of course, small business owners part company with workers in at least as many ways. Workers' wages are business costs, as are the costs of complying with health, safety, and environmental standards often championed by workers. On these questions, and in the general defense of private property interests, the middle class of small business owners is drawn to the side of big business. But it can also happen that big business will promote certain government regulations knowing that they alone can afford to abide by them, using regulation on purpose to put smaller competitors at a disadvantage.

In short, small business owners are caught in the middle. They share with working people a common vulnerability to market forces dominated by large corporations, but they share with those same big businesses an interest in keeping the power of working people to a minimum.

Supervisors and Managers

Supervisors and middle managers make up another large part of the middle class. Think about a foreman or supervisor. This person is the company's front line of management, there to make sure the work gets done, responsible for pushing the workforce to perform. Foremen and supervisors are often promoted from the ranks of the workers themselves, often have a detailed knowledge of the work, and sometimes even continue to work alongside those they are supervising. But they are an extension of management, although at the lowest level, with layers of management above pushing them to perform, just as they push the workforce below.

The foreman has a notoriously nasty job. He or she takes grief both from the workers being supervised and also from those in higher management who are suspicious of any laxness in the performance of managerial duties. This is what supervisors at all levels are in the middle of. This distinction has long been recognized in labor law, which usually requires supervisors to be in a different bargaining unit from nonsupervisory employees, and in the way the Department of Labor reports wages and other information separately for "supervisory" and "nonsupervisory" employees.

Of course, class position is based on the reality of the work situation, not the job title. I had a student who was an "assistant manager" at a shoe store in a local mall. All this meant was that she had a key to open the store in the morning (so the boss didn't have to come in early), and she had the authority to count the money. These extra duties brought her a slightly higher wage than her coworkers, but she didn't manage anything. She was in the working class despite her managerial title.

Some workers do take on what may seem like supervisory duties. "Lead workers," for example, give direction to coworkers with less experience or skill and often get premium pay for their abilities. These more senior workers are not middle class managers, however. They don't discipline fellow workers or act in other ways as direct representatives of management authority, duties that are central parts of any supervisor's work life.

Over time, court rulings have reduced the legal definition of who is an employee with rights to union organization and membership protected by law. In private universities and colleges, for example, the Supreme Court ruled in the Yeshiva decision in 1980 that faculty should be considered on a par with upper management because they participate in hiring and firing decisions, even if only by advising upper management in peer-review tenure deliberations.[28] Ever since, lacking the protection of law, it has been almost impossible for faculty in private colleges and universities to organize into unions except in rare instances when the college president voluntarily accepts a union for the faculty. Faculty at public colleges and universities, on the other hand, are covered by state laws that sometimes allow faculty unions (and sometimes prohibit them), unlike federal laws, which cover only private sector employees. Public university and college faculty have organized themselves into unions for collective bargaining in many states.

Professionals

A third section of the middle class is made up of the millions of professional people such as doctors, lawyers, college professors, and accountants. These people tend to have considerable authority and flexibility in their jobs, whether they are self-employed or work in a corporate department. They often put in long hours, and they do their work in accordance with rules that guide their actions. But on the whole they function within professional associations that exert considerable influence in setting the rules and standards to which the members of the profession are subject. In this way, the discipline professionals face is not the same as that experienced by workers.

Young professionals just starting their careers can be subject to intense supervision and long hours and have no control over their work. Medical residents or first-year associates in a law firm may experience these conditions. At universities, young adjuncts face conditions much closer to those of the skilled working class than to those of tenured professors. But worker-like conditions do not put young professionals into the working class. Rather, the conditions are part of an apprenticeship or even hazing. The hope and expectation are that full professional status will come. One's sense of class, and the reality of class, is therefore not just a question of one's current work setting. It is related to the trajectory of future prospects connected to the current work.

If a medical resident were told that she would have to live that harried life for the next forty years, she would think differently about her situation and her supervisors and employers. People with new PhD degrees may be willing to put up with temporary employment for a year or two before settling into a tenure track job with an academic future. But in recent years, as it has become apparent that tens of thousands of adjuncts will *never* find a regular place in the professional life of the university, their attitudes as adjuncts have been changing. Their militancy and interest in union protections have increased, and their feelings of estrangement from the regular professorate have grown as well.

As corporate management practices penetrate deeper into professional life, professionals are increasingly finding themselves in the middle of social forces they have little experience with. I have identified classes according to the degrees of power and authority people have at work. But power relationships are not fixed over time. They can change, and as they change, people's class position can change, too. We saw evidence of this especially among middle class professional and managerial people caught in the changing structures of work that began in the 1990s and have continued into the 2010s.

There can be no better example of the traditional middle class professional than the family doctor. Traditionally a person of authority and independence, the doctor at work is clearly removed from the work life of the secretary or mill hand. The doctor's class standing is not directly a result of the years of training required. A skilled machinist or auto mechanic can take years to train, too. The doctor is different from the machinist because no one tells the doctor what to do. The doctor is in control of her time and effort as well as the treatment of her patients. That is, until recently.

Now that HMOs have brought cost control, reengineering, and corporate management practices to the medical sector, doctors are increasingly subject to a discipline and control unknown in their ranks in the entire history of the profession. Managed care was supposed to be a way to "bring competition to the health industry." What this has actually meant is the penetration of big business and capitalist methods into the medical work process, in the doctor's office as well as the hospital. Under this regime, doctors are increasingly being changed into—many would say, "reduced to"—employees, more like skilled artisans, less like independent agents. In response, some doctors are turning to unions for protection. To some extent they are concerned about their incomes. But in most of these unionization efforts, the real spur driving doctors to unions is the question of power and autonomy in their work life. As doctors have come under these management practices, their political views have changed as well. [29]

Beginning lawyers now often find themselves in large firms where they work in bullpen conditions on repetitive, routine matters. They are assigned cases and intensely supervised for efficient use of time, and share more in common with skilled workers than with the independent lawyers of the traditional professional middle class.

In recent years, even managers have been subject to the discipline of capitalist labor relations. When the *New York Times* ran a weeklong series called "Downsizing in America" in 1996,[30] the stories were of middle managers as well as skilled workers. During the corporate restructuring of the early nineties, millions of workers lost their jobs. But in fact production workers were not losing jobs any faster than in the 1980s. What had changed was the increase in layoffs for managers and supervisors, long cushioned from the discipline of the labor market.[31]

The fervor the media had for this story reminded me of the 1968 garbage strike in New York City. After many days of growing piles of garbage on the sidewalks, a TV reporter tried to convey the seriousness of the situation: the rats, he said, had been seen leaving Harlem, crossing over the Triborough Bridge into largely white areas of Queens.

Rats shouldn't go into Queens. But neither should they have been in Harlem in the first place, and it wasn't news when they were. It is a serious matter that middle managers and professional people are treated badly, stripped of their dignity at work, and subject to the raw power of capitalist authority. But for working class people, such treatment is no news at all.

The fact that middle class professionals are increasingly exposed to capitalist power does not immediately put them into the working class. This can occur, however, if the basic nature of the work and work relations in a profession changes drastically enough. That is what happened to skilled craftsmen as mass production drew them into capitalist work settings in the last part of the nineteenth century. It was this proletarianization of skilled craft work that led those workers to form the first long-lasting trade unions, the basis of the American Federation of Labor.

In the opening years of the twenty-first century, public school teachers have been the primary example of this process. Fighting for authority, they are caught between pressures from school boards wanting to apply corporate management strategies to control their work, on the one hand, and reluctance among many to identify too closely with unions and the working class, which can be seen as unprofessional. At the same time, teachers face increasingly impatient demands from working class parents that their children get a better education.

The corporate attack on teachers demands that teachers give up "special privileges" that professional people share but working class people lack. High on the list is tenure. With tenure, teachers have greater job security than most workers, even though tenure does not really guarantee a job for life. Teachers can still be fired or laid off for many reasons. The main benefit of tenure is that it protects academic freedom and helps shield the curriculum from outside political interference. Parents might envy tenure, or believe that it keeps lousy teachers on the job. But they share with teachers a common interest in resisting corporate practices in the schools and universities and a common interest in allowing teachers to apply their expertise, in association with parents, to construct professional standards that serve the interests of students. This is a typically complicated condition of middle class existence.

It has always been true that the process by which professional people are brought into the working class is not smooth. It involves intense conflict. We see that most clearly now in the education reform movement that challenges the legitimacy of teacher unions across the country, claiming that they are the biggest impediment to school reforms that would help children get a better education.[32] The imposition of corporate management practices into the schools, central to much of the reform agenda, requires the freedom of principals and school boards to impose their decisions upon the teachers. Management has increasingly subjected teachers to the sorts of discipline and regulation that typify the conditions of skilled workers. As *New York Times* business columnist Joe Nocera approvingly explained the process, New York City schools chancellor Joel Klein "empowered principals, making them, as he puts it, 'the CEOs of their buildings.'" [33]

In response, the American Federation of Teachers and the National Education Association, the two major teachers' unions in the United States, representing over four million people, have insisted that teachers should play a central role in guiding curriculum reforms and other changes in school operations. In doing so, the unions are trying to preserve the professional status of their members, to distinguish the work life of the teacher from the experience of the cafeteria worker or janitor. The idea is to avoid a situation in which the school board, principal, or curriculum consulting firm decides what should be taught in each class and what teaching methods should be used, and then hires teachers only to tell them "here's the job, now go and do it." As the school reform movement has come to dominate the public education system, teachers have often been on the losing side of this conflict.

The imposition of detailed control over teachers involves subjecting them to quantitative measures of "output," using students' scores on standardized tests of basic skills as indicators of teacher performance in creating "value added" in their work. The corporate model of education requires the teacher to hone the student into the desired market-ready product with appropriate skills, much as the machinist shapes work into a product for sale in the market. A key distinction between a professional and a skilled worker is the degree to which the person has control over the design of the work. When the teacher loses control of the lesson plan and becomes subject to evaluation based on externally determined quantitative measures of output, the teacher leaves the realm of professional life and enters the world of skilled work.

There is no question that this process is well along after ten years of No Child Left Behind, and two years of the Race to the Top as implemented by the Obama administration. As a result, teachers across the country are being transformed from professionals into skilled workers, moving from the middle class into the working class as the dynamics of capitalist development play out in their part of the economy. A natural part of this agenda is weakening or destroying teachers' unions.

But this process is not uniform across the entire teaching profession. Some schools and teachers are subject to rigorous control, others much less so. As a general rule, for teachers and other professionals, changes in their economic and social circumstances are closely tied to the experience of those whom they serve. Those professionals whose work and lives are most closely linked to working people have tended to do badly as the standard of living and social standing of the working class has declined. Those professionals most closely associated with the capitalist class have tended to do much better. Compare the experience of public defenders with corporate lawyers, or the experience of doctors who practice in HMO clinics in working class towns with that of high-priced doctors who don't have to hassle with insurance companies because their well-to-do patients can afford to write checks for services rendered. These differences reflect the "middle" position of the professional middle class.

For public school teachers, following this approach suggests that it is reasonable to conclude that by 2010 the school reform movement had gone far enough that about 60 percent of teachers could be counted as skilled workers, roughly in proportion to the size of the working class in the country (see Table 1). These are teachers in "failing schools" or schools judged in need of strong intervention, typically in working class areas of cities and suburbs. But teachers in other public schools, particularly where the children of middle class professionals and others who are relatively secure economically get an education, have generally escaped these pressures.

Nursing is another profession increasingly subject to the rigors of skilled work without the independence of professional life. One indication is the prevalence of overtime, even forced overtime, in nursing work. Reviewing 5,317 eight- and twelve-hour nurse shifts, one study found that two-thirds of full-time nurses worked overtime at least ten times in two two-week periods, one-third reported overtime on every shift, and 10 percent of the shifts involved forced overtime.[34] The prevalence of overtime for nurses is one of the leading reasons that nurses leave the job. The desire to protect patient care and sustain nursing levels has led sixteen states to impose legislative or regulatory restriction on overtime for nurses.[35] In the calculations underlying Table 1, I've counted three-quarters of nurses in 2010 as members of the skilled working class, one-quarter as middle class professionals.

Similar questions arise in higher education, where the erosion of tenure and the increasing employment of contingent academic labor—part-time adjuncts and full-time non-tenure-track lecturers—have dramatically changed the academic workforce. During the rapid expansion of higher education in the

United States in the 1960s and 1970s, two-thirds of faculty were tenured or on tenure-track lines. A decade into the twenty-first century, the proportions have reversed—only one-third of faculty are in relatively secure positions while 70 percent of undergraduate instruction in public institutions is done by part-time adjuncts, who make up 47 percent of all teaching faculty (not counting graduate students).[36]

The challenge to professional standing among academics is not only a question of tenure. As modern corporate management practices gain ground in universities, faculty members are increasingly subject to bigger teaching loads, larger classes, and other forms of speedup. Research activity is less and less supported by the university itself; rather, faculty are required to seek outside, often corporate, support for research, casting the professor in the role of part entrepreneur, part subordinate and supplicant to those with the money to control the research agenda. The life of the mind, individual research and scholarship: these professional aspirations are being replaced by expectations that the professor is there to generate a certain number of market-ready students, the "product" of higher education institutions, and to do research that corresponds directly to the needs of business. As university administrators treat faculty more like employees and less like colleagues, as faculty tailor their research more and more to corporate needs, they come to resemble the skilled working class. The characteristics of middle class professional life slip away, with telltale changes in power.

The imposition of corporate management practices at colleges and universities sometimes extends to changing the content and process of teaching itself, by which faculty teach courses they do not design (using curricula and teaching materials developed by other faculty, sometimes at different institutions), and administering standardized tests they do not create and sometimes do not grade. These tasks are sometimes done by others in a process called "unbundling," in which the variety of tasks a professional faculty member does is split apart and assigned to different people in a new division of labor in higher education.

John Sperling, the founder and then-president of the University of Phoenix, the largest private for-profit institution of higher education in the United States, vividly described this process in an address to a conference of the National Center for the Study of Collective Bargaining in Higher Education in March 2000. Speaking to an audience of professors and university administrators who bargain union contracts, Sperling began his remarks with an extended quote from *The Communist Manifesto*, by Karl Marx and Friedrich Engels.

> The bourgeoisie [capitalist class] cannot exist without constantly revolutionising the instruments of production, and thereby the relations of production, and with them the whole relations of society....Constant

revolutionising of production, uninterrupted disturbance of all social conditions, everlasting uncertainty and agitation distinguish the bourgeois epoch from all earlier ones. All fixed, fast-frozen relations, with their train of ancient and venerable prejudices and opinions, are swept away, all new-formed ones become antiquated before they can ossify. All that is solid melts into air, all that is holy is profaned, and man is at last compelled to face with sober senses his real conditions of life.[37]

Looking up from the lectern, Sperling said that he didn't usually agree with Karl Marx, but that he did want his audience to understand that capitalism was coming to higher education, that all that was solid would melt into air, and that all that was holy would be profaned.[38]

There is no precise measure of the degree to which this process has penetrated colleges and universities. As with all other professionals, those academics most closely connected to working class students—in community colleges and private for-profit colleges—are most subject to these pressures, while academics in university centers are much less affected, although not immune. The transformation of academics from professionals to skilled workers is furthest along in the private for-profit institutions that exercise the greatest control over their instructors. The widespread use of adjuncts in community colleges also carries the academy along this path.

Management employs adjuncts to avoid paying benefits, to escape the requirements of tenure, and to secure classroom instruction at per-course pay far less than regular faculty receive. But low pay and bad working conditions are not the basic markers of class; authority and autonomy are. Many adjuncts retain authority over their work, and college administrators often lack the resources to supervise adjunct instruction as closely as they might prefer. Nearly 40 percent of adjuncts have nonacademic jobs;[39] they teach a course or two for personal or professional reasons—business owners teaching accounting, judges teaching law school courses, practicing engineers teaching something of their field at the local community college. While the process of subjecting academic labor to capitalist control, forecast with such relish by John Sperling, has begun, most academics retain sufficient control over their work to remain in the professional middle class, though under ever-increasing pressure. The class standings reported in Table 1 count only 5 percent of academic labor as skilled workers, the rest still in the professional middle class.

Some teachers, social workers, and other professionals whom I place in the middle class already think of themselves as workers and show increasing interest in unions and collective bargaining for protection. Others resist any association with people who are not "professional" and identify more closely with the capitalist class in their values and political leanings. In politics, as in economics, people in the middle class are in the middle, and tend to identify themselves with labor or with capital depending on their particular situation and depending on the relative power of working class movements compared with the power capitalists can demonstrate.

The Working Class

The working class is large and diverse. Pursuing our economic approach to class, we can get a picture of it by looking carefully at the occupational structure of the U.S. economy. But the specific work of a particular job is not the only question to consider. Since class is a matter of relationships and power, not of job title, a person with the same job will be in one or another class depending on the circumstances of the work. A truck driver who owns his own rig, for example, is in the middle class as a small entrepreneur, but a truck driver employed by a freight shipper is in the working class. A plumber operating as an independent contractor counts in the middle class, but the same plumber working for someone else is in the working class.

The U.S. Department of Labor publishes detailed information about the numbers of people employed in hundreds of different occupations.[40] These occupations are grouped into nine broad categories: management, business, and financial occupations; professional specialty; sales; office and administrative support; services; construction, extraction and maintenance; production; transportation and materials moving; and farming, forestry, and fishing. After examining the detailed occupational content of each job title in each category, I have assigned employees to the working class or to the middle and capitalist class according to the degree of authority and independence the employee typically has on the job. The results are shown in Table 1.

For example, in 2010 15.4 million people were employed in sales occupations. Of these, 8.1 million had working class jobs, including 3.1 million retail cashiers and 3.3 million retail sales workers, as well as telemarketers, rental clerks, and others with similar titles. But stock traders and real estate agents, also counted by the Department of Labor in the broad "sales" category, have enough authority and independence to be counted in the middle class. By going through each occupation in the sales category in this way, I conclude that of these 15.4 million people, 8.1 million are in the working class, and 7.3 million in the middle class.

The professional specialty category divides the other way: of the 30.8 million people in these jobs, 62 percent are middle class. People counted as professionals hold such jobs as engineers, computer scientists (not computer operators),

TABLE 1   Employment by occupation, 2010 (in thousands)

OCCUPATIONAL GROUP	TOTAL	MIDDLE CLASS	WORKING CLASS	WORKING CLASS (% OF TOTAL)
Management, business, financial operations*	20,938	20,656	282	13.0
Professional and related	30,805	19,025	11,780	38.2
Service (including health support)	24,634	2,213	22,421	91.0
Office and administrative support	18,047	1,507	16,540	91.6
Sales and related	15,386	7,324	8,062	52.4
Construction, extraction, and maintenance	12,086	1,040	11,046	91.4
Production	7,998	702	7,296	91.2
Transportation and material moving	8,182	498	7,684	93.9
Farming, fishing, and forestry	987	44	943	95.5
TOTAL EMPLOYED	139,063	53,009	86,054	61.9
Unemployed**	13,605	2,858	10,747	79.0
TOTAL	152,668	55,867	96,801	63.4

*includes 1,505 CEOs
**only with past employment
Source: U.S. Department of Labor, *Employment and Earnings,* January 2011, Table 1 (Household data).

doctors, lawyers, and the like. These are middle class people, given the degree of independence and authority they typically have at work, and they are a clear majority of this occupational category. But this broad category also includes many working class people. For example, the Department of Labor includes respiratory, speech, and physical therapists among professional specialists, as well as emergency medical technicians, clinical laboratory technicians, teacher assistants, and broadcast sound engineers. Given the specifics of these jobs, I think it is appropriate to count those who do them as highly trained and skilled working class people, even with their professional qualifications, except when they are self-employed. Similarly, the Labor Department counts all nurses as professionals, but the conditions of their work lead me to believe that perhaps three-quarters are working class, while the rest have the authority and independence that characterize middle class jobs. Similarly, as discussed above, 60 percent of K–12 teachers counted by the Department of Labor as professionals, and 5 percent of academics, are best considered skilled workers. Adding them all up reveals that 38 percent of people classified as professionals by the Department of Labor are working class.

The remaining seven occupational categories are fairly homogeneous. The "executive, administrative, and managerial" category includes essentially no working class people (except insurance claims examiners and appraisers). These are such jobs as property managers, financial managers, and educational administrators. At the other extreme, almost all of the office and administrative support personnel are working class: secretaries, information clerks, file clerks and other records-processing occupations, postal clerks and mail carriers, computer equipment operators, and teacher aides, among others. The middle class is found among the supervisors. The same is true of transportation and material moving occupations, production jobs, and construction, extraction, and maintenance. Table 1 shows that service occupations are overwhelmingly working class. These include firefighters, dental assistants and nursing aides, private guards and police officers, hairdressers and cosmetologists, janitors, and waiters. But service occupations also include some middle class positions such as supervisors and restaurant chefs (though not short-order cooks, who are typically working class).

In addition to those working in 2010, the labor force included 13.6 million unemployed people who were actively looking for work but had no job of any kind. Data are available showing the last-held occupation of the unemployed.[41] Not surprisingly, the unemployed tend to be from those occupational groups with a larger concentration of working class jobs. Using Department of Labor data, we find that 79 percent of the unemployed in 2010 came out of working class jobs.

Once each occupational group is analyzed and separated into working class and middle class jobs, it is a simple matter to add up the pieces and find the total class composition of the labor force. In 2010, the labor force numbered 152.7 million people (employed or unemployed but actively looking for work). Of these, 96.8 million were working class; 55.9 million were middle class and above. In other words, in 2010 the working class was 63 percent of the labor force. This is why I say we live in a country with a working class majority.

By the way, the Department of Labor comes up with an even larger number for what might be considered the working class than I do. It notes that 82 percent of the 108 million private sector employees in the United States in 2009 were "non-supervisory" employees.[42] This includes such professionals as doctors, accountants, and professors who do not supervise others, whom I count as middle class.

It may seem surprising that so many people are in the working class, given the declining relative size of manufacturing in the U.S. economy. But images of the working class too closely identified with goods-producing blue-collar workers miss the point. Only 14.8 percent of people counted by the Department of Labor as "nonsupervisory employees" in the nonfarm private sector are in goods-producing industries (mining, construction, and manufacturing).[43] Over 70 percent of all private sector nonsupervisory employees hold white-collar jobs in wholesale and retail trade, finance, insurance, and real estate, and a wide variety of business, personal, and health-related service industries.[44] But even in 1950, in the heyday of American manufacturing strength, no more than a third of the nonagricultural workforce was employed in manufacturing.[45]

Old images of the working class need correction in other ways, too. Identifying the working class with factories may foster the notion that "working class" means men, or even just white men. Think again: less than half of those in the working class labor force, about 40 percent, are white men. Minorities have always been an integral part of the working class, a good number of women have always worked in factories, and today women are a slightly higher percentage of the working class workforce than they are of the labor force as a whole. In 2010, women were 47.2 percent of the employed workforce. Sorting through the data by detailed occupational category to look at gender composition, I find that women were 50.1 percent of the working class, and 42.6 percent of the middle class (Table 2).[46]

But this does not mean that women have broken out of traditional job categories in a big way. Women are still grossly underrepresented in the more-skilled blue-collar jobs that traditionally have been held by men. In 2010, women held 27.6 percent of production jobs in the United States, but were only 3.9 percent of machinists and 0.9 percent of tool and die makers. Women were overrepresented in lower-paying jobs such as bakers (57 percent) and sewing machine operators (78.5 percent). In sales, women are disproportionately in low-paying working class occupations such as cashier and retail clerk, and underrepresented in high-paying professional sales positions such as stockbrokers and financial service professionals. Among the professions, women are the majority (57.4 percent), but they are overrepresented among nurses (91 percent), teachers (73.8 percent), and other predominately working class jobs, and underrepresented among engineers (12.9 percent), lawyers (31.5 percent), computer scientists (30.5 percent), and other relatively well-paid positions.[47]

If we look at racial and ethnic composition, we see that blacks and Hispanics are overrepresented in the working class and underrepresented in the middle class, patterns similar to women, but even more pronounced. From Table 2 we see that in 2010, blacks were 10.8 percent of the total employed labor force, but they were 12.7 percent of the working class and only 7.6 percent of the middle class. Hispanics were 14.3 percent of all those with jobs, but held only 8.6 percent of middle class positions and 17.8 percent of working class jobs. Asians, on the other hand, were disproportionately represented in middle class positions, particularly the sciences, engineering, and higher education. Non-Hispanic whites were also overrepresented in the middle and capitalist classes.

We see from all these numbers that women, blacks, and Hispanics are a larger proportion of the working class than they are of the labor force as a whole. They are by no means absent from middle class positions of authority, but generally women and minorities are in the lower-paid sections of the working class and in the lower ranks of management and professional life, compared with men or white people. Following this pattern, women and minorities are also found

TABLE 2 Percentages of employed labor force by gender, race, and ethnicity, 2010

	WOMEN	MEN	BLACKS	ASIANS	HISPANICS	NON-HISPANIC WHITES
Employed labor force	47.2	52.8	10.8	4.8	14.3	70.1
Working class	50.1	49.9	12.7	4.1	17.8	65.3
Middle class*	42.6	57.4	7.6	6.0	8.6	77.8

*includes CEOs and other senior executives in capitalist class
Source: Author calculations based on U.S. Department of Labor, *Employment and Earnings*, January 2011, Table 1.

among capitalists, but their businesses are small by national standards.[48] The largest black-owned business in 1998 had sales under $400 million.[49]

A look at census data showing the number of people of different races, genders, and nationalities in hundreds of occupations reveals a surprisingly mixed labor force at all levels. Economist Doug Henwood wrote of the 1990s:

> The largest occupational category for white men in 1990 [the single occupation employing the largest number of people] was salaried managers and administrators, a title that also appears on the top ten list for black men (#8), Hispanic men (#7), and white women (#6). Secretary is the leading job label for white women—but it's also number one for Hispanic women and number three for black women. Truck driving is the leading employer of black men—but it's second for both Hispanics and whites. "Janitors and cleaners" is the biggest occupation for Hispanic men, and second for black men—but sixth for white men. More black women are nurses' aides and orderlies than any other occupation—but it's the ninth biggest employer of white women. The privileged titles usually appear higher and more often for whites, especially men, but there's no shortage of gritty jobs for white folks either.[50]

The 2000 census data revealed a similar landscape of common occupations within genders. "Driver/Sales Workers and Truck Drivers" was the largest occupation for white, Hispanic, and black men and the seventh largest for Asian men. Janitor was the third-largest occupation for black men, fifth for Hispanic men, and eighth for white and Asian men. Secretary was the largest occupation in the United States and the largest category for white women, third for black and Hispanic women, and fifth for Asian women. Cashier was the second-largest occupation for Hispanic, black, and Asian women, and fourth for white women. With 3.1 million people, it was the fifth-largest job category in the workforce.

Occupations are often sex-segregated, however. There were almost 1.5 million carpenters in 2000, the largest construction occupation. Ninety-eight percent were men. Of the thirty-one occupations with more than one million workers in 2000, auto service technicians and mechanics, carpenters, construction laborers, drivers/sales workers and truck drivers, and grounds maintenance workers all were more than 90 percent men. For women, child-care workers, receptionists and information clerks, registered nurses, secretaries and administrative assistants, and teacher assistants were at least 90 percent women. In only five of the top thirty-one occupations was the difference between the percentage of men and women less than fifteen points: accountants and auditors, cooks, marketing and sales managers, miscellaneous assemblers, and postsecondary teachers.[51]

Neither the working class nor the middle class is uniform in gender, racial, or ethnic composition. Each class presents a mosaic. Looking at the mosaic another way, we see that gender, racial, and ethnic groups are also not uniform. Each is divided by class, as reflected in Table 3. We see that the working class is the majority of every ethnic and racial group, but there's quite a bit of variation in class composition among them. The working class accounted for 53 percent of Asians in 2010, but 77 percent of Hispanics. At the same time, 73 percent of blacks and 58 percent of non-Hispanic whites were in the working class. Compared with the employed population as a whole, men, Asians, and non-Hispanic whites were disproportionately overrepresented in the middle and capitalist classes, while women, blacks, and Hispanics were overrepresented in the working class. While women and nonwhites were virtually unknown in the capitalist class fifty years ago, there are now quite a few women and black chief executives of major corporations, although still greatly underrepresented at that level compared with their numbers in the labor force.[52]

This complex set of relationships and identities is what we have to sort through to make sense of and then influence the politics and economics of U.S. society.

Race is not just a numerical category in a demographic division of the population. Race is a central feature of social dynamics in the United States. It has a long

TABLE 3   Class composition of racial and ethnic groups, 2010

	TOTAL EMPLOYED IN MILLIONS	PERCENT IN WORKING CLASS	PERCENT IN MIDDLE CLASS	PERCENT OF CHIEF EXECUTIVES
Women	65.7	66	34	25.5
Men	73.4	59	41	74.5
Black	15.0	73	27	2.8
Asian	6.7	53	47	3.2
Hispanic	19.9	77	23	4.8
Non-Hispanic White	97.7	58	42	89.2
TOTAL	139.1	62	38	100.0

Source: U.S. Department of Labor, Employment and Earnings, January 2011, Table 1.

history as the foundation of slavery, and then as the basis of the Jim Crow laws of legal segregation and racial discrimination that followed formal emancipation. This history has had profound implications for all Americans, not just those of African descent.

A rich literature has developed since the 1970s demonstrating that the social meanings of race are not tied to physical traits, nor is racism psychologically innate. We have come to understand that race has played, and in many ways continues to play, a role as an instrument of social control, dividing "white" from "black" in a workforce that from early colonial days threatened rebellion, and, from the point of view of ruling elites, needed discipline. The English colonial ruling elites of the seventeenth and eighteenth centuries gave special social meaning to the idea of race as they created the reality of chattel slavery for people of African descent. They used racism and the new institutions of slavery to divide from each other the indentured laborers of English and African descent who were working in the colonies.[53]

AFL-CIO President Richard Trumka addressed the legacy of this history in the 2008 presidential campaign in an address to the convention of the United Steelworkers union meeting in Las Vegas as the U.S. presidential campaign was heating up. Trumka spoke directly to the racist attitudes that some workers continued to express in their resistance to voting for Barack Obama:

> A lot of them are good union people; they just can't get past this idea that there's something wrong with voting for a black man. Well, those of us who know better can't afford to look the other way. I'm not one for quoting dead philosophers, but back in the 1700s, Edmund Burke said: "All that is necessary for evil to triumph is for good people to do nothing." Well, there's no evil that's inflicted more pain and more suffering than racism—and it's something we in the labor movement have a special responsibility to challenge. It's our special responsibility because we know, better than anyone else, how racism is used to divide working people. We've seen how companies set worker against worker—how they throw whites a few extra crumbs off the table—and how we all end up losing. But we've seen something else, too. We've seen that when we cross that color line and stand together no one can keep us down. That's why the CIO was created. That's why industrial unions were the first to stand up against lynching and segregation. People need to know that it was the Steel Workers Organizing Committee—this union—that was founded on the principle of organizing all workers without regard to race. That's why the labor movement—imperfect as we are—is the most integrated institution in American life.[54]

I have left out of this discussion of classes any mention of the "underclass," a term often used in popular and sociological discussions of poverty. We will look at poverty and the so-called underclass in detail in chapter 4. But for our purposes here, to the extent that we are talking about people engaged in the illegal drug business as the "underclass," there is no reason to believe that the class composition of that industry is any different from that of legal ones. The drug trade includes owner-entrepreneurs and managerial and supervisory personnel who have the same authority as their small (and sometimes not-so-small) capitalist and middle class counterparts in the legal economy. And the business includes people engaged in the making and distribution of products who are working class in every sense of the word. Illegal gambling and prostitution operations may be smaller and may typically lack the layers of middle management characteristic of larger businesses, both legal and illegal, but the class divisions between business owners and those who work for them reflect the class divisions of the comparable visible economy.

If anything, the power differences that characterize class division in illegal sectors must be greater than those we see in legal businesses, where working people have recourse to the protections of labor law. There is, in short, no reason to think that the illegal sector is different enough in its organization to make class differences any less striking or important.

Class Ambiguities

Class is not caste, a social status acquired at birth from one's parents and indelibly marked on the person for life. As we will see more fully in the next chapter, there is limited mobility across class lines. Yet, some cross-class mobility and ambiguities at the boundaries between classes should not lead us to conclude that classes don't exist, or are arbitrary divisions among more-or-less equal human beings. Classes are central elements in our society, growing out of and in turn shaping our economy, politics, culture, and history.

The majority of people are in the working class, those who do the direct work of production and who typically have little control over their jobs and no supervisory authority over others. The working class is the clear majority of the labor force, 63 percent. At the top of the class order, controlling the big business apparatus, is the capitalist class, about 2 percent of the labor force. A small fraction of the capitalist class operates on a national scale, and an even smaller network of several tens of thousands of interlocking directors among the largest of businesses is the core of the national ruling class. Between the capitalist class and the working class is the middle class, about 35 percent of the labor force.

While each of these classes is distinct from the others, all members of a particular class do not, of course, have the same degree of power, the same income, status, or lifestyle as others in the class. Each class is diverse—in skill, authority, occupation, race, gender, ethnicity, and every other characteristic that human beings possess. It even happens that individuals in one class can have attributes most often identified with another class, as when some skilled workers make more money than some professionals, or some managers work longer hours and have more stress than some production workers. Because some working class people go in and out of business, with small stores or contracting outfits that mostly serve their working class neighbors, a degree of overlap exists between working class and middle class experience. In many neighborhoods, there is more than a little personal identification across this porous class boundary.

Faced with such diversity and apparent incoherence, it may be tempting to give up the idea that class is a meaningful category and just focus on each individual, or fall back to the common belief that there are simply the rich, the poor, and the broad middle class in between. But an analogy with water—though a bit of a stretch—will help explain why it makes sense to keep class categories as I am defining them, despite the variety of individual experience within each class.

Water takes different forms, ice, liquid, and steam, even though in each state it is still H_2O. Each state is distinct, yet within each wide variations can occur. Liquid water can be cold or hot or lukewarm. Ice can take different forms too, and under different conditions of pressure and volume, steam can vary in temperature and other properties. The three states of water are even fuzzy at the edges, when it is not clear exactly what is going on. Is slush ice or liquid? How many bubbles have to form at the bottom of a pan of water, and how many have to rise to the top and roil the surface, before we say the water is boiling? Yet these variations within states of water, and ambiguities at the edges, don't stop us from knowing that water takes different forms, even if it's all H_2O.

Thinking along these lines tells us about class as well. We are all people. The capitalist, the worker, the middle class professional or business person, all flesh and blood, all with hopes for ourselves and our children, most of us trying to do the best we can. But this underlying sameness, which is terribly important to remember and respect, in no way means that we are all equally powerful or that no systematic differences exist among us. Our different class standings cause us to act differently, live differently, and have different experiences and life chances, despite our underlying resemblance in a common humanity.

Within classes, people are different. An unskilled factory sweeper is in the same class as a radiology technician, a postal letter carrier, a bank teller, a machinist. The professionals, managers, and entrepreneurs of the middle class vary widely not only in the content of their work but in their social status, income, power. Among capitalists, too, are the big and the small, national and local power brokers, the well-connected and the relatively isolated. But despite the variations among people within each class, it still makes sense to view the world as made up of distinct classes, because, in the end, workers do not have the power of the middle class, let alone the capitalists, either big or small.

In the last decade of the twentieth century and through the first decade of the twenty-first, nonstandard work arrangements spread. Instead of holding a regular job, more and more people were working as temps, as independent contractors, as franchise operators. These new work relations were often forced on people after they had lost a regular job to downsizing or a company move or failure. These new arrangements usually brought with them a reduction in living standards, increased insecurity, an end to employer-provided pensions and insurance. Depending on how narrowly or broadly we define "temporary" or "contingent" jobs, in 1997 anywhere from 1.9 to 4.4 percent of the labor force was in nonstandard employment. Fewer than half were employed part-time.

A February 2005 government survey revealed that the fraction of workers in on-call, temp service, and contract-provided positions had remained unchanged since 2001, but the number of independent contractors had risen. While all these categories of employment are considered "contingent" (with no expectation that the job would continue), the people holding them, and their attitudes towards their employment, differed dramatically. The 10.3 million independent contractors tended to be professionals, older, white, and men, with 82 percent reporting preference for their job status compared with regular employment. The 4.5 million temp services, on-call, and contract workers, on the other hand, tended to be women, African-American or Latino, and younger, and only 32 percent reported preference for their work situation over a regular job.[55]

The largest category of people with nonstandard work relations is the category of independent contractors, consultants, and freelance workers. Many of these are professionals and people involved in managerial or sales work and thus part of the middle class. But some "independent contractors" and "franchise operators" are not the middle class people their titles suggest.

In 1998, forty thousand limousine drivers (not taxi drivers) were working in New York City. Some had traditional employee status, but many were independent contractors, forced to lease their cars from car service companies. In these lease arrangements, which have the appearance of a business contract between two independent parties, the driver takes on the status of a franchise holder, but in reality is completely controlled by the car service company.

What class does the "independent" limo driver belong to? The question is not rhetorical; the answer controls whether the drivers can organize a union and force the company to negotiate a collective bargaining agreement. In 1997, when drivers at one company wanted to organize, the company claimed they were independent contractors, not employees, and so not protected by labor law that gives workers the right to organize unions and requires their employer to negotiate in good faith. But the National Labor Relations Board, the federal agency that decides these disputes, dismissed the company's claim and ordered a union representation election. The drivers overwhelmingly voted the union in.[56]

The story of these limousine drivers is repeated wherever employers try to mask power relations with the veneer of a professional or entrepreneurial title bestowed on workers. Class is not in the name. Class is in the power relationships people experience.

In which class is a secretary who also has a Mary Kay franchise on the side, supplying and managing three other women? What do we call an electrician who works for his city's board of education but also has his own contracting business? In what class do we put a family with a husband who works in an auto plant and a wife who is a pediatrician? Is a person who owns a machine shop employing twenty-five people on two shifts and who works side by side with his employees on the floor two mornings a week while taking care of the business the rest of the time, a capitalist or in the middle class as a small businessman?

The ambiguity of such borderline cases, and the wide variety of experience within classes, is testimony to the fact that classes are not simply boxes or static categories into which we pigeonhole people. Classes are formed in the dynamics of power and wealth creation, and are by their nature a bit messy. Classes are more complicated, more interesting, and more real than the arbitrary income levels used to define class in the conventional wisdom.

WHAT WE THINK ABOUT WHEN
WE THINK ABOUT CLASS

Why Has the Working Class Disappeared
from Public View?

Even though the middle class is only about 35 percent of the workforce, almost every aspect of politics and popular culture, with help from the media, reinforces the idea that "middle class" is the typical and usual status of Americans. Four strands of thinking have combined to promote the idea that we're all middle class and to dissolve working class identity: 1) ideas about upward mobility, 2) the promotion of consumerism, 3) the politics and ideology of the Cold War, and 4) media coverage of class and economic issues. Let's look at each in turn.

Upward Mobility

Upward mobility is a central feature of the American story, although belief in the American Dream was deeply shaken by the chronic unemployment and millions of home foreclosures that marked the economic crisis beginning in 2008. Almost everyone wants opportunity for advancement, for themselves and for their children. But we should be aware that those who discuss upward mobility sometimes speak condescendingly of working class people. Too often they imply that there is a stigma attached to being in the working class, as though the only legitimate aspiration of working people is to escape their class as soon as possible. Working class people are often proud of the work they do and the contributions they make to society. Their aspirations may include the desire for more time with family, better pay, opportunities for their children, and better treatment at work, rather than to become a professional or a business owner.

In many periods of U.S. history, the dream of upward mobility has come true for millions of American families, in the working class and throughout society. The possibility of upward mobility has often been taken as a sign that classes don't exist in the United States, or that class position is at most temporary and unimportant in such a fluid situation. But it turns out that not everyone can be upwardly mobile, and those who are often have luck to thank for their success. In any case, upward mobility does not wipe away the class divisions characteristic of U.S. society and capitalism more generally.

One common understanding of upward mobility is rising family income. Since working class families now earn much higher incomes than they did fifty and a hundred years ago, who can question the reality of upward mobility and the good life workers have under capitalism? This argument is often made in terms of lifestyle: almost everyone lives a "middle class lifestyle" now (except the rich and the poor), so most people, including workers, must be middle class.

It's true that over a longer sweep of history the working class standard of living has improved greatly, even though it has stagnated and even declined since the 1970s. Despite the consequences of the 2008 economic crisis, many more workers now than in 1945 own their own homes, have new cars and home media centers, take vacations with their bass boats. In 1945 only capitalists and middle class professionals, entrepreneurs, and managers enjoyed such comforts. The working class had enough to cover basic needs and that was about it.

Working class families have raised their standard of living when they have been able to take home in higher pay (or shorter work hours) a share of the increased wealth they have helped to create with their higher productivity. But an increase in personal possessions doesn't catapult workers into the middle class. The lifestyles of the middle class have also improved dramatically—to say nothing about the capitalists. It makes no sense to compare the workers of today with the middle class of 1945.

What is considered a typical standard of living also changes from one period to another. Partly this reflects the new possibilities of a more productive society. Partly it happens when the definition of "basic needs" changes as a society becomes differently organized. For instance, in 1945 workers could often walk to work or take the bus. Now, given how we organize our transportation systems, almost everyone needs a car, and has to be paid enough to buy one.

The working class has neither disappeared nor caught up with the middle class. Compared with middle class families today, most working class families continue to live very different lives, in very different parts of town, with very different life chances. Once again, class is determined not by income and lifestyle but by relative standing in power relations at work and in the larger society.

The myth of a classless society endures nonetheless because of individuals who have risen from modest beginnings to own their own business or lead a prosperous, respected professional life. The American Dream of upward mobility is promoted relentlessly in the popular culture. This exciting story line has captured our imaginations far beyond its reality. The Dream becomes the Myth when we focus only on the one who makes it rather than the many who do not.

The U.S. class structure is certainly not a rigid caste system. When we know personally or read about working class parents doing three jobs to put their children through college, who then become doctors or financial analysts, the power of class to define us seems to disappear. When we know of working class kids who work hard, scrape a stake together, and, with imagination and guts, set up a successful business, the claim that class counts might seem like the whine of the lazy and the losers, a throttle on initiative and hope. Individual striving for a better life is a central part of the American Dream. But the desire to get ahead is not necessarily incompatible with an acute awareness of class distinctions. Many of my working class students have gone to college because they want to get away from the life they've seen their parents endure. They want professional training or their own business because they believe that it is better to "be your own boss" than to have someone else bossing you around.[1]

Individual upward mobility rests on individual effort, but also on something mentioned much less frequently: luck. No one is more closely associated with the legend of upward mobility than the American novelist Horatio Alger (1834–1899). Alger wrote 135 novels in the last third of the nineteenth century, just as the country was becoming more urban and industrial. These tales for boys often followed the same pattern: a poor boy works hard, lives a clean life, and goes on to success and sometimes riches. But the crucial element of luck is too often forgotten in today's retelling. Every hero of a Horatio Alger story may have exemplary character and work hard, but that alone is never enough. The hero is also always incredibly lucky. The boy Ragged Dick saves from drowning just happens to be the son of a rich banker. The person who finds Phil the Fiddler and rescues him from death under a snowdrift early on Christmas morning is—guess what—a wealthy doctor. It is the well-to-do savior who guarantees our hero's success.[2]

In putting luck at the heart of the story, Alger was true to life. It is simply not possible for everyone who works hard and lives an exemplary life to rise above working class roots. Hard work and honest living may be necessary ingredients for success (though much in life seems to contradict this claim), but they are certainly not sufficient.

The fact that luck is part of most success stories is a reflection of a deeper fact about upward mobility: it is limited by the structure of the economy. The fact that some individuals move up, even far up, in the class hierarchy does not mean that all of us can. Who makes it and who doesn't—that's a matter of luck as well as hard work and honest dealings (or cunning and backstabbing, as the case may be).

The way society and the economy are organized limits mobility the same way the rules of any game limit what the players can do. A baseball team can't have lots of shortstops or center fielders. It doesn't matter how much money those players make, how glamorous or important their jobs, or how many people want to play those positions. The structure of the game is what determines how many players of different sorts there are.

Likewise, there can be no capitalism without a working class that constitutes the majority of the labor force. That's the structure of the game. Modern capitalism cannot have "too many chiefs." Once the days of small farms and artisanship vanished, the working class became as fixed a feature of capitalism as were the capitalists themselves. This structural fact explains why no amount of upward mobility can erase the reality of deep and permanent class divisions in society. It also limits what we can become as individuals.

Class differences are not the only structural barriers to mobility. Racial, ethnic, and gender discrimination also limit opportunity, and they operate within every class. As we saw in the previous chapter, and will see again in this and following chapters, classes have important racial, gender, and ethnic characteristics, just as these groups have class differences within them. Each of our life chances and experiences develops in this complex mix.

Some people do move up the ladder, of course. Families of almost every nationality that has come to America can tell stories of immigrant success, of people who arrived as common laborers but rose to professional and business achievement in a generation or two. In these stories, both hard work and luck play their parts. But no amount of hard work could have achieved these results if the structure of the economy and its needs for labor hadn't changed dramatically, too.

Through the course of the twentieth century, the occupational mix of the labor force changed along with changes in the industrial composition of production and the way production was organized. Farming gave way to manufacturing, manufacturing to services. In the process, farming skills and jobs have almost disappeared, and, after relatively stable numbers of goods-producing jobs through the last thirty years of the twentieth century, at the start of the new century the number of blue-collar goods-producing jobs declined as white-collar service employment rapidly expanded. In this context, it is not surprising to find that the children of blue-collar workers had moved into white-collar jobs.

But what does this tell us about class and social mobility? Since the working class includes both white-collar and blue-collar people, the fact that the son of a steelworker is now a bank teller says nothing about the disappearance of the working class through upward mobility. Some may believe that standing behind a bank counter is a better job than standing in front of an oxygen furnace, although it pays about half as much. But such occupational mobility is not mainly the result of the hard work and good character of the person who has gotten the better job. Rather, it comes from structural changes in the economy that have shrunk the steel industry and opened up the financial sector. This is a process over which no one has direct control, a process that destroys some kinds of jobs and creates others.

The same workings of the economy contribute to the fact that some children of the working class have made it into the professional and managerial middle class. These occupations have grown somewhat in relation to the overall labor force, so it would not be possible for all the people who are currently middle class to have been born that way. No amount of hard work and good character could have made as many working class kids upwardly mobile if the "higher class" jobs had not been created by economic changes that had nothing to do with individual strivings.

Scientists, for example, are a greater fraction of the labor force today than sixty years ago because, after Sputnik, the Cold War race against the Soviet Union created a demand for scientists. The increase in science jobs didn't just happen because a lot of smart kids saw science as a way up and worked hard to become professionals. Those interested in science at the time were lucky to be alive and in the market just then. Today, with the demand for basic science on the skids, luck has run out for many young people with an aptitude for science who are looking for a way up through study and hard work in that field.

We can get a sense of future structural limits on upward mobility by looking at the projections the U.S. Department of Labor has made for the occupations that will offer the most new jobs in the first years of the new millennium.[3] Between 2008 and 2018, the ten occupations with the largest number of new jobs are expected to be registered nurses; home health aides; customer service representatives; food preparation and serving workers, including fast food; personal and home care aides; retail salespersons; office clerks; accountants and auditors; janitors and cleaners, except maids and housekeeping cleaners; nursing aides, orderlies, and attendants; and post-secondary teachers. Of these, only 17.8 percent are middle class jobs (if we count one-quarter of all nurses and 95 percent of higher education faculty as middle class, as we did in chapter 1). Twelve of the twenty occupations expected to add the most jobs to 2018 require only on-the-job training; just seven, less than 30 percent of the new top-twenty jobs, require any postsecondary education. People in ten of the twenty occupations with the largest numbers of new jobs earned less than the national median wage in May 2008.[4]

Not everyone can be the "symbolic analyst" former labor secretary Robert Reich proposed in the early 1990s as the bright future for the U.S. labor force in a global economy, with low-paid work to be done in other countries.[5] Actually, a relatively tiny number of such jobs will exist in the future. As the economy moves on, the working class will not disappear. Within the working class, more new jobs will be at the low end of the skill and salary scales than at the top. This is the restricting economic structure young working class people are entering.

Occupational mobility in the United States did increase in the twentieth century, compared with the nineteenth.[6] But structural changes seem to have slowed and will provide fewer opportunities for class advancement in the foreseeable future.[7] Young people coming into the labor force after 1979, the "baby bust" generation, did worse overall in terms of income and occupation compared with the earlier "baby boom" generation, despite strong growth in the number of jobs available. The reasons have to do with changes in the kinds of jobs available to the different generations of young people.[8]

A recent study found that a child born into a family in the bottom 10 percent of the U.S. income distribution has less than a 2 percent chance of making it into the top 10 percent as an adult.[9] While it is still true that a child of the working class is far more likely to remain in the working class than to move up to the professions, let alone the ruling class, the slow spread of college education among working class youth has made the trip up more possible for some. In fact, there seems to be no relationship at all between the occupation of college graduates and the occupation of their fathers,[10] suggesting that a college education can provide a ticket out of the working class.

In 2009, however, only 29 percent of all people over twenty-five in the United States had at least a bachelor's degree. Among those aged twenty-five to twenty-nine, those most likely to have graduated from high school and had sufficient time to graduate from college, 31 percent had four-year college degrees.[11]

College students are drawn disproportionately from middle and upper class families, and success at college is disproportionately greater for those from families with higher incomes. In 2009, the college participation rate (the percentage of the population between ages eighteen to twenty-four attending college) for students from families in the bottom quartile (income below $36,080 in that year) was 41.4 percent, but only 8.3 percent of students from families at the bottom graduated from college with four-year degrees by age twenty-four. College participation and graduation rates climbed steadily as incomes rose, to the point where for families in the top quartile of income—above $108,294—84.2 percent attended some college, and 82.4 percent graduated with bachelor's degrees.[12]

These results echo earlier experience. In 1992, two out of three high school graduates who came from families in the top quarter of the income distribution (above $67,000 that year) went on to a four-year college, while only one in five high school graduates from the lowest quarter (incomes then less than $22,000) did so. Looking just at those graduates who went on for more schooling of any kind, in 1992 three out of four from the top end of incomes went to four-year colleges and universities, while only four out of ten students from the lower end did. The rest went to community colleges and post-secondary technical and vocational programs. Differences in who finishes with a degree were even greater. Over 40 percent of college students from the upper end of the income distribution who started college in 1989 got a four-year degree within five years, while only 6 percent of the low-income students did.[13]

These figures indicate that while higher education can be a path to upward mobility for the working class, in reality it mostly helps to stabilize classes and reproduce them across generations. Working class kids go to college, when they do, mainly to get an associate degree, useful for a variety of skilled working class jobs. Middle and upper class kids tend to go on for training that prepares them for professional and managerial roles, not unlike those their parents have played.

As long as people with college education are relatively scarce in the labor force, it will continue to be an important channel for upward mobility, although no guarantee. But if college education becomes universal, an economy that requires the continued existence of a working class will demand that a janitor have a college degree. When education cannot help sort out classes, something else will be used to separate people and limit their chances.

In a society whose overall class structure remains relatively unchanged, upward mobility for some must be matched by downward mobility for others. Some children of professionals and business-owning parents do fall to lower levels of power and influence, although they are far more likely to remain in the upper reaches of the class structure. Again, a college education greatly improves the chances of continuing success, but not all children from upper reaches go to college, and not all who do can establish themselves.

In the United States today the child of a maid can become a doctor or a business executive, and the child of an executive can end up selling shoes. But it remains true that the single most likely occupation of a child is that of the parent.[14] Of those who were in the bottom 20 percent of income at the end of the 1960s, less than 1 percent had made it into the top 20 percent by 1990, while 54 percent remained at the bottom. Of those who started in the top 20 percent of income, 46 percent stayed there, and only 7 percent fell to the lowest 20 percent by 1990.[15]

While education, which is associated with advancement, has become somewhat more widespread in recent decades, structural mobility has declined. Those with university and professional degrees often do not find positions up to their skills, and spend years underemployed in working class jobs.[16] This means that while personal opportunity from education is expanding, structural opportunities are contracting, and the economy will continue to require a working class majority as long into the future as anyone can see.

This is where luck comes back into the picture. Who will make it into the relatively few good jobs? Luck will play a part in everyone's story, and the most important piece of luck, good or bad, is the family you happen to be born into. Those born into the capitalist class were born on third base (though some may think they personally hit a triple).

The labor market is a chancy place for the working class. Few people can win in the upward mobility sweepstakes. Therefore we have to be careful how we think of the people who are the winners and the losers, not to put too much weight on market success or failure in our judgments of them. We will return to this question in chapter 5 in a discussion of the limits of individualism. Here, to conclude our discussion of upward mobility, we should remember that it does not operate to the extent most people seem to believe. Mobility does not wipe out class distinctions in most people's personal work experience through their lifetime or in the chances for family improvement in class standing across generations.

Consumerism

Over a hundred years ago novelist Henry James depicted the habits of the upper classes in his account of summer life at Newport: "'An American woman who respects herself,' said Mrs. Westgate...with her bright expository air, 'must buy something every day of her life. If she cannot do it herself, she must send out some member of her family for the purpose.'"[17] Sociologist Thorsten Veblen coined the phrases "the leisure class" and "conspicuous consumption" to describe people like Mrs. Westgate.

We consume to live, but also to say something about who we are. Over two-thirds of all production in the United States is destined for personal consumption, as opposed to investment or government use,[18] and it is not only the upper classes, and certainly not only women, who seem to need to buy something every day to have a sense of purpose and identity.

How do we know who we are unless we know what we have? Advertising is based on getting us to identify a product with some characteristic we would like to have: sexiness, power, smarts, happiness, status. The ever more relentless introduction of advertising into every nook and cranny of our daily lives constantly reinforces a sense of identity through possessions that tends to crowd out other identifiers, such as class.

Identity through possessions rather than work was reinforced in the decades following World War II, as leisure time increased, the consumer boom flourished, and "keeping up with the Joneses" seemed to become the very purpose of life. As jobs have become more routine and deskilled (an increasingly common fact of working life throughout the twentieth century and continuing into the twenty-first), we have tended to identify ourselves less with work and more with other aspects of our lives. And, as incomes have risen to the point where we have some discretionary income beyond the bare necessities, questions of consumption have taken on more immediate meaning. In recent decades, working hours have increased and real incomes are down, but consumption still holds our attention as people try to find fulfillment and identity in life beyond work.

Meanwhile, the consumption patterns of the middle class are taken as a model and presented through advertising, films, television, the Internet, and other popular entertainment.[19] This middle class, middle-income standard of living is close enough to what many in the working class can afford to serve well both as a magnet and as a source of ready comparison, at least through copycat products of lesser quality, often bought only through greater debt. (The lives of the rich and famous are available, too, for another purpose: to satisfy a certain voyeurism, rather than to provide a daily role model.)

The improved living standard the working class has achieved over the past century has bought a wide array of consumer goods. The middle class and the better-paid, unionized working class have experienced a rough equality: most own a house, a car or two, a home entertainment system; they both go to the movies and take paid vacations. To many people, it makes no difference that the money to buy these things has come from very different work environments with different degrees of power. And the fact that the middle class family will tend to have a bigger house, a fancier car, a more complex entertainment system, and a longer vacation seems like a minor point against the argument that the working class, through consumption, is essentially the same as the middle class.

Once again, class differences in power at work and in the political arena are eclipsed, lost from view in the glitter of lifestyle. If you want power and status, live like the powerful. Consumption cannot change anything in the economic power that working class people exert, of course. It can only mean the fake power of imitation and make-believe, which ultimately must be empty and unsatisfying— as so much consumption actually is.

The power of consumption is central to economic theory as well as to Madison Avenue. Every introductory economics textbook speaks of "consumer sovereignty." The idea is that all production decisions are guided by consumer desires, since producers can sell only to willing buyers in a free market. In this view, consumption is the ultimate purpose of economic activity; consumers rule the economy by expressing their desires for goods and services, which producers scramble to satisfy.

In this view, all are equal as consumers, except that some people have more money than others and so have more power in the market. It makes no difference if the consumer is a worker and got her money from a wage, or a capitalist who got her money from profits. A middle class professor, a union bus driver, and a business owner, each making $50,000 a year, have achieved equality, since the money each has is as good as the money of any of the others. Class distinctions, however real they are in the world of production, disappear from the economic analysis of markets.

The emphasis on consumption leads to one of the more common ways of measuring class: to divide the population based on income. The bottom fifth of the population are poor, the top fifth are upper middle class and rich. This leaves the middle three-fifths to form the middle class. In this way of counting, middle class people make up the majority, leaving the working class nowhere to be seen.

When the working class disappears, it leaves serious practical consequences to the disadvantage of working class people, whatever their incomes. A couple of examples will illustrate the point.

When workers go on strike, the issues at stake are often important far beyond the immediate parties to the dispute. The United Auto Workers strike at General Motors plants in Ohio in 1996, for example, was an attempt by workers there to limit GM's practice of outsourcing work to nonunion shops to cut costs. The conflict over outsourcing was central to labor-management relations throughout the country, in all kinds of industries, in the 1990s.

The strike was an important test of strength, with implications for workers and their employers everywhere. Yet news coverage often overlooked the power issues and focused instead on the effect the strike was having on consumption. Daily reports emphasized dwindling supplies of vehicles and the inconvenience the strike was imposing on consumers of new cars. Many reports focused on the strikers' high incomes, implying that they had nothing to complain about. The strike showed that even a powerful company could be humbled by workers' application of concerted force, yet these implications were lost in coverage that treated the event as consumer news.

Workers are consumers too, of course. But when our identity as consumers *takes the place of* our identity as workers, we lose something vital. For workers wanting to buy a GM vehicle, looking at the strike as a consumer instead of as a worker meant seeing the strike as a problem rather than as a source of strength in their own attempts to hold on to their jobs. A steady, consistent representation of workers as consumers undermines working class identity and weakens solidarity, to the disadvantage of workers everywhere. The weaker working people are in their confrontations with employers and with the capitalist class in the larger society, the less will they be able to improve their wages. Ironically, this in turn will undermine their ability to consume.

Another common example in which the confusion between worker and consumer plays out to the detriment of working class people has to do with the call to privatize government services. This appeal takes two forms: Why do we all have to pay for services even if we don't all use (consume) them? And why do we have to pay so much for the government services we do use?

Both questions appeal to us as consumers, with the government cast as supplier. If I go to a supermarket, no one can make me buy pears. So why should government force me to pay taxes for a public transportation system if I never ride the bus? Why should we pay for schools if we don't send our own children there? Why should I pay for someone else's retirement benefits through a social security system? Let those who use the services of government pay for them, and leave the rest of us alone.

The second complaint extends the idea that the government is just another supplier of goods and services by insisting that the government be subject to market competition. If the government wants to be in the school business, or to supply transportation, or to manage pension funds, let it compete with private firms for our business. If the government can do it cheaper, we'll buy there. If not, let the private sector do it.

In chapter 8, we will see why privatization is almost always an attack on the living standards of working class taxpayers. Here the point is that working people are called to support privatization with appeals to their identity as consumers. When this identity dominates our stance toward government, the purpose of government shrinks and the political process is trivialized into a question of consumer choice.

The idea that as consumers we can exercise control over government in ways that we cannot do as workers or as voters rests again on the idea of consumer sovereignty. But the fact is that consumers are not powerful in their relations with business in the market. Corporations decide what to produce and limit the choices we find in the market. Advertisers manipulate us psychologically in ever more sophisticated ways, as advertising uses up ever greater shares of business budgets and creative talent. Even brand names, which give the appearance of promoting competition, actually work to limit competition.

The whole idea of brands is to build loyalty to a particular product—Coca Cola, for example, so that consumers will not be tempted to buy Pepsi. When it establishes brand loyalty, the company with faithful customers faces less competition, not more. Advertising does more than manipulate our desires. Even though aggressive ads appear to be the essence of competition, they actually are designed to end competition by making us loyal to one brand and less interested in competing brands. The bewildering apparent competition among dozens of brands of cigarettes or automobiles is in fact a process by which only a handful of huge tobacco and auto companies market many brands on behalf of a single parent company.

Ideology and Politics of the Cold War

In the context of the Cold War and strident anticommunism in the decades following World War II, it was difficult to sustain a discussion of class divisions in the United States in the last half of the twentieth century. Explicit talk of the working class was widely identified with alien and enemy forces, as had also been true in the 1920s. In the years following World War II, right-wing pro-business legislators attacked union organizers, writers, and others who held on to the ideas that the working class existed, had interests in conflict with those of the capitalists, and should be organized as a class to challenge the power of capital. These "un-American" ideas were ridiculed, and those who promoted them and organized accordingly suffered complete marginalization in politics, in the country's cultural life, in academic circles, and even in unions. Class talk was just not tolerated.

This attack came in the context of the longest sustained increase in living standards for the American people, including the working class, in the history of the country. The twenty years following World War II were extraordinary, as workers, aided by a host of government programs, bought their own homes, moved to the suburbs, made more money, took longer vacations, and in general came to enjoy some of the stability that had until then been known only to the middle and capitalist classes. (The gains were not uniformly distributed, of course. Women, who had come into the workplace in "Rosie the Riveter" roles during the war, were pushed back into the home to make way for the returning men. Blacks were forcibly excluded from suburban growth, barred from owning homes in Levittown, New York, and hundreds of other new subdivisions throughout the country.)

Those who continued to talk about the working class as an important identity and potential social force seemed stuck in an earlier era. Appeals to upward mobility, middle class status, and consumerism seemed entirely natural in this new world of general prosperity, especially in comparison with the years of Depression.

In a departure from earlier times, hostility to class talk penetrated deep within the labor movement.[20] In the 1940s and 1950s, under intense pressure from congressional investigations in a hostile Cold War climate, most unions purged left-leaning organizers and officials. The craft unions of the American Federation of Labor (AFL) had never had much use for talk of broad working class interests, and remained focused only on the well-being of their own members. But the unions that were organized by industrial workers in the 1930s did have a sympathy for class struggle, enough so that in 1936 the Congress of Industrial Organizations (CIO) that housed them broke away from the AFL that had given them birth to follow a more radical and militant course. By 1955, the purge of the left from the CIO unions had gone far enough that it was possible to consolidate the two federations into one, the AFL-CIO. Although it was hailed at the time as the creation of a powerful new force for labor, the AFL-CIO steadily declined in strength for the next fifty years and more; 1955 marked the high point in the percentage of private sector workers belonging to unions.

As unions came to represent fewer and fewer workers, they grew more isolated politically. On the defensive and without a sense of themselves as part of a broader working class movement (an idea that had been largely purged with the left), union leaders spoke less and less for working people as a whole and more and more for the members of their own unions only. This played into the hands of those who wanted to further weaken and marginalize the labor movement. Unions came to be known as just another in the constellation of "special interests" seeking favors for a select few at the expense of the country as a whole. Rather than being recognized as the majority of the country, working people—in the form of their principal organizations, unions—were portrayed as a small group laying claim to the hard-earned livelihood of the broad middle class majority.

After the right wing mounted its intense attack on working class identity and class talk in general, liberal politicians in the Democratic Party—traditionally "the party of the working man"—followed suit. We will look more closely at this process in chapter 6.

In the 1960s even much of the radical left became estranged from the working class. No better symbol of this estrangement exists than the day in 1970 when construction workers beat up demonstrators who had gathered at New York's City Hall to protest the war in Vietnam as it escalated into Cambodia. Images of the City Hall beatings were broadcast around the world and became emblematic of the mutual hostility supposedly felt between all unionized workers and all student activists.

The building trades workers were also among the most hostile opponents of racial integration, another social movement of the 1960s that gave rise to a radical left. The building trades completed their hat trick of reaction at that time when opposition to the new women's movement became widely characterized by the image of the construction worker whistling and leering at women passing by. Much was made at the time of the "reactionary worker," enemy of social progress, or, from the other side, the patriotic worker, true to the American cause, standing against the communist foe.

With anticommunist leadership, the labor movement moved to the right. As class-conscious workers' voices were silenced, the simple-minded right-wing stereotypes of the working class were more easily picked up in the media and came to dominate the thinking of many young sixties student radicals. They, in turn, often came to think of themselves outside the long tradition of progressive intellectuals' support for the working class.[21]

Unions and working class people did come to the antiwar movement, well after students and college faculty initiated it. The antiwar movement came to include thousands of members of Vietnam Veterans Against the War, who were overwhelmingly working class. As the war continued, more and more unions, and more and more workers, joined the opposition. But their participation was never seen as a shift within the working class, a difference among working class people on a major question of the time. Working class people who didn't fit the stereotypes were given other identities: veterans, antiwar activists, marchers. The image of the City Hall fight continued to dominate popular representations of the working class.

The antiwar, civil rights, Black Power, and women's movements developed in the context of a history of union hostility to the needs and interests of women and minorities. Even among progressive unions and left-wing political people, some believed it would be wrong to pursue a feminist or antiracist agenda too strongly, for fear of alienating white men and splitting the working class—as though disregarding racial and gender issues didn't itself divide the working class.

These new movements of the sixties developed radical critiques of society and in their analyses often challenged capitalism itself. But for many the working class came to be identified as only reactionary white men. Activists in these movements, and those who developed social theories to understand and guide them, often dismissed the working class as a backward, hostile enemy, and recast politics solely in terms of race and gender. Radical politics of the 1970s and 1980s were increasingly dominated by identity politics.

The social movements of the sixties and seventies won important gains for women and minorities. They contributed to a deeper understanding of society and of oppression, enriching everyone's knowledge and offering all people, including the working class, valuable lessons on which to build more powerful justice movements. Yet on the campuses, despite the anticapitalist and anti-imperialist talk, the working class tended to disappear from the map, replaced in the theories of many radical opinion leaders by a combination of race and gender. This happened in one of two ways. Sometimes the working class came to mean white men. This has continued with those stuck with the image of workers on the construction sites of the sixties and seventies. Other times, in the triumvirate "race, class, and gender," class came to mean "the poor," who were in turn said to be women and minorities. In these formulations, white men are either irrelevant or the enemy, and white working class men are stripped of their legitimate standing among those who suffer wrongs in this capitalist society. This type of politics is a recipe for alienation and anger among white men, dividing the working class and creating needless hostility toward the justifiable demands of women and minorities.

Identity politics of one sort or another is nothing new in the United States. Reaching far back into the nineteenth century, as the working class grew and developed, working class identity faced competition from a host of other identities, most important among them race, nationality, craft, and religion.[22] What was potentially a source of strength—respect for each other's histories of struggle, enriching traditions, stimulating diversity—became mainly a source of division. Many a populist movement and union organizing drive has ended in defeat as a result of divisions in the working class based on other identities, especially race. But the identity politics of the last forty years has had its own particular dynamic and left its unique legacy for this time. Unlike the early years of the twentieth century, when in some cities the working class had its own newspapers, theaters, and clubs, in recent years no organized voice with any significant following has asserted working class identity alongside and intertwined with the other identities that now dominate our thinking.

Media

Representations of class and social issues in the popular media reflect and also help to create the misconceptions that erode our awareness of the working class and promote the idea of the United States as a middle class country. Even when the media report on working class people's lives, the story is usually cast in terms of middle class identity.

A typical example appeared in the *New York Times* as a feature story about the Irizarry family,[23] chosen to show that "it is difficult for many middle class families to achieve the American dream." Here is the story: Amancio Irizarry lives in the Bronx and works two jobs, at night as a janitor in one school and by day in another stocking shelves as a kitchen aide. His wife Brenda works too, as an assistant teacher in a day-care center. They have a daughter, Michelle, in community college, with a part-time job doing telephone surveys to help pay her tuition. Thirteen-year-old Amelia occasionally helps her father clean his school and sometimes sweeps the floors in her own school to earn pocket money.

The Irizarry family income from four jobs just tops $38,000 a year, two and a half times the poverty level for a family of four at the time. For all that, the story tells us, the Irizarrys have never taken a vacation together, have never owned a new car, go out to dinner at most once a year, never spend more than ten dollars for a Christmas present, and have no savings, which means they cannot come up with a down payment for a house of their own. They are, as the reporter so tellingly puts it, "on the cusp of hard times and making it," yet earning enough for John Mollenkopf, director of the Center for Urban Research at the City University of New York Graduate Center, to assure us that they are "in the solid middle." Andrew Beveridge, director of the Program in Applied Research at Queens College, CUNY, also attests to their middle class status, albeit at the "low end."

The Irizarrys have a middling income, it is true (a bit below the national median family income of $41,000 that year), but their jobs are working class. Their life circumstances are typical of the working class, not the managerial and professional middle class. When Michelle Irizarry thought about her parents' lives and her own future, she said, "I don't want to live like this the rest of my life. I feel sorry for my mother. I mean, unless they hit the Lotto, this is how it's going to be for the rest of their lives. And it's sad, to think that's it." This way of asking "Is this all there is?" is not the existential angst of a middle class intellectual. It is the worry and alarm of a young person looking at a life of unrelieved hard work for not much reward in the richest country in the world.

There is value in such a story, one that highlights the lives of working people. But the value is diminished when the characters are misidentified as middle class. We learn something about the individuals and their aspirations, but we learn nothing helpful about the society in which they, and we, make our lives. The working class disappears as a category that can help us think about workers' experience.

Political reporter Andrea Bernstein conveyed the same message in her analysis of the 2010 midterm elections. Speaking in an extended radio interview, Bernstein reported the experience and views of a "middle class voter" in Tampa, Florida, whom she described as a welder for the past forty years who had recently lost his job and then his house.[24]

Even the labor press routinely refers to workers in unions as middle class. Readers of the United Auto Workers publication *Solidarity* learned about "the economic squeeze on middle-class Americans" in a story featuring a fork lift operator, a warehouse worker, and members of a local representing machine operators and metalworkers. The article defines the middle class "loosely" as "families with good jobs that allow them to have health insurance, own a home, send their children to college and save for retirement." But "these things are getting out of reach for working Americans," who are being squeezed to the point that they "live paycheck to paycheck," don't eat out or take vacations, and worry about the debt their children accumulate when going to college.[25]

Union leaders often proudly claim that the union has brought its members into the middle class, referring to gains in income and benefits and greater respect at work that come from union representation. Resisting rollbacks of previous gains, union leaders often declare that they are trying to save the middle class, their members and others like the autoworkers of the previous paragraph. But unionized workers are still workers—except that through collective strength they are workers who live better than they could without the union.

The mainstream media can display sympathy for individual workers and their families. But when it comes to working people as a whole, it's another story. Organizations of working people, especially unions, are systematically ignored or attacked. Hostility to organized labor permeates every part of the mass media: newspapers and magazines, film, television.[26] The media attack on workers has not been the work of conservative political forces alone. In a process paralleling the retreat from the working class by sixties radicals, liberal media personalities have also stereotyped or abandoned workers. The television show that most lampooned the working class in the 1970s and 1980s was produced by Norman Lear and starred Carroll O'Connor, both active and influential in liberal political circles. *All in the Family*'s Archie Bunker was the worker as reactionary white male, disrespecting his wife and opposing the antiwar, antiracist ideas of his son-in-law, whom he called Meathead. Although Meathead was from a working class family, he was never presented as another way for us to think about *workers*. He had progressive ideas; he became a student. Archie's buffoonery gave him a certain charm, perhaps, but in the popular culture of the time he served as a means to dismiss the working class as a serious or reasonable force.[27]

It will not be a simple matter to turn around the media bias against labor. The major television networks are owned by Fortune 500 conglomerates whose executives have an interest in downplaying workers' sense of themselves as workers. These executives are in a position to skew not only entertainment but the news we see. And they do.[28] Corporations and unions are treated very differently by the media. Public television was created in 1970 to allow for broadcasting free from commercial pressures and interests, but in 1997 the executives at PBS decided that any program dealing with working people that is produced with substantial funding by unions will be treated as a special interest piece, not suitable for broadcast.[29] Yet Kaiser, one of the leading corporate operators of health maintenance organizations in the United States, began in 1998 to sponsor health coverage within the nightly *PBS News Hour,* and Wall Street firms sponsor a number of programs for business news and analysis.[30]

PBS News Hour is prominently sponsored by Archer Daniels Midland, "supermarket to the world." In 1996, ADM paid a fine of $100 million to settle a suit brought by the federal government for illegal price-fixing that cost consumers millions of dollars in higher food prices. In mid-1998, three top executives of ADM were facing personal trials on federal criminal charges related to the case.[31]

Yet the sponsorship continued, associating ADM in the public mind with objectivity and public service. By contrast, and to get a flavor of the double standard applied to public TV sponsorship, think how strange it would be to have *PBS News Hour* prominently sponsored by the International Brotherhood of Teamsters, and how impossible it would have been to continue such a connection after a money-laundering scheme was uncovered in the 1996 Teamsters internal election campaign, resulting in the resignation of the union's president.

The newspapers, television, and Internet news sites may occasionally run a human interest story on the life of a particular working family in hard times. But rarely do they attempt any analysis of what these stories tell us beyond the individuals shown. Workers are seen, when they are seen at all, as faces in a crowd or in sound bites, rarely as people with thoughtful things to say about their condition and their country. In the media, the working class is truly the silenced majority.

Working Class Identity Survives

Given all the ways in which working class identity tends to be denied and displaced, it is perhaps amazing that working class identity continues to be widespread in the United States. As recently as 1996, a majority of Americans responding to a *New York Times* poll identified themselves as members of the working class rather than the middle class.[32]

This survey gave people four choices in response to the question "What class are you?" People could choose upper class, middle class, working class, or lower class. Fifty-five percent said working class. Thirty-seven percent said middle class, 6 percent lower class, and 2 percent upper class. This is remarkably close to the actual class composition of the labor force that I showed in chapter 1.

In the prosperity following World War II, *Fortune* magazine cheered the arrival of middle class America and the end of the working class by citing poll results in which the vast majority of people identified themselves as "middle class" when offered the choices "upper class, middle class, and lower class." Challenging this conclusion in 1949, sociologist Richard Centers introduced "working class" as a survey choice and dramatically changed the results.[33] Most "middle class" people identified themselves as working class when they had the choice. And this is still happening.

In another recent survey, when the choice was limited to a face-off between "middle class" and "working class," the result was 53 percent working class, 45 percent middle class (and 2 percent no opinion).[34] Researchers at the University of Chicago have consistently found over the past twenty years that, when offered "working class" as a possible identity, along with "middle class," "rich," and "poor," about 45 percent of people think of themselves as working class, the same fraction as middle class. Not surprisingly, in the early 1970s, when this survey question was introduced, working class identity was even stronger.[35]

Other findings go further to show that identities other than class have less influence than one might suppose given the conventional wisdom on class and identity politics. Within the African American population, appeals to racial identity are significantly more accepted among middle class blacks than among working class blacks.[36] Black workers know they are black, of course. But there is no indication that black workers are less inclined to working class identity than are white workers. In the poll just cited, 51 percent of white respondents, but 71 percent of black respondents, identified themselves as working class. Unpublished details from the *New York Times* poll also show that blacks more closely identify with the working class than do whites, even though the majority of both groups say they are in the working class.[37]

The effect of income on class identity is also less than one might imagine, given the emphasis so often placed on income as the basis of class. Men with working class occupations making relatively high, "middle class" incomes tend to continue to think of themselves as working class. On the other hand, relatively low-income managers tend to identify themselves as middle class.[38] Even life in the suburbs doesn't erase working class identity. Living in the suburbs, as opposed to cities, has a small effect on workers' perception of themselves as members of the working class.[39]

Despite four powerful factors operating against it, working class identity has managed to sustain itself in at least some minimal way quite broadly in the United States, an indication, perhaps, of a gulf between mainstream "opinion makers" in the media, universities, and politics on the one hand, and the working class majority on the other. Workers do not view working class identity as a foreign concept or something limited to some marginal radicals.

Just what workers *mean* by "working class," who beyond themselves they include in it, and how closely they associate their lives and chances with others they put in the working class: these are complicated issues and little seems to be known about them. We will return to these questions when we consider the prospects for a working class politics in the United States. For the moment, we can conclude that talking about class as we go further into the twenty-first century is not a recipe for social isolation. On the contrary: most people have a pretty good sense of who they are and where they stand in the larger society. Class talk can strike a chord among working class people.

WHY IS CLASS IMPORTANT?

I can think of at least four reasons why it is important to understand that the majority of people in the United States are working class. First and foremost, quite simply, it is true. From this, all other benefits of class analysis flow. Any study of society that hopes to capture what is going on in the world must approach its subject with categories that reflect reality. Any plan of action that hopes to influence events must be rooted in reality.

Beyond this, we will look at three consequences of looking at the world through the lens of class: its contribution to the basic dignity of working people; the insights it sheds on important economic issues, including wages and the distributions of income and wealth; and the clarity it brings to the way power works in our society. Let's look at each of these in turn.

Dignity

When society fails to acknowledge the existence and experience of working people it robs them of an articulate sense of themselves and their place in society. We know from the vibrancy of other identity movements that to silence and leave nameless a central aspect of people's identity is to strip them of a measure of power over their lives. A full, realistic self-identity is a basic requirement for human dignity.

The importance of dignity should not be underestimated. When I was growing up in Detroit, the autoworkers would sometimes go out on strike. One local newspaper would immediately begin to print a daily front-page chart showing the amount of pay the strikers were losing and how much of a raise they would have to get to make up the loss over the life of the contract. It didn't take long before the losses could not be made up. But, for the workers involved, the issues of the strike could not be reduced to a straight financial accounting; the newspaper's approach missed the point and had little influence among the strikers. Pay was important, but the strike was really an insistence that the company treat the workers with respect for the work they did and for their humanity. Similarly, almost every union organizing drive revolves around dignity and the many ways employers rob their workers of it.

During the last half of the nineteenth century and the first half of the twentieth, the United States had a vibrant working class culture: theater, magazines, and a whole literary world dedicated to working class life. Working class newspapers with broad circulation addressed all questions of society. Working class social clubs and political parties brought working people together. All these helped define their lives and assert their interests.

Most of these independent institutions are gone, and with them, the identity of working people has also suffered eclipse. A resurrection of working class social, political, and cultural life, proudly defined as such, would contribute to the strengthening again of working people's sense of dignity, as well as increasing the power and authority of working people in the larger society.

Understanding the Economy

Another reason to acknowledge class distinctions has to do with the power of class analysis to help us understand what is happening in the economy. Through the rest of this book, I will show what this means for a number of issues. Here, let's consider three widely reported developments of the last forty years and see how our understanding of them changes when we look at them through the lens of class: the widespread decline in real wages, and the increasing inequality in the distributions of income and of wealth.

Back in 1983, Jim Ramey earned $11.83 an hour assembling ATM machines at the Diebold Corporation in Canton, Ohio. By 1996, his hourly pay had dropped to $9.93—in 1996 dollars.[1] He was not alone.

Weekly earnings haven't increased since the 1970s, except for an occasional up followed by another down. The median weekly wage (the point at which half make more and half less) for all full-time wage and salary workers in 1979 was $335 (in inflation-adjusted 1982–1984 dollars). It was $337 in the first quarter of 2011. In the first decade of the twenty-first century, when unemployment was—until 2008—relatively low, wages averaged $336 per week in 1982–1984 dollars.[2]

Through the last quarter of the twentieth century and through the beginning of the twenty-first, family incomes increased only because the number of wage earners in the average family increased, especially for families with children at home. By 1992, 57 percent of all families had two or more wage earners, while three out of four married-couple families with children at home had both parents working. In 1972, that had been true for only half of such families. Between 1972 and 1992, the percentage of "traditional families" (Dad working, Mom at home with the kids) fell from 23 percent of all U.S. families to 9 percent.[3] Since the 1990s, the fraction of women in the labor force has fluctuated closely around 59 percent, where it was in 2011, having risen from 44 percent in 1972.[4] By 2010, the fraction of "traditional families" had also not changed much since 1992.[5]

For most working people, life has gotten harder. Families are working longer hours and have less time for one another. Parents can't be home for the children. Stress levels are high. On top of falling incomes and extra jobs, companies making record profits keep laying off more workers. Increasingly, working people feel that no one is safe in their jobs, no matter how hard they work or how much they contribute to the success of their company. Economic insecurity permeates life for tens of millions of people, more than at any time since the Great Depression three generations ago. The recession following the financial crisis of 2008 officially ended in mid-2009, after which business profits rebounded to record levels. But unemployment remained above 9.5 percent for another year, home foreclosures continued for millions of working people, and the pain of widespread economic suffering contributed to the defeat of many Democratic Party candidates in the 2010 elections.

In March 2011, there were 26.2 million part-time workers in the United States, with over 8 million involuntarily working reduced hours because they were unable to secure full-time employment, or their employers had cut back on hours.[6] Even those who prefer to work part-time pay a heavy price. In 2007, almost 94 percent of part-time workers earned less per hour than their full-time counterparts.[7] In 2010, 14 percent of part-time employees participated in some form of health insurance plan, compared to 67 percent of full-time employees. Seventy-nine percent of full-time workers had paid sick leave but only 28 percent of part-time employees. Eighty-six percent of full-time workers had paid vacations but only 36 percent of those working part-time.[8] As employers have moved increasingly to part-time work forces, the conditions of millions of working people have deteriorated.

To help maintain living standards during the period of declining real income, Americans resorted to debt. From the mid-1970s until the financial crisis of 2008, personal debt rose steadily as a percentage of disposable income (income after taxes). The Federal Reserve reports that most of the increase was in home mortgage debt, but installment and credit card debt rose from 17.5 percent of disposable income in 1975 to 21 percent in 2010.[9] The increase in household debt that fueled personal consumption in the 1990s and the beginning of the twenty-first century, and also fueled the housing bubble, was unsustainable. It contributed to the 2008 collapse and painfully slow recovery from it, as consumers grappled with the loss of jobs, income, and homes, as well as the end of easy credit.

The broad decline in living standards has been well reported, but not in terms of working class experience. A typical example, still relevant to the political language common in 2011, was a 1998 *New York Times* story under the headline "The Middle Class: Winning in Politics, Losing in Life."[10] The article talked mostly about workers, but not at all about the working class. As usual, class was reported in terms of income alone, and workers were said to be in the middle class, the middle three-fifths of the income distribution. The middle class is "winning in politics," according to the writer, because everyone from Newt Gingrich to President Clinton was trying to help them with "middle class tax cuts," but they were "losing in life" because their earnings were down.

The fall in real wages has occurred in spite of continuing increases in output and productivity (output per hour of work). Figure 1 presents a dramatic picture: The top line shows increases in output per worker hour, a measure of productivity. The lower line shows what happened to average hourly earnings for production and nonsupervisory workers in the nonfarm business economy, adjusted for inflation.

After World War II, workers shared in the growing wealth. Until 1972, workers' wages increased about as fast as productivity did. But since 1972, as Figure 1 shows, wages have fallen even though productivity and output have continued to rise.[11] Workers have been producing more but getting less.

Even taking benefits into account doesn't change that fact. As real wages began to decline in the 1970s, workers traded lost wages for employer contributions to pension, health, and other benefits so that for a few more years total compensation (wages plus the cost of benefits paid by the employer) continued to keep up with productivity. But by the early 1980s even total compensation began to decline as productivity continued to go up. The gap has widened ever since.[12]

In the last half of the 1990s, real wages (wages adjusted for inflation) began to rise again. By 1999, the strong labor market and the increase in the minimum wage finally brought up the incomes of the bottom 20 percent.[13] The improvement led many to believe good times were back. But it wasn't until 1998 that real weekly earnings returned to the level of 1989 for the average worker, who is still far away from the peak earnings of the early 1970s. Through the first decade of the new century, real wages continued to stagnate for most workers

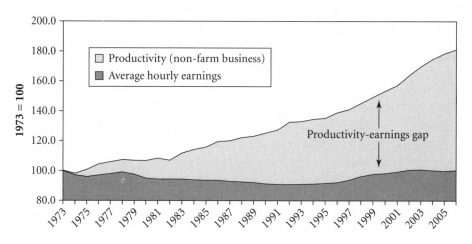

FIGURE 1.   Workers stopped sharing economic growth after 1972.
Source: Dean Baker, *The Productivity to Paycheck Gap: What the Data Show,* Center for Economic and Policy Research, April 2007, Table 1

as productivity continued to grow. Workers are far from regaining their historic share of total output.*

Where did the increased income and wealth go? The stark picture of workers unable to benefit from their own increased productivity has another side: spectacular increases in corporate profits, and income and wealth for capitalists and for those most closely associated with them in business dealings.

Changes in the Distribution of Income

Between 1980 and 2008, production of all goods and services in the United States increased 126 percent (after correcting for inflation). You might think, therefore,

---

*It may seem that at times when both productivity and wages are increasing by the same percentage, workers are getting the whole increase in their output. But this is not the case, because output is always divided between workers and capitalists. To see this, suppose that total output is 100 and workers get 70 while capitalists get 30. Now suppose that output increases by 10 percent, to 110. If wages go up 10 percent, too, then out of the 10 units of increased output workers will get 7 more (not 10 more), and the capitalists will get 3 more. The new, larger output will be divided 77 to 33, and the share of the total going to workers will remain unchanged. But if workers do not get a raise to match their increase in productivity, the distribution of income will change. Suppose workers get a raise of only 5 instead of 7. Their income will rise to 75, which is a smaller share of the 110 total than they had before, while the capitalists will get 35, an increase in their share. In other words, workers can receive a smaller share of total income even if their wages are going up, if the wage increases don't match productivity gains. Between 1972 and 1996, as productivity and output went up, workers' wages actually went down, which corresponded to the dramatic changes in distribution of income in the period. In the strong labor markets of 1997 to 1999, this trend ended, at least temporarily, as real wages sometimes increased more quickly than productivity.

that the average person improved his or her living standards by something close to that amount. But it didn't happen. That's because the increased income from production was distributed very unevenly. The average household of the top 1 percent of earners saw its income increase 281 percent (after adjusting for inflation) between 1979 and 2007, from $347,000 in 1979 to $1.3 million in 2007. Those who fell into the middle quintile (the 20 percent of all earners who fell in the middle of the income distribution) had their income go up 25 percent over the same period (far less than the increase in production), from $44,100 to $55,400. The poorest 20 percent of income earners saw even more modest gains. They went from an annual income in 1979 of $15,300 to $17,700 or 16 percent (all figures are in 2007 dollars).[14]

Contrary to myth, it's not that low-income people weren't working hard. The poorest fifth of the population worked 4.6 percent more in 1989 than at the beginning of the go-go eighties decade, but they got 4.1 percent less for their efforts.[15] A Miller beer ad in the late eighties promised "more taste, less filling" to people whose life experience was "more work, less money."

The distribution of income in the United States has become steadily more unequal since 1968, and especially after 1980. Economists commonly divide the population into five layers based on income: the highest-earning 20 percent, the next-highest 20 percent, and so on (these are called "quintiles"). Figure 2 shows the share of total income (not counting capital gains) that went to each 20 percent layer of U.S. households in 1968 when the distribution of income was the least unequal of any year since World War II, in 1992 just before President Clinton came into office, in 1997, and in 2009, the latest year for which information is available[16]

Compared with 1968, every layer of the population has lost ground except the top. In 1968, the poorest 20 percent of the population (in 2009 dollars this would be households with income of less than $20,453) received 4.2 percent of all income. But by 2009 their share had fallen to just 3.4 percent. This amounted to a 19 percent decline in their share. The next 20 percent layer (with an average annual income of $29,257 in 2009) experienced the greatest decline, their share falling by 23 percent (from 11.1 percent of all income in 1968 to 8.6 percent in 2009). In every case, the trend to greater inequality that characterized the Reagan and George H. W. Bush years continued and even accelerated during the Clinton, George W. Bush, and early Obama presidencies. Even the next-to-highest quintile (average household income $78,694 in 2009) lost ground. It's only when we come to the top 20 percent (average household income of $170,844 in 2009) that their share of income has increased, by 18 percent between 1968 and 2009.

The increase is more dramatic the higher up the income scale you go. We've seen that the top 1 percent increased their incomes by 281 percent between 1979 and 2007. But the top one-hundredth of 1 percent (0.01 percent), fewer than fifteen thousand households making at least $11.5 million in 2007, took home 6 percent of all U.S. income (including capital gains), their highest share since such records began in 1913.[17] It's especially at the top layers of the elite that we find the people who have made out like bandits during this period. But who are all the people in these quintiles?

I explained in chapter 1 that class is not based on income. But income has a great deal to do with class. I have used occupation as a way to approximate the real determinant of class: power. But occupation tells us about more than power. In general, the more authority and power, the higher the income the occupation carries. So while income doesn't determine class, class is strongly related to income.

Not every worker earns less than every middle class professional or small business owner. Some workers in skilled, unionized jobs who work a lot of overtime can earn $100,000 a year, placing them in the top 10 percent of incomes. But they are few and far between. For the most part, workers make less than the middle class, and those in the capitalist class have incomes higher than those who work for them, whether as workers or as professionals and managers.

The working class is 63 percent of the labor force. The bottom 60 percent of the income distribution certainly contains some middle class managers and professionals. And the next-to-highest 20 percent of the income distribution, and even the top

FIGURE 2.   The rich got richer and everyone else got poorer. Percent shares of income, 1968–2009.

Source: Income, Poverty, and Health Insurance Coverage in the United States, 2009, U.S. Bureau of the Census, Series P-60, no. 238, September 2010, Table A2

quintile, includes some workers. But the fact that the bottom 60 percent and more of households in the United States lost ground relative to the top tells us a great deal about the experience of the working class, just as the gains at the top reflect the experience of the capitalist class and of those in the middle class most closely tied to their fortunes as high-level managers, lawyers, and other professionals.

In other words, the dramatic shifts in income distribution have not been, as so often reported, simply a case of the rich getting richer while the middle class suffers. The changes in income distribution have been gains by capitalists and those closely associated with them, on the one hand, at the expense of the working class, on the other. Not every capitalist made a fortune, of course. But most workers have lost ground. Some unionized workers have managed to stay even or make modest gains, but millions of union jobs have been wiped out and the percentage of workers covered by union contracts has fallen. As union power has declined, millions of workers, union and nonunion, have been forced to take wage cuts, whether in their contracts or simply by decree of the boss.

The experience of the middle class has been decidedly mixed. Some professionals, lower-level managers, and small business owners have lost ground. These tend to be people more closely associated with the working class—social workers, teachers, store owners in working class neighborhoods, community college faculty. Others have prospered dramatically—corporate lawyers, sophisticated tax accountants, professionals in the financial industry, people closely involved in the maneuverings that have brought vast fortunes to those at the very top.

Social critic Barbara Ehrenreich has described the political conflicts that characterize the middle class because of its position in society. She writes: "[T]here is not, ultimately, an objective answer to the question of whether the middle class is an elite or something less exalted—an extension, perhaps, of the working class. And hence there is no easy answer to the much harder question of whether it is 'naturally' inclined to the left or to the right. Is the middle class, by nature, generous or selfish? Overindulged or aggrieved? Committed to equality or protective of privilege? These are not only possible answers, but *choices* to be made."[18]

For members of the middle class, these choices will depend largely on whether their connections and identifications are more with labor or with capital.

Since the early 1980s, one especially galling sign of the growing inequality is the explosion in executive compensation. In the year Ronald Reagan was elected, *Business Week* reported that the average large-corporation CEO was paid 42 times an average factory worker's wage. By 1995, the ratio had risen to 141 to 1: $3.75 million for the CEO and $26,652 for the worker. And that counts only direct compensation, not income from investments. Executive pay continued to explode during the Clinton years, so that by 1998, the CEO earned 419 times the pay of the average blue-collar worker.[19] In other words, if in 1994 workers making

$25,000 a year had gotten this rate of pay increase, in 1998 they would have been making $138,350. Instead, by then the average big-time CEO was making more in a day than the average worker made in a year.

This is the kind of thing that gets people mad. While Jim Ramey's pay at Diebold in Ohio was going down, and the company laid off hundreds of workers, Robert Mahoney, Diebold's CEO, was doing fine. He pulled down $2.37 million in 1995, up from $464,250 in 1990. Mr. Ramey didn't like it. "I begrudge Mahoney his big salary. I begrudge his bonuses when workers are hurting." But the Diebold board had other concerns. They gave Mahoney and other top executives these huge raises to keep up with increases in executive pay at competing companies.[20] Into the early Obama years, the same mismatch between stunning and still rising executive compensation at the top and lower wages, unemployment, and foreclosure for working people continued with no sign of letting up.

It doesn't have to be this way. U.S. executives are the highest paid and lowest taxed of any in the industrial world.[21] And, more generally, income is distributed far more unequally in the United States than in any other industrial country.[22]

Changes in the Distribution of Wealth

So far, we have been looking at income: what people make in a year. Personal wealth is something different: the value of money and other assets someone has managed to accumulate up to a given point in time. A person who makes $50,000 a year in income may have some wealth in the form of savings, or accumulations in a 401K plan, or equity in a house. The components of wealth are valued on a balance sheet reflecting the situation on a specific date, like December 31 of a given year. Many people who have incomes have no wealth, especially low-income people. People at higher levels of income tend to have more wealth, and their wealth is in a greater variety of assets, such as real estate and corporate bonds.

Wealth is distributed even more unequally than income. People with low incomes spend all they get and have very little in assets. Those with wealth tend to be people with higher incomes, so as income has become more unequally distributed, it is not surprising that wealth, too, has become even more concentrated in the hands of a relative few.

In the words of one headline, "Rich Control More of U.S. Wealth, Study Says, as Debts Grow for Poor."[23] Although the article dates from 1996, the story continues. In 2007, the wealthiest 10 percent of households (as measured by net worth— the value of all assets, less all debts) owned 73.1 percent of household wealth, up from 68.2 percent in 1983. If we subtract personal homes from this account to look only at business and financial assets, the top 10 percent owned 82.9 percent of the nation's nonhome personal wealth in 2007, up from 80.3 percent in 1983. In dollar terms, in 1983 the wealthiest 1 percent of Americans had an average net worth of $9.1 million (adjusted for inflation to 2007 dollars). By 2007, the average had more than doubled to $18.5 million.

Meanwhile, the bottom 40 percent of households saw their average net worth (including homes) fall by 62 percent, from $5,900 to $2,200. Their indebtedness excluding homes increased by 160 percent, to $10,500 in 2007, as people scrambled to make ends meet and sustain their consumption on an average income of $20,200 a year (in 2006).[24]

Between 1983 and 2007, after adjusting for inflation, the top 1 percent of households received about one-third of all new net worth, the next 4 percent gained another third of newly created wealth, and the rest of the top quintile (15 percent of all households) gained about 20 percent of new wealth. In other words, the top 20 percent of wealth holders gained about 89 percent of wealth created between 1983 and 2007. The remaining 80 percent of households gained just 11 percent.[25]

Excluding personal residences to look only at moneymaking assets—stocks, bonds, real estate, and business assets—the top 1 percent of Americans own many times more than the bottom 90 percent put together. For example, in 2007 the wealthiest 1 percent of households owned 49.7 percent of all individually owned income-producing assets, four times the amount (12.2 percent) owned by the bottom 90 percent.

The greatest disparities in asset ownership are in financial securities and business equity. In 2007, the wealthiest 1 percent owned 62.4 percent of business equity (remember that there are over fifteen million individual businesses in the United States), while the bottom 90 percent of Americans heldz just 6.7 percent. At the same time, the top 1 percent of Americans owned 60.6 percent of financial securities, compared with just 1.5 percent owned by the bottom 90 percent. [26]

As in so many areas of life, wealth and income are different for blacks compared with whites. In 1982, median non-Hispanic black income was 56 percent the level of non-Hispanic whites. The ratio had climbed to 60 percent by 2006. When we consider net worth, median levels in the non-Hispanic black community fell from 7 to 6 percent of non-Hispanic white levels in this period: $91,000 for whites, compared with $6,000 for blacks. A similar picture emerges when comparing non-Hispanic whites with Hispanics. These inequalities expanded further into 2009, when median wealth of Hispanic households had fallen by 66 percent since 2005, while black median household wealth dropped by 53 percent and that of white households by 16 percent. [27]

Even within the top 1 percent, wealth is concentrated among the most rich, the top half of 1 percent of the population. This is the part of the population with names like Rockefeller, Gates, Kennedy, Carnegie, Mellon, and a few thousand others who seldom make it into the news. If we look at the business assets owned in 1992 just by the top 1 percent, 85 percent of them are in the hands of the top half of that 1 percent. The same for stock: half of the top 1 percent of households in 1992 owned 72 percent of the stock owned by that 1 percent.[28]

Given the market reports every half hour on all-news radio and the daily price movements featured on every nightly TV news show, one would think that stocks were important to almost everyone. Without question, stock ownership is more widespread now than it was forty years ago, before financial deregulation and the spread of Keogh and 401(k) plans. But the skyrocketing stock prices of the 1990s left 60 percent of the population entirely untouched in their personal finances. Working class people do own scattered shares of stock and mutual funds, but this hardly amounts to "people's capitalism." In 2007, the top 1 percent of households owned 38.3 percent of all individually owned stock (stock not owned by corporations), more than four times the amount owned (8.9 percent) by the bottom 80 percent. But not everyone owns stock. In 2007, 51 percent of U.S. households owned no stock. In the bottom 80 percent of American asset holders, 40 percent owned stock. In the bottom quintile stock ownership was only slightly more than 15 percent.[29]

The business press occasionally lets us know whom they consider to be the little guy, the "everyman" involved in the market. In a story about the stock market turmoil of August 1998, the *New York Times* reported that the flighty actions of institutional investors were being tempered by the steady confidence of the "small investor." The article tells us that a small investor is someone who trades fewer than ten thousand shares at a time![30]

When the market had recovered and was reaching new highs in the spring of 1999, the *Wall Street Journal* also focused on the growing role played by individuals. Without explicitly mentioning class, of course, the story acknowledged that 60 percent of the population owned no stock whatsoever, but that "ordinary people" were more deeply involved than ever. Who were the ordinary people described? They were high-level corporate executives and investment managers, Washington lawyers and lobbyists, a senior U.S. marshal, and a fitness trainer for the wealthy—"ordinary" only among the readers of the *Wall Street Journal.* The one working class person in the story, a cafeteria cook who was standing in line at the Department of Motor Vehicles, owned no stock. She expressed some annoyance at the airs some people put on with their new wealth. "It's not like people earned all that stock market money. It, like, happened while they slept."[31]

Working class people often do have personal assets in a house and car and some savings. This is especially true at middle age, in peak earning years, before major health and retirement expenses begin. But even paid-off houses are now being remortgaged in ever greater numbers to pay the expenses of the elderly, eating up the most common form of working class asset.

By the time workers die, there is usually nothing left. We can get a sense of this by looking at the number of households who receive inheritances. In 1993, 90 percent of Hispanic households with a person aged 51–61 had received no financial inheritance. For blacks, it was 89 percent; for whites, it was 66 percent.[32]

Except for rare cases where parents disinherit their children, lack of inheritance means either that both parents have not yet died, or that they died but had nothing left to pass on. Taking into account different life expectancies at different incomes (people with lower incomes die younger), and factoring in the proportion of people who are white, black, and Hispanic, I calculate that about 45 percent of the population receives no financial inheritance from their parents. Most of these people are in lower-income families, part of the 63 percent of the population who are the working class.

In other words, well over half of American working class families have nothing left to give when the last parent dies. Maybe they were able to help their kids buy a car or some furniture or contribute to a down payment on a house when they were in their prime earning years. But these days, with real wages down, that basically just allows the kids to get by. The sad fact is that after a lifetime of work, most working class people have no assets left to show for it, only their kids to take their place.

In the last decades of the twentieth century, then, production and worker productivity continued their historic climb. But real wages for working class people fell, and both income and wealth shifted away from workers to capitalists. Income and wealth are now more concentrated at the top than at any time since before the Great Depression. These experiences show starkly that economic growth alone is no guarantee of a more prosperous country for all. In a world with such differences in class power, a rising tide does not lift all boats. To switch metaphors, it is not enough just to make a larger pie. We have to ask, who gets to eat it? And that's a question of power.

Understanding Power

Beyond economic issues, analyzing class allows us a better understanding of power. The economic trends just discussed reflect shifts in the relative power of workers and their bosses, labor and capital, both at work and in the political process.

Although most people do not look at social issues in class terms, many business leaders have a keen appreciation of the matter. As we will see in more detail in chapter 9, for forty years they have mounted a deliberate and public attack on working class wages and power, by 2011 reaching a point where democracy itself seemed threatened by the extreme and accelerating imbalances of class power in the United States. While working and middle class people have been disregarding class, others have been astutely conducting class struggle—on behalf of capitalists.

Since the 1970s, employers have argued continuously that workers get paid too much, that unions put too many restrictions on management (either directly or through their influence in politics), that workers have to give up past gains to help business regain competitiveness. Politicians complain that labor is a "special interest" that threatens the middle class. Any talk of the working class and class conflict is considered a ridiculous throwback to outworn dogma. These assertions are all direct attacks on labor by capital. It is class struggle, but only one side seems to know it.

In fact, the long decline in working class living standards coincides with the gradual and now almost total avoidance of the working class as a subject of public discussion. As part of the attack on labor, the working class has been disappeared. As part of a renewed and vigorous defense of labor, the working class must reappear.

My insistence on identifying a working class is not a word game. It is not just a matter of semantics to say that workers are in the working class, not the middle class. It is a question of power.

To exercise power, you need to know who you are. You also need to know who your adversary is, the target in the conflict. When the working class disappears into the middle class, workers lose a vital piece of their identity. In political, social, and cultural terms, they don't know who they are any more. To make matters worse, they also lose a sense of the enemy, as the capitalist class vanishes among "the rich." As the capitalist class disappears from view, the target of struggle disappears, too.

Rich people are not the problem working and middle class people face. Real wages haven't fallen, unions aren't weaker, multiple wage earners aren't a necessity in almost every working class household because Derek Jeter and 50 Cent are rich. If we look at the movie stars, big-name athletes, and musicians among the rich (although they are hardly typical of the rich or of all actors, athletes, and musicians), we find that most of them are rich because, through their talent and work, they have made other people even richer—the team owners, the owners of studios and recording companies, in short, the *capitalists* among the rich. (Of course, some of these stars become capitalists themselves.) Thinking of class in terms of "rich, middle, and poor" or "upper, middle, and lower" wipes out this vital distinction.

Capitalists tend to be rich, yes, but more important is the fact that they are capitalists. When Vice President Dick Cheney assembled a task force to formulate the Bush administration's energy policy in early 2001, its members were rich, but the real point was that they were mostly top executives of major oil, gas, and mining companies.

When the capitalist class disappears, the middle class, and particularly workers, who are thought to be middle class, seem to confront…whom? The rich? It is relatively easy to trivialize and ridicule class politics when it appears to be a knee-jerk attack on the rich. Not least, this is because most people would like to become rich themselves, to live the good life with ease. To attack the rich is to attack what many hope for in their own futures. It seems to rob people of their aspirations.

Thinking about class in a more appropriate way helps clarify the proper target of struggle. Economic problems arise not because some people are rich but because private profit and the power of capital are the highest priorities in the economic system.* As history and current experience show us, the pursuit of profit leads too many business owners to too easily abuse workers, ruin the environment, and corrupt the political process. Economic problems come from the economic system, and the structure of power within it, that favors one class and disfavors others. Too few people have too much power over culture, education, the economy, and the institutions that affect the life chances of us all. Beyond economic problems, the concentration of power in the high citadels of the capitalist class is a serious threat to political democracy.

With the disappearance of the terms "capitalist" and "working class" from public discussion, politics in the late twentieth and early twenty-first century has meant the substitution of a host of other targets for the wrath of working and middle class people. As the capitalists disappeared, we saw poor people, immigrants, foreigners, the government, and even the workers themselves and their unions proposed as targets for our anger. Even when "Wall Street" earned villain status after the 2008 crisis, the term referred almost exclusively to the financial sector, and then mainly to greedy individuals among the executives. Even so, by 2011 no executive of a major bank, investment house, hedge fund, or other financial institution had gone to jail for his or her role in creating the frauds and deceptions that sent the lives of millions of people into ruin as a result of the crisis. The results have been bad for workers, good for capitalists.

The potential forms and content of a *class* politics are the subject of the last chapters of this book. Leading up to that discussion, we will look at what happens

---

*Being and aspiring to be "rich" do present serious problems in regard to the environment. Unlimited consumption, especially in the rich countries, places an unbearable load on the environment over time. While capitalists will oppose efforts to limit their markets, controlling consumption to sustainable levels is a requirement that challenges all people.

when politics and social policy take on the false targets that politicians and opinion leaders have presented to the American public. We will see that confusion about issues of class has led to greater gains for the capitalists, mixed results for the middle class, and more problems for the working class. Clarity about class will help to reverse these developments.

LOOKING AT THE "UNDERCLASS"

The "angry white guy" is something of a cliché in American politics, a cartoon representation of the working class person as anyone from camouflaged militiaman to hard-hat Reagan Democrat to Tea Party activist. The angry white guy is mad at people on welfare, foreigners, the government. The angry white guy is mad at gay people and resents women and minorities who have improved their social standing in the past forty years. Like any good cartoon character, the angry white guy is alternately scary, righteous, ludicrous.

And, like any good cartoon character, he also reflects something real. Tens of millions of white guys have plenty to be angry about (although some of them have been happily laughing all the way to the bank). Lower wages, fewer chances, less time for family, demeaning culture, alienating politics: it really is enough to get a person angry, not just white men. The economic, social, cultural, and political suffering of the last quarter of the twentieth century and first decade of the twenty-first knew no bounds of race, gender, ethnicity, sexual orientation, creed, or geography.

Anger needs a target. Hope needs a way out. As the conditions of working class life have become harder, a crueler politics has come to prevail. Anger has been focused on the poor, and people on welfare in particular. In the years following the welfare reform legislation of 1996 that ended Aid to Families with Dependent Children (AFDC), replacing it with Temporary Assistance for Needy Families (TANF), poor people and the very existence of poverty have largely faded from public discussions. Instead, anger has been directed at a new target: foreigners, whether immigrants in the United States or cheap foreign labor abroad. And anger has been heaped upon government agencies at all levels.

Whatever hope arose with the prospect of punishing, banishing, or shrinking these targets has proven false and empty. No one's life is better because fewer people are on welfare, immigrants can't get medical treatment, and government services are cut to get the federal and state budgets closer to balance. Our children do not have a brighter future because our anger has found these targets, provided to us by opinion makers and political leaders. The opposite is true. In each case, the way the problem has been defined and then "solved" has brought more difficulty into the lives of working people, not less. Meanwhile, with each attack on the wrong target, capitalists have gained more freedom, more power, more resources, within the United States and around the world. We need to get a sense of how class politics has been operating without our being aware of it.

The Poor as Real People

Even though poverty has largely disappeared from public acknowledgment in recent years, poor people have not disappeared. Poverty rates fell in the strong economy of the late 1990s to 11.3 percent of the population in 2000, then rose and remained around 12.5 percent of the population after 2001, until increasing sharply to 14.3 percent by 2009 in the wake of the economic crisis.[1]

The passage of "welfare reform" generally ended the utility of the poor as a target of public anger and, by extension, a subject for political campaigns.[2] Increasingly, immigrants have taken the place of the poor in this role. Before considering attitudes toward immigrants, though, it is important to recall that poverty remains an acute and growing problem in the United States. This should command our continuing attention, and we should remember that poor people can easily reappear as targets of anger in the midst of widespread economic hardship.

After years of neglect, for example, poor people and those who cater to them returned as villains in some explanations of the financial crisis of 2008. Deflecting responsibility from banks, insurance companies, and lax financial regulation, some instead blamed the spread of sub-prime loans, the housing bubble, and subsequent financial crisis on poor people who took mortgages they could not sustain, and federal policy that encouraged home ownership for minority families. While this story had failed to gain widespread favor by 2011, the fact that powerful political and media voices put it forward suggests that a renewed focus on the poor as scapegoats may again become important. With high poverty rates in hard economic times and governments at all levels straining to limit spending and avoid tax increases, we can expect more voices to call for limiting outlays for the poor as a way to "save the middle class."

Through the years, the poor have been blamed for most of the problems of people in the United States. They have drained our pockets through welfare and blighted our cities by living in the center of them. They have corrupted the nation's morals by having children out of wedlock, refusing to work, and otherwise setting a bad example. The drumbeat slogan "end welfare as we know it" summed up a twenty-five-year-long attack on the poor finally culminating in the 1996 "welfare reform" legislation passed by a Republican Congress and endorsed by President Clinton.

When the law passed, the president's senior advisors on welfare policy, Mary Jo Bane and David Ellwood, resigned in protest. Welfare reform, perhaps more than any other policy initiative of the 1990s, came to symbolize the scapegoating of the weak and defenseless for political gain.

Two central facts should guide our understanding of the welfare debate and policy regarding poor people. First, poverty is something that happens to the working class. Attacks on the poor are attacks on the working class. The poor are not some marginal "other"; the poor are typically working class people who don't make much money, either because they aren't working or because they make low wages. When we talk about poverty and welfare as part of the world of the poor, we are talking about the conditions of life for a sizable part of the working class. Yet much of the discussion of poverty in the United States has been framed in terms of an "underclass," wrongly removing the poor from the mainstream of American life and values.

This leads to the second important fact of the welfare debate: that so much of the attack on welfare was based on myth, stereotype, and distortion about the people receiving aid. The image of the "welfare queen" popularized by President Reagan was deeply misleading, but it served an important political purpose, making it possible for many people to attack welfare without realizing that they were attacking themselves.

To see how this worked, and to help prevent such wrongheaded attacks in the future, it pays to look back at the highlights of the welfare debate. When President Clinton declared it time to "end welfare as we know it," he was talking about the "welfare queen," which by then was how most people had come to "know" welfare. Based on the popular image to which the president appealed, it was time to cut off people who refused to work and preferred to rip off the taxpayers for their televisions and Cadillacs. It was time to end payments to irresponsible single mothers, often teenagers, who kept having children to get the benefits. It was time to stop feeding personal irresponsibility and social dependency transmitted from generation to generation by mothers on the dole—transmitted to their children, who knew no other life and were unable to make it in the world of work, in the unlikely event that they even wanted to work. It was time to disown women who thought they could get by without a man, raising children outside of the standard family. It was time, in short, to save the people on welfare by destroying welfare; the politics of tough love as preached by the president joined with the politics of meanness as practiced by the Republican majority in Congress.

Thrown into this mix was a racial element. In media representations and in the public imagination, the "welfare queen" was usually black. The attack on welfare was one piece of a long-term Republican strategy that has promoted a sense of outrage among whites that they are being made chumps by blacks trying to get something for nothing at their expense. To many, "end welfare as we know it" meant an end to white people paying taxes to support lazy black people.

The realities of the welfare population, and of the poor in general, were dramatically different from the stereotypes. To start with, two-thirds (68.5 percent) of all poor people in the United States in 2009 were white (42.5 percent of the poor were non-Hispanic white), while three-quarters of all black people were not poor.[3] Tens of millions of white people have also received benefits from "means-tested" government programs, in which the recipient must prove a low income to be eligible (for example, food stamps, Medicaid, and housing assistance). In 2005, non-Hispanic whites were approximately half of all those who received TANF, food stamps, and Medicaid; non-Hispanic blacks were 30 percent of recipients, and Hispanics 20 percent.[4]

The stereotype that welfare recipients typically stayed on the dole for very long periods as part of a "culture of dependence" was also wrong. Yes, some individuals who receive aid lie around drinking beer and watching television all day, paying no attention to their children, with no intention of ever working as long as the welfare check comes in. Every community has its examples of pathological behavior, including the capitalists. But these people were not typical of welfare recipients, nor are they typical of TANF recipients. Long-term spells on TANF are unusual. From 2001–2003, nearly 75 percent of TANF recipients collected payments for less than a year, and 49.6 percent for four months or less. Only one in six recipients collected TANF payments for twenty months or more.[5]

An easy way to understand the confusion about long-term welfare dependence involves an analogy to a hotel. Think of a hotel with a hundred rooms. The hotel serves some long-term tenants and some short-term guests. For argument's sake, suppose seventy rooms are taken by tenants with long-term leases, and thirty rooms are rented to people for an average stay of one week. On any given day, 70 percent of the people in the hotel will be long-term tenants. But if you look at the hotel occupancy over the entire year, a very different picture emerges. Each of those thirty short-term rooms has been home to fifty-two people, each staying a week. Over the year, 1,560 people have stayed in the hotel for a short time, and only 70 for a long time. In this example, what had been a 70 percent long-term occupancy on a given day becomes a 4 percent long-term occupancy rate when measured over a year.

As with the hotel example, some people received assistance for a long time, some for a short while. If you looked at the welfare population on a given day in 1995 or in any other year, most of the people were long-term recipients. But looking over a longer period, the great majority of people who received welfare received it for a relatively short time.[6] Welfare dependence stretching across generations from mother to daughter was not common, either. One typical study found that 20 percent of daughters of welfare-dependent mothers (defined as mothers being on welfare in each of the three consecutive years of the first phase of the study) were themselves on welfare for three years or more in their twenties, while 64 percent of daughters of welfare-dependent mothers received no welfare at all in the final three-year period of the study.[7] Contrary to popular myth, the same study showed that when welfare dependence did stay with a family across generations it was much more likely to be in white families, not black.[8]

Myths about welfare involved money as well as people. At the time of the mid-nineties welfare debate, AFDC payments were less than 1 percent of the federal budget, not at all the budget-busting myth. Similarly, TANF payments in 2010 were $17.1 billion, less than one-half of 1 percent of federal budget outlays that year.[9] Even counting food stamps, now named the Supplemental Nutrition Assistance Program (SNAP) and much loved by farmers, who benefit directly from the program as much as poor people, the total was less than 2.3 percent of the budget.[10] States pay administrative costs for the food stamp program, but the federal government picks up a major portion of those costs. In 2007, the year for which the latest data are available, state administrative overhead came to $2.9 billion, or 0.2 percent of state expenditures. State TANF outlays were budgeted in 2007 at $17.6 billion, just 1.1 percent of state government spending. The fiscal crisis did not arise from caring for the poor.

Nor did people on welfare and other poor people live high off the hog. Consider Frank and Carla Ricci, a family with one child living in St. Louis at the top poverty level income in 2009, $17,285 for the year. The U.S. Department of Labor publishes detailed information on the way an average urban working family spends its money.[11] What would the Riccis have been able to buy if they spent their income on goods and services in the same proportions as an average family, but in amounts scaled back across the board to get by on poverty wages? Frank and Carla could spend seventy-one cents per day per person on meat. They could spend $2.15 a day for all food and beverages per person. For each month they would have $311 for housing, not including utilities, appliances, furnishings, or household operations. To spend more on any of these things, they would have to make do with less elsewhere, less, for example, than $120 per year for shoes for the entire family.

And that's the good news. The Riccis' income equaled what the government calls the "poverty threshold." In 2009, nearly 44 percent of all poor persons were in families with incomes *less than half* the poverty threshold.[12]

Recognizing the harsh realities behind the official poverty measure, policy analysts have come up with more realistic incomes required to provide families with a minimum acceptable standard of living. Using actual costs for basic housing, food, transportation, health care, and other necessities (but excluding such extras as eating out or taking vacations), one such analysis for 2010 found that a family requires roughly three times the official top poverty threshold income "to survive and meet its basic needs" in the United States.[13]

The decline in income support for the poor during the Reagan and Clinton years increased hardship from what had been a pretty dismal starting point at the end of the 1970s. In 1977, the poverty budget provided a family no more than "an even chance of … a diet meeting two-thirds of the recommended dietary allowances of the National Research Council."[14] It has been getting worse ever since. Despite the rhetoric of excessive living by the poor, hunger and malnutrition are widespread in the United States. In 1995, about four million children under the age of twelve didn't get enough food. As many as half of all children in poverty ate significantly less than the federally recommended level of calories and nutrients needed for normal learning and thinking.[15] At the same time that President Reagan was imagining the welfare population as "welfare queens," his first administration famously tried to have ketchup declared a vegetable so that school lunch programs could be cut back.

During the period of mounting outcry over aid to the poor, from Reagan's election in 1980 to Clinton's 1996 reform, the cash value of the AFDC payment was falling steadily, from $685 to $497 per month (in 2006 dollars). In 2006, the average family TANF payment was $372. In Mississippi, the state with the lowest payments, the maximum a family of three could collect per month was $170.[16]

In 2009, the U.S. Department of Agriculture found that almost 15 percent of Americans suffered from food insecurity within the past year. Almost 5 percent of American households experienced bouts of very low food security, meaning that someone in the household had to reduce their intake of food and had their normal eating patterns disrupted because of lack of money or other resources. About 4.2 million households with children, or 10.6 percent of such households children, were "food insecure" at some time during the year. Households usually shield children from disrupted eating patterns, but in 469,000 households children were directly affected by food insecurity. The study found that the poor pay a third more for food than the prices paid by people who are not poor. And despite these problems, 43 percent of households experiencing low food security did not participate in any of the three largest federal food and nutrition assistance programs.[17]

In 2009, 15.5 million young people lived in poverty, 20.9 percent of all those under eighteen years old. They made up 35 percent of those living below the official federal poverty level. Another 8 percent of the poor were 65 years or older. In other words, 43 percent of the poor were not working age while 57 percent were working-age adults. Why didn't they work? Actually, many did. Forty-one percent of those between the ages of sixteen and sixty-five living in households earning less than the federal poverty level (26.2 million people) worked in 2009. Of those 10.7 million who did work, 2.6 million worked full-time, year-round.[18]

When poor people do not work, it is often because they are ill, disabled, or unable to find work, conditions that afflict the poor more frequently than the nonpoor. In 1990, nearly a quarter of all working-age poor people who were out of the labor force were sick or disabled (compared with 15 percent of the non-poor). Forty percent of poor working-age people who were out of the labor force stayed home to take care of family (compared with 45 percent of the nonpoor who were out of the labor force).[19] For millions of poor adults, it is simply not realistic to shout "Get a job!"

Despite the level of need among the poor, large numbers of them receive no government support of any kind. Fewer than half of poor people received any means-tested cash assistance at all in 1992. Only 51 percent received food stamps, and only 56 percent of poor households had one or more people covered by Medicaid.[20] Even before welfare reform dramatically reduced the numbers of people receiving government assistance, millions of eligible people were getting nothing, and the pattern continues. In 2005, only 40.4 percent of eligible families received TANF payments, and 59.1 percent of eligible households participated in the food stamp program.[21]

Immigrants in Place of the Poor

In many ways, immigrants have replaced the poor in the stories some people tell to explain the economic hardships so many Americans face. Again, facts don't seem to matter. We need to examine in some detail the realities that contradict the easy assumptions that so often lead to popular hostility toward immigrants. Let's consider three common claims: that immigrants cost native-born Americans their jobs and drive down wages; that immigrants, especially those in the country without proper documents, are a major drain on public finances; and that immigrants are poor people with criminal inclinations.

Concerning criminal activity, "There's a real disconnect between emotions and facts when it comes to the border," says El Paso, Texas, city council member Beto O'Rourke. "You've got a lot of politicians exploiting this fear that the Mexicans are coming over to kill us." Yet, as reported in *Time* magazine, "According to the FBI, the four large U.S. cities (with populations of at least 500,000) with the lowest violent crime rates—San Diego, Phoenix, and the Texas cities of El Paso and Austin—are all in border states. 'The border is safer now than it's ever been,' U.S. Customs and Border Protection spokesman Lloyd Easterling told the Associated Press [in June 2010]."[22] Looking at the country as a whole, studies by the Justice Department and the U.S. Commission on Immigration Reform document lower crime rates among immigrants compared with native-born residents.[23]

If immigrants were a significant source of crime we would expect to find that communities with the fastest growth in immigrant populations would have faster-growing crime rates compared with other areas. But the opposite is the case. University of Colorado sociologist Tim Wadsworth examined crime rates for murder and robbery in nearly 450 U.S. urban areas with populations over fifty thousand and found that "cities that experienced greater growth in immigrant or new immigrant populations between 1990 and 2000 tended to demonstrate sharper decreases in homicide and robbery."[24] Comparing 2006 with 1999, the eighteen states with the highest immigration influx experienced a 13.6 percent decline in crime, compared with a 7.1 percent decline in the rest of the country.[25] If all you know is that a crime has been committed, and nothing else, your best bet is that a native-born U.S. citizen is the guilty party, not an immigrant.

Hysteria about immigrant crime rates blends into the claim that immigrants drain our communities of resources and strain our public finances. Again, ample evidence documents the opposite. Most immigrants, even those without papers, work in jobs where the employer deducts income and social security taxes. (Some immigrants working in the informal cash economy as day laborers pay no income or social security taxes, but the same can be said of native-born workers in the cash economy.) Adding further to government revenues, all immigrants pay the same state and local sales taxes as the native-born. Immigrants pay local property taxes, too, even when they rent, because landlords pass the cost of property taxes (and other costs of ownership) on to their tenants, immigrant and native alike, in the rent they charge.[26]

On the expenditure side of public finances, immigrants without papers, the focus of much public hostility, will never collect on their Social Security contributions when they provide false papers to secure work. Undocumented immigrant workers contribute $8.5 billion dollars every year into the Social Security and Medicare trust funds, payments they and their children will never see as benefits. These payments are pure gains to the funds, making them more secure for native-born workers who rightly expect benefits upon retirement or disability.[27]

More generally, the claim is also false that immigrants unfairly drain public resources with claims on welfare, food stamps, and other assistance to the poor. U.S. law requires, with almost no exceptions, that even immigrants with legal residence wait at least five years after entering the country before they are eligible to apply for food stamps, Section 8 housing, SSI, and other income support programs.[28] Immigrants without documents are never eligible. States can impose further restrictions on Medicaid and TANF benefits. The only government expenditures immigrants can claim as a matter of right are emergency hospital medical treatment and public education for their school-age children. But these are paid for through state and local taxes, which, as we have seen, immigrants pay together with their native-born neighbors.

We often think of immigrants as being poor and working low-end jobs. It is true that immigrants tend to have disproportionately lower education levels and work in lower paid jobs than native-born workers. In 2000, 39 percent of immigrant men had less than a completed high school education, compared with 12 percent of non-Hispanic white men, 27 percent of non-Hispanic black men, 10 percent of non-Hispanic Asian men, and 31 percent of Hispanic men. Similar disparities existed for women. But immigrant men also had higher rates of master's degree and PhD completion (11 percent) than native-born workers.[29]

This distribution of educational background is reflected in the jobs immigrants hold. In 2009, foreign-born people made up 18 percent of the workforce, 27.8 of 155.6 million. Roughly eight million immigrants, less than 30 percent, were undocumented. (There were almost 12 million undocumented people in the U.S., but many were children or others not in the labor force.) Immigrants were overrepresented in seven of fifteen major occupational categories tracked by the Department of Labor, mostly paying relatively low wages. Of all workers in farming, fishing, and forestry, for example, 69 percent were immigrants. Among cleaning and maintenance workers it was 44 percent. But, reflecting the high education levels of many immigrants, they were 24 percent of all science and engineering employees in 2009.[30]

It is not clear what impact immigrants have on the employment and wages of native-born workers. These questions have been the subject of an extensive scholarly and technical literature stretching more than twenty years in which there is no consensus. Disagreements arise because of different methodologies based on different plausible assumptions. The limits of statistical methods are another source of disagreement because it is difficult to distinguish the specific influence of immigration from the many other factors that affect employment and wages in particular industries, occupations, and parts of the country.

New immigrants entering the labor market can tend to push wages down and take jobs from existing workers with whom they directly compete. Some evidence suggests that low-wage workers who haven't completed high school are particularly vulnerable, although the effects seem to be quite limited. While native-born workers, especially African American men, experience some of these effects, most downward pressure on jobs and wages impacts earlier immigrants, not the native-born, since new immigrants typically enter into labor markets for employers where previous immigrants have found work.[31]

A couple of ironies are worth noting in this respect. First, while negative effects on the lives of poorly educated African American men should be a real social concern, the needs of these men are hardly the priority of anti-immigrant activists. And the problems of wage and job competition are actually made worse by tightening border controls and making movements in and out of the United States more difficult. This is because the competition for jobs is more intense when the economy is in recession. If it were easy for immigrants to come into the country when times are good, it would be easy for them to leave when economic opportunity shrinks and many want to return to their native places. Making it risky to enter the United States only increases the resident immigrant population in bad economic times because immigrants, once in the country, will not want to risk the inability to return should they leave.

It is also true that immigration can push employment and wages up for some native-born workers. Immigrants contribute many hundreds of billions of dollars in market demand each year for all sorts of products that are produced in the United States, generating jobs. And if employing immigrant workers requires employing other workers in complementary jobs (like architects, skilled tradespeople, and construction managers whose jobs come along with laborers), immigrant employment supports the employment of native-born as well.

The poverty rate among immigrants is somewhat higher than among the native-born, but the gap is much less than that between native-born black and white poverty rates. Immigrant poverty is concentrated among the newly arrived. After immigrants are in the United States for at least five years, as they gain language skills and better knowledge of employment opportunities, and as the less successful return to their native countries, their poverty rate falls to about the same as that for the native-born. Consistent with research findings that immigrants have a negligible impact on native-born wages, there is "little evidence of an effect of immigration on native poverty through immigrant-native labor market competition," Steven Raphael and Eugene Smolensky write in an Institute for Research on Poverty report. [32]

One area in which immigrant experience is dramatically different from the native-born is the extent of employer violations of wage, hour, and safety laws. Undocumented workers especially are regularly victimized by employers who pay no overtime premium as required by law, pay less than the legal minimum wage, or even pay no wages at all. Employers regularly deny these workers required safety equipment. The widespread abuse of undocumented workers is a major focus of worker centers that mobilize immigrant workers and address their needs. Far from the stereotype of people entering the United States to mooch off the system, undocumented workers experience a well-documented life of illegal abuse by their employers.[33]

Images of immigrants in the media and the popular imagination are as full of inaccuracies, myths, and racial biases as are images of the poor. These misperceptions persist in part because the supposed presence of an "underclass" plays a particular role in the culture that we turn to now. We will return to the immigrant story in chapter 7.

The Function of the "Underclass"

If the poor are not, in reality, eating up vast resources, and if immigrants are not a financial drain and moral threat to the country, why have immigrants and people on welfare been targets of such vicious attacks? Why have the myths dominated the debate, despite so much evidence that shows the stereotypes are false? The answers to these questions tell us much about the way class works in America. To see how, let's look first at the claim that there is an "underclass" in the United States, and then at the relationship of the poor, immigrants, and the so-called underclass to the working class.

Since the term came into widespread use in the early 1980s, "underclass" has been defined in different ways: the inner-city poor, the chronically unemployed, those involved with illegal drugs and prostitution, violent criminals, those on welfare, or the poor in general. But policy makers' vagueness hasn't stopped the concept of the underclass from playing an important part in American social discourse. In all its meanings, this concept serves the same function. It defines a group of people as outside the mainstream of society. Once the group is on the outside, its members become an "other," different from the rest of us. The "others" can then serve important political and psychological functions. They can become a social lightning rod, grounding vast amounts of anger and fear.

The idea of an underclass fits well with the idea that most Americans are in the middle class. The underclass, as the name so well suggests, is at the bottom, below most of us. Unlike the rich, who are presented as role models whose lives we should seek for ourselves, the poor are to be shunned, feared, changed. We don't drive through their neighborhoods for fear of being robbed. We want their grasping hands taken out of our pockets. Calling the poor an underclass separates them from society in a way that allows and even encourages everyone else to treat them in dehumanizing ways. Demonizing undocumented immigrants has the same effect. The actual facts of their lives become irrelevant when the poor and immigrants take on a social and psychological role in the popular imagination. They stop being people and become symbols, freighted with the baggage of fear and loathing.[34]

Often the hostility we express toward the poor is disapproval we cannot express toward ourselves or those with real power in society. If we have doubts about the value of the work we do, we reject any notion that we might be looking for a leisurely life and condemn the poor instead for being the lazy ones. When we cannot admit that we live in dysfunctional families, we condemn the poor as dysfunctional instead. If middle class teenagers are having sex, it cannot be because sex is a normal thing for all teenagers to want to do; it must be because of the wicked influence of the poor. If the values expressed in the dog-eat-dog world of the capitalist marketplace undermine our sense of community and self-worth, how much easier it is to see the source of moral decay in the poor, and so escape the need to confront the powerful. If we cannot find work, we find it easier to blame powerless immigrants than to imagine taking on an economic system that throws tens of millions of people out of work. Even the story of the "good immigrant" is a challenge: the immigrant who, according to employers, often works more diligently than the native-born and takes the "dirty" jobs most native-born workers are unwilling to do, certainly at the low wages typically paid. We displace onto immigrants and the poor our own weaknesses and those parts of ourselves we find most threatening and frightening.

Certainly lazy people exist, who take maximum advantage of the welfare system, cheating the taxpayers to lie around on the dole. Anyone living in a poor neighborhood has known a few personally, and resents them as much as others do. But the cheats are a tiny fraction of the poor and hardly characterize welfare recipients as a group.

Besides, every section of society has its tax cheats and frauds, stretching every rule, playing every angle. In 1999, eight Medicare contractors paid $275 million in fines to the government after admitting to defrauding the health-care system they were supposed to administer.[35] And then came the far more extensive Enron, WorldCom, and other scandals of the early years of the new century, followed by the frauds leading to the financial crisis in 2008, and then Bernie Madoff. Compared with this level of fraud, the poor are again poor indeed. Even more insidious, some people have the political power to write the rules on their own behalf, as we have seen in the financial crisis. Then their self-serving use of the government turns into something perfectly legal and bureaucratically appropriate, rather than the massive cheat it actually is.

When they are shamed and punished through welfare reform, the poor serve the important psychological function of the scapegoat. It doesn't matter if what we "know" about the poor and immigrants isn't true. Facts alone don't overcome myths. Saving money is not really the point of the attacks, anyway. Deeper symbolic issues are in play.

Conservatives aren't the only ones who have defined the poor as "other." It is ironic that awareness of poverty as a serious problem in the United States began with the publication in 1962 of *The Other America* by socialist and Catholic activist Michael Harrington. The "other" in the title were the poor, then invisible in a country much taken with its power and affluence compared with the rest of the world and compared with the United States itself not twenty-five years earlier, when the Depression seemed endless. Harrington wrote of the poor with passionate concern, not with disdain, and sought to include them in the broader society, not punish them. Lyndon Johnson's War on Poverty followed within three years, a central part of the liberal agenda.

But as different as the liberal and conservative agendas for the poor have been, one thing unites them. Each looks at the poor from the outside. For members of the capitalist elite and often for the middle class professionals who write about social questions, the poor are literally other. The liberal approach to poor people involves no small amount of mythologizing, too. "Blessed are the poor," through whom we redeem our worth, after our success in the soul-destroying market system, by doing good on their behalf. Blessed are the poor, pure victims of the juggernaut that we ourselves have managed to negotiate successfully. Are we not then also blessed in our ability and desire to help the poor among us? "Liberal guilt" and patronizing attitudes can distance the poor as much as conservative "meanness."

So for conservative and liberal alike, the poor become objects for use in psychosocial dramas of one sort or another. The beatification of the poor by liberals in the 1960s turned into the demonization of the poor by conservatives in the 1990s; the War on Poverty in the sixties and the war on the poor in the eighties and nineties were two sides of the same coin.

Poverty Happens to the Working Class

Fortunately we have quite a lot of information about who the poor and people on welfare really are. Getting past the myths, we come to see that poverty mostly happens to the working class. Understanding this basic fact tells us something about the practical effects of the assault on welfare. The attack on the poor is an attack on the working class, not some marginal "other."

In 1995, nearly 14 percent of the U.S. population was counted as poor.[36] But most of the poor don't stay poor for long periods. They cycle in and out of poverty, depending on employment, family situation, changes in earnings on the job. Through the 1970s and 1980s, the chance that a poor person would escape poverty within a year was about 50 percent, and after a year out of poverty, a previously poor person had about a 25 percent chance of falling back among the poor.[37] A 2009 Census Bureau study found that over a four-year period (2003–2007) 31.6 percent of the population had at least one spell of poverty lasting two or more months. Meanwhile, "chronic poverty was relatively uncommon, with 2.2 percent of the population living in poverty all 48 months of the period."[38] An earlier Harvard/MIT study, which followed the population over a ten-year period, found that 40 percent experienced poverty in at least one year.[39]

In other words, more than half the working class experiences poverty in a ten-year period.[40] The poor are not some persistent lump at the bottom of society; they are working people who have hit hard times.

The cycling of working people into and out of poverty is reflected in the experience of many welfare recipients. A large fraction of people who were on welfare for long periods of time in the seventies and eighties actually experienced many shorter spells of welfare interrupted by spells of work. As Mary Jo Bane and David Ellwood have explained, most were "people who have tried to leave welfare, often repeatedly, but who seem unable to maintain full independence. They obtain a job or find additional support elsewhere, but the improvement is only temporary. Their child becomes ill or they miss a day of work, and they are back on welfare."[41]

Poverty is not evenly distributed across the working class; it is relatively concentrated among blacks and Hispanics, and among women. In 2009, 14.3 percent of the U.S. population lived below the poverty line. Among white non-Hispanics, 9.4 percent were poor; among blacks, it was 25.8 percent; among Hispanics (of any race), 25.3 percent; and among women householders without a husband present, it was 29.9 percent. The poverty rate among single women in 2009 was 24 percent; it was 20 percent for single men.[42] While it is certainly true that women, either living alone or as heads of households, endure a disproportionate share of poverty, men are no strangers to being down and out.

Sadly, the situation is even worse for children. In 2009, when just over 20 percent of children lived in poverty, among white non-Hispanic children 11.9 percent were poor; for black children it was 35.7 percent, and for Hispanics (of any race) it was 33.1 percent.[43] Half of all children living in female-headed households were living in poverty in 1996.

The fact that minorities are poor in greater numbers than their share of the total population contributes to the misconception that the face of poverty is black or brown, not white. The continuing legacy and practice of racism in the United States helps explain the disproportional number of minority people who are poor. But it is wrong to say that poverty itself is solely the result of racism. Racism cannot directly explain the poverty of the 18.5 million white Americans who make up 43 percent of those who live below the federal poverty threshold.[44]

Confusion on this point can lead to unfortunate political consequences. When John Edwards tried to make poverty the hallmark of his 2007–2008 campaign for the Democratic Party nomination for president, he opened his campaign in the Lower Ninth Ward of New Orleans, an all-black neighborhood that had been devastated by Hurricane Katrina in 2005. Surrounding himself with dispossessed black residents, he declared his goal of ending "two Americas," by which he meant rich and poor.

In the southeastern Louisiana region severely damaged by Katrina, 30 percent of working blacks had jobs paying less than $9 per hour when the hurricane struck, a poverty wage for a family of three. But 24 percent of working whites had such jobs, too, and they outnumbered the black working poor in the region, 85,000 to 65,000.[45] Associating poverty with blacks, who endure it disproportionately, while ignoring the larger numbers of white people living in poverty (often in the same area), develops a politics that ignores and therefore affronts many whites. We fail to make the linkages that must be made across racial lines to mount a full campaign against poverty, linkages that class analysis brings forward and makes possible. At the same time, making those class connections endure requires us to recognize and address the disproportionate suffering borne among communities of color and women.

Within the working class, racism and sexism operate to push minorities and women into the lower-paying, more unstable jobs, and they experience longer spells of unemployment. (The same kind of thing happens in the professional and managerial jobs of the middle class and in the capitalist class as well.) That's why they experience poverty in greater numbers than they "should," and why it can appear that the problem of poverty is really a problem of race and gender.

Affirmative action and other programs designed to reverse the operation of discrimination are important tools to correct the imbalance of poverty across race and gender, but they do not address the problem of poverty as such. If we address the problem of poverty exclusively with tools that focus on minorities, and do not look at it in the context of class, we ignore the bulk of the problem, and mistake the source of it as well. We tend to neglect the white poor and divide the working class against itself. To get at poverty effectively requires improving the conditions and increasing the power of the working class as a whole and, within that, addressing racism and sexism so the advance can be shared by all.

Wrongly Dividing the Poor from Workers

It may seem surprising, given the concerted attacks on the poor in recent years, that it has not been the poor among the working class who have taken the biggest hit to their standard of living. We saw in chapter 3 that between 1968 and 2009, the poorest 20 percent of the population saw a 19 percent decline in their share of society's income. But the core of the working class, the second lowest 20 percent, lost 23 percent of their share in the same period. Despite their relatively greater losses, these people were not generally eligible for programs available to the poor. This helped fuel the resentment many workers felt about welfare and government in general.

To treat the poor in isolation from the experience of the entire working class is to obscure what has been going on. Two results follow. First, by making the poor seem fundamentally different, poor people are more easily subject to abuse and disregard. And when the poor appear in the popular imagination not as workers but as minorities, racist attitudes are reinforced, just as racist attitudes tend to make the false claim credible in the first place.

Second, when we push the poor into a separate category outside of "regular society," the problems of the poor are more easily explained by the supposed deficiencies of the poor themselves, rather than the workings of society and the economy. We come to believe that poverty is poor people's fault.

This all-too-human tendency to blame the victim is extremely powerful. For conservatives, it can justify hard-heartedness toward the poor, together with calls for the poor to transform themselves, their attitudes, their culture and values, before they can expect to be treated with respect. For liberals, it can justify a charitable and paternalistic attitude, and policies designed to help the poor through education and training, and by teaching the poor proper work attitudes and behavior, all good things to do. Our society would be much worse off without the liberal impulse to help the poor. But for conservatives and liberals alike, the lack of a class context for poverty leads to a variety of programs designed to change the poor, to make them more mainstream. In one way or another, the idea is that if only the poor could be like "us," their problems would be solved. Then they could have jobs and everything would be fine.

As hopeful as this recipe appears, it is simplistic because the premise is largely wrong. The poor *are* workers. Even the bulk of the destitute and long-term unemployed of the inner city ghettos are workers whose jobs have disappeared from the cities around them, as sociologist William Julius Wilson has shown.[46] These potential workers will work if the jobs are there. Many commentators had written off young black men in the inner cities as hopelessly lost, but in the unusually strong economy of 1999, with the national unemployment rate at a thirty-year low, these potential unemployed outcasts were drawn into regular jobs.[47] The experience of urban black working families left without jobs when companies fled to the suburbs parallels the experience of Appalachian coal miners in the 1950s and 1960s, when the shift from coal to oil destroyed hundreds of thousands of jobs and created hundreds of thousands of poor rural white workers sunk into long-term unemployment. It was the poverty of these white workers that first drew the nation's attention when the War on Poverty began. At the beginning of the twenty-first century, it remains true that poverty is disproportionately rural rather than urban.[48]

The idea that the welfare poor are lazy leeches with terrible work habits misses the actual possibilities and limitations of the lives of the working poor. People unfamiliar with the daily life imposed by poverty have a hard time understanding the life circumstances that often make the "culture of poverty" a reasonable set of behaviors. Leaving welfare and Medicaid for a low-paying job with no medical benefits is hardly a rational economic choice. For anyone with children, it is an irresponsible choice. The chaos of personal life in crowded quarters (no place to study); no money for regular health care and a host of illnesses that come with poverty (days lost to long and unexpected waits in hospital emergency rooms); sick children and elders to take care of (hard to keep a regular work schedule); unreliable cars or long bus commutes to work or school (if public transportation is even available)—these and other everyday life circumstances of the poor, including the working poor, are obstacles that no capitalist family and few middle class families have to confront.

Yet those who condemn the poor for nonstandard behavior expect "mainstream" behavior to arise from nonmainstream conditions. For example, in the late 1990s, it became fashionable to condemn poor and working class young people who did not graduate from college in a "standard" amount of time. They were called dropouts and quitters who should have been excluded from college in the first place, unworthy of access to public higher education and a possible way out of poverty.

Sociologist Herbert Gans has well identified the problem:

> Unlike the affluent, the poor cannot mask their occasional inability or unwillingness to practice mainstream behavior, which is why the affluent imagine the poor have bad values. For example, while middle

class people who become jobless generally have family connections, networks, and other resources to fall back on and usually even remain home owners, the working poor who lose their jobs often go on welfare, and some eventually become homeless, or show up in the street crime statistics. If the better-off use drugs, they do so in their living rooms. And if the more fortunate fail repeatedly in their marriages, they can still hope that the next one will succeed. Poor women who have rarely met men with decent and secure jobs learn to expect from the start that marriage is not in the cards for them, and government data collectors frequently make sure that the illegitimacy of their children becomes public knowledge. Poor women who sour on marriage are stigmatized while their middle class peers become the stuff of TV sitcoms, not evidence of moral failure.[49]

The poor are ruined workers, pushed out of the economy or to its lower reaches. In the early history of capitalism, the poor in Europe were mainly ruined peasants and small farmers pushed off the land into urban slums, in the initial process that created the working class. This process is still going on as capitalism extends more deeply into Mexico, China, India, Brazil, and other developing countries. There today, as in Britain and the United States in earlier times, the newly created working class includes a very high percentage of women and children. In past centuries, the hardships of early capitalism pushed European poor people to immigrate to the United States, where they became part of the lowest echelon of the working class. The immigrant story is repeated today as capitalism penetrates further into the developing countries of Asia and Latin America. But within advanced capitalist society, where traditional society has already been destroyed, the home-grown poor also come from another source: the working class already in existence.

In the hard times working people face, they are often told to believe that their difficulties could be relieved if the poor led less cushy lives. This can appeal to the millions of working people just above the poverty line who are not eligible for welfare, housing assistance, food stamps, or Medicaid, yet suffer all kinds of difficulties because they too don't have enough money. The "angry white guy" lives in this milieu.

More recently, in the fiscal crises that hit local governments, states, and the federal government after 2009, new false targets were created to deflect the frustration and anger of ordinary people away from the corporate elites who had dominated the policy making that led to the crises. We once again saw people with supposed privileges—teachers, firefighters, and other public sector workers—vilified for having what others do not. But in this case the anger settled on people with pensions and medical coverage won through collective bargaining by public sector unions, while those benefits had been wiped out for millions of private sector workers whose unions were weakened or destroyed. We will return in chapters 6 and 9 to Wisconsin Governor Scott Walker and his 2011 attack on public sector unions that touched off such a furor.

Going after false targets misses the real target. Poor jobs, poor education, poor prospects, weak unions, corporate elites demanding to make and keep more money while starving public services, private sector workers losing jobs and pensions: these things aren't caused by poor people or immigrants or public sector workers. They are part and parcel of a social and economic system run for the benefit of the capitalist.

Economic grievances belong at the boss's door. This is true on the shop floor and it is true in the political system. But the ability to carry those grievances to the capitalist requires the power of an organized and united working class, and a clear understanding of the proper target. While many were aiming at the false target of welfare reform, the real one went unnoticed, and divisions among workers by race, gender, and relative economic standing were intensified.

Giving voice and power to the poor and immigrants requires giving voice and power to the working class, bringing into focus its reality in a class-conflicted society. In chapters 6 through 9, we will investigate the prospects for an explicit working class politics in the United States. But first it will be helpful to explore the values that underlie political action. In doing so, we will see that class can help us understand how "family values" have been another false trail, and how thinking about class can help us define a different set of values that are more useful for the lives and needs of working people.

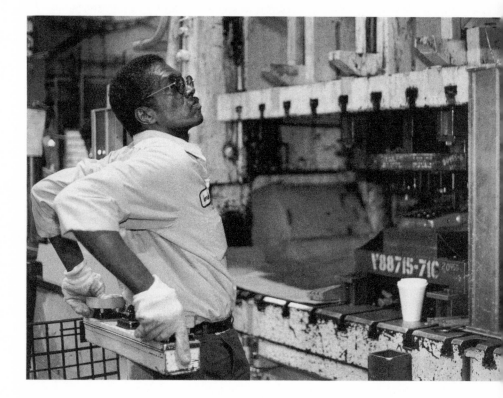

LOOKING AT VALUES—FAMILY AND OTHERWISE

I am a volunteer in a fire department on the North Fork of Long Island, about a hundred miles east of New York City. All of Long Island's population of nearly three million people are served by volunteer fire and rescue companies. Big cities across the country are served by professional firefighters and EMS workers, but throughout rural and suburban America, volunteers do the work.

The nearly one million men and women who each volunteer many hundreds of hours a year to this service confront in their activity the moral and ethical issues we need to consider when thinking about the economy. These volunteers confront in a very vivid way the question of the proper balance between self-interest and the needs of the community.

Fire and EMS volunteers go through rigorous training to learn the technical skills required for the work. Their teachers are often professionals from nearby city departments. But before technical skills are taught, the training stresses a first principle of service: your first responsibility is to yourself.

This may seem an odd emphasis for people whose purpose is to serve others. People join fire and rescue squads for many good reasons beyond the desire to help their neighbors: a social life, excitement, personal challenge. But these self-serving aspects of the work are not what "your first responsibility is to yourself" is about.

The point is that you cannot serve others if you are out of service yourself. If you are down and in need of rescue, you cannot do what you are at the scene to do. In fact, you become part of the problem. To be of service to others, you must first of all be physically and mentally able to serve.

The search for the proper balance between self-interest and service to others suggests the basis of an ethical evaluation of the market economy and capitalism, because capitalism poses the very same problem: What is the connection between self-interest and service to the community? The pursuit of self-interest may be an essential life priority, but it comes with a critical question: When does following self-interest stop being a legitimate priority of business and keep companies from serving the larger community? And what happens when self-interest becomes the whole point of economic activity?

It's fine to pursue narrow self-interest, except when it cuts us off from or disrespects the social connections and responsibilities that help to define us as we participate in the larger society. Just as a firefighter pursues self-interest as a priority, but not as an end, self-interested economic activity needs to be understood as a priority, perhaps, but not as an end. The end is playing a constructive part in the larger society, not out of a misty sense of altruism, but to nourish the relationships that give us our character, place, and meaning in the world.

We need ethics and values to guide our public and private lives. Because values must be an essential foundation of politics, before going on to explore what a working class politics might be in the United States, we should try to establish a moral compass for the discussion. In doing so, we need to identify the proper place for self-interest, both of the capitalist class and of the working class. We will see how working class self-interest in the context of community responsibility advances family life far more effectively than the "family values" agenda as defined by the right wing.

Self-Interest Is Not Enough

The conservative agenda asserts the superiority of the capitalist market system. In this view, self-interest is the dominant motive for economic activity, and private ownership of business with minimum restrictions is necessary to allow people to capture for themselves the benefits that come from their economic activity.

It is no mystery that this view should appeal to capitalists, who are the core supporters of the conservative cause. But the implications of such a market society for ethics and values are grim indeed. Let's look at three ways the exaggerated assertion of individualism and self-interest breaks away from reality: how it disregards the connections among us, ignores the role of luck, and denies the social origin of wealth.

Connectedness

Seeing the world in terms solely of the market ignores the complex interconnectedness of human beings. Even Adam Smith, the great original champion of early capitalism, wrote of the conflict between market exchange and morality. Over two hundred years ago Smith described how the capitalist division of labor ended self-sufficiency and how the market brought people together to coordinate their activities. He pointed out:

> It is not from the benevolence of the butcher, the brewer, or the baker, that we expect our dinner, but from their regard to their own interest. We address ourselves, not to their humanity but to their self-love, and never talk to them of our own necessities but of their advantages.[1]

Smith, a professor of moral philosophy when he founded the modern study of economics, tells us here that self-love and humanity are in opposition. He tells us that in a market economy each of us acts without concern for others, with a concern only for ourselves. Each person appeals to others' self-interest, but actually only as a means to serve his or her own ends.

This approach defeats "humanity," as Smith calls it, or community responsibility as I have called it, because it undermines and denies true mutual concern. The point of ethics and morality in social conduct is to find ways to guide our responsibility toward others. If the only thing that counts is me, there is no place for ethics of any sort as a guide to my behavior, because social ethics are about relationships between people, the terms of mutual responsibility, a guide to each of us about our obligations to others.

An overriding belief in the market and reliance on self-interest defeat morality. They trivialize ethics by making true concern for others irrelevant or, worse, self-defeating, as in "nice guys finish last." Even the idea of "enlightened self-interest"—in which we appear to behave altruistically now only as a means to a longer-term self-interest that would be undermined by immediate selfishness—doesn't solve the problem. In the world of "enlightened self-interest," we still see ourselves as isolated individuals in a sea of other isolated individuals. This way of thinking about society fails to recognize the ways that individuals are also social, created and sustained in a network of other people. It cannot guide us to recognition of our interdependence and of the moral emptiness of individualism.

We are social beings. But the usual way we think about the social nature of human beings doesn't fully capture what is going on. Everyone knows that "no man is an island," that we live in groups, that we need one another to survive. As Adam Smith put it: "In civilized society, [a person] stands at all times in need of the cooperation and assistance of great multitudes, while his whole life is scarce sufficient to gain the friendship of a few persons."[2] The strength Adam Smith found in the market was exactly its ability to coordinate the economic connections among us so that, through buying and selling in the market, we could get what we need from one another without knowing one another. Through the market, we can reach beyond the personal connections and personal obligations that were the limits of earlier societies—a positive result of the growth of markets.

But people are social in different and more complicated ways. We are each distinctive beings, but each of us is also a set of relationships. We are created in relationships; our ideas and values and needs arise in our connections with others, not solely out of our minds and bodies fully distinct from others. We are social because we as individuals emerge only in the context of social connections.

Adam Smith was right to point out that in the modern, capitalist world, these connections extend beyond the immediate circle of family, friends, and coworkers we know directly. These are the people who immediately come to mind when we think of the communities that have shaped us. But in the modern world, our very nature as people and the very content of our individuality is also created in an extensive and impersonal network of relationships. Our life chances and experiences are not just our own doing and they are not just the making of our family's influence, they are also the product of the entire structure of society as it bears on each of us.

This is why we cannot protect ourselves individually by referring only to our immediate self-interest. We have to be concerned with the relationships we have to the broader community as well. To protect ourselves, we need to protect and nurture and make healthy and look after the interests of all those in society with whom we jointly make a life on this planet, and look after the health of the planet as well.

When I talk with people about this view, they raise objections. One friend, a computer technician, told me he could see how his family and long-time friends shaped him, but beyond that, society was all a blur. For him, the broad community is just an abstraction. Even if we are not aware of broad social relationships, though, they act upon us, define us, create us, lift us up and cast us down, call out to us for attention.

It is easy to see how the lives and ideas of our parents and even our neighbors and coworkers define us, because we know them and experience their influences directly. But what about those we don't know and will never even meet? The influence these remote individuals have on each of us is about zero, as individuals. But we have seen that people make up classes, sharing with others common degrees of power in the structures that shape society. Our relationships with others whom we don't know are formed within these contours of power. As all these individual strangers together give force to class—as well as to race, gender, nationality, and other defining aspects of who we are—their collective presence in our lives is substantial. We are, each of us as individuals, created not only in relation to our families and immediate influences but also in our relations with the operation and reproduction of the class structure and social dynamics of the larger society.

We are not used to thinking of ourselves as social in this sense, so another example may help clarify the point. When I was in college, I thought history was what happened before my time, completely separate from the here and now. I thought of it as a curiosity or at most a source of lessons about past behavior to be avoided or copied. Whatever the lessons, the past, I thought, was not the present.

But history *is* in the present, as is the potential of the future. The present has within it history reaching forward to help create it, and seeds of what may come. Our lives and the functioning of the society around us are not just a series of individual moments. The current moment exists because of the momentum of the past. The past shapes the present as the present reaches into the future.

Similarly, social relationships reach into our lives and create us, become a vital part of us. Self-interest includes an interest in these relationships, not as arm's length market transactions with completely separate others, but as defining connections in which we are responsible for others as we are to ourselves. We ignore or disrespect these defining relations at great peril to ourselves. This fact should guide our politics and be the foundation of our values.

This knowledge also helps us to understand the proper limits of individualism and self-interest, beyond which responsibility to oneself turns to corrupting greed. The trick is to find the right balance: to avoid self-assertion to the degree that it poisons the relationships that create, nurture, and sustain us as individuals, but also to resist demands of others that stunt our individuality and hinder our self-expression.

Individuality, privacy, and self-interested behavior are essential ingredients of Western life. No political or ethical system that denies them can be effective. We wouldn't want the stifling of individual initiative that so often characterized collectivist societies in the twentieth century. But neither can the kind of individualism that capitalism fosters play a positive role. By separating the individual from social connections, raw individualism becomes dysfunctional because it is false to the reality of our mutual dependence and mutual responsibilities.

Individual responsibility and safeguarding oneself and one's family and friends are central to healthy self-interest. These parallel the rule that firefighters' first responsibility is to themselves. But how are we to exercise this self-centered responsibility in a socially responsible way?

Champions of the market and the politics of individualism think that we take care of our responsibilities to others by paying them for what they provide us, in a market exchange. They think that after we pay, we owe nothing to anyone.

Without a market transaction, there is no connection. If money isn't involved, there is no obligation. In this view, the market is the channel of connectedness; accounts payable and receivable are the only measure of mutual obligation.

This is too narrow; it denies the many ways we are connected outside of markets. The market is a mechanism that facilitates buying and selling, but it is neither the whole economy nor the whole society. The actions of people and companies in the market need to be limited by values that respect and enhance the whole social network. Those values cannot come from the rules of the market, since it is those very rules of self-interest that need restrictions. Our obligations to others form the basis of respect, compassion, sympathy, caring, nurturing—all that we associate with the humanity that, as Adam Smith taught us, market behavior disregards.

I am talking about more than altruism here. Meeting our obligation to others is not a selfless giving. It is recognition of mutual involvement. It is a giving of self out of a sense of responsibility to others that expects responsible behavior from others as well. But I am also not talking about a ledger-keeping expectation of reciprocal favors. We need to be caring toward people we will never meet, who will never be in a position to reciprocate directly.

If this sounds utopian, it is because it's hard to imagine a world different from our own, one motivated by the ethic of social responsibility. This ethic is not a denial of self-interest or "human nature." It is a guide to behavior that fits the realities of who we are as social creatures in modern society.

People set up businesses to make a living and to be their own bosses. In addition to the good life the owner may enjoy, this self-interest can result in a genuine contribution to the community, in the product or service provided, jobs created, taxes paid. In fact, this is the standard claim that capitalists make to justify the role business plays in society.

But there is nothing automatic about the contributions a business makes, beyond the creation of wealth and power for the owner. If its product is poorly made or dangerous to the consumer, if its workforce is treated disrespectfully, if the community and environment surrounding the business suffer without compensation, if the business escapes taxes and instead demands various subsidies and other special favors just for existing, then self-interest has crossed the line into greed.

For any business, making a profit—staying in business—is the first priority, just as self-protection is the first order of business for a firefighter responding to an emergency. But when making money means harming the community, that's when social trouble begins. We cannot know where the line between self-interest and greed lies in any particular situation without looking at the details. So there is no easy rule to guide us into ethical economic behavior. But we can be sure that market success cannot be the measure of moral social conduct. Economic activity should be organized toward the goal of public service, in the form of quality products, respectful treatment of workers and the environment, and paying taxes to support the social structures each business requires for individual success. Beyond the return to shareholders, business activity must be fully accountable to social purposes.

In short, any discussion of values in society has to include the terms on which we limit the activity of private business. Of course, many owners oppose limits on what they can do with their businesses and resist the idea that business has any purpose beyond making money. They are only too happy to welcome the recent emphasis on family values as a matter entirely separate from the marketplace, because it lets them off the hook and puts greedy, predatory business practices beyond the reach of moral review.

Luck

"There but for the grace of God go I." Whether you take life's chances as the work of God, or as the effect of social and natural processes beyond our powers to control, or as the result of random events, it remains a fact that we do not fully control our destiny. Luck of all sorts plays an enormous role. Successful athletes and artists often talk about luck. Successful business leaders also acknowledge it on occasion. As one mutual fund manager put it, "When you're younger, you are more inclined to believe that the profits you make in the market are due to your own wit or talent. When you get older, maybe you get a little wiser and discover that it's exogenous [external] forces that are making you all that money."[3] We saw in chapter 2 that even Horatio Alger put luck at the heart of many rags-to-riches tales that became icons of the American Dream.

Of course, being in the right place at the right time does not guarantee success. A person has to be able to make something out of a lucky break, and that ability comes from the successful person's own skills and talents. But the central place of luck in our lives cannot be denied. This knowledge requires humility from the successful, as well as compassion for those who fail. And it certainly rules out any conclusions about the relative moral worth of those who succeed compared with those who fail.

The place of luck in our lives has other ethical consequences. The Golden Rule, "do unto others as you would have others do unto you," is not a call for tit-for-tat reciprocity, like "an eye for an eye and a tooth for a tooth." It involves recognition that you might well *become* the other. Social ethics need to reflect the risky reality we all face. Laws and regulations need to be acceptable no matter who you are, no matter who you might become.[4]

A philosophy of individualism that ignores the place of luck and the shaping power of social relationships beyond the individual accentuates the hubris of those who succeed and intensifies the sense of worthlessness of those who fail. The widespread lack of self-esteem among poor and other working class children and young adults is a serious problem, reaching almost epidemic proportions. It holds back their learning and their productivity, as well as causing deep personal suffering. But the successful can also suffer from the effects of extreme individualism. Their often overblown sense of self-importance has its own unreality, which leads to the self-doubts that gnaw at many of the rich and powerful, and to the personal despair that follows the fall from power many of them experience at one time or another.

The Origins of Wealth

A third problem with market individualism that leads it to moral bankruptcy is its failure to acknowledge that private wealth is socially created. Here again it helps to look at the problem through the lens of class. In chapter 3 we saw the importance of identifying the capitalists among the rich. Their wealth is not just money; it is based on capital, which is created by workers.

To see how this is true, it may help to take the discussion away from capitalism for a moment, with all the controversies that a frank discussion of it brings, and look instead at slavery. No one doubts any longer that the wealth of the slave owner originated in the work of the slave. Whatever the slave received in the way of sustenance came from the work of the slaves themselves, given back to the slave only after the owner took it from the slaves who had produced it in the first place. In fact, the slave owner took everything the slaves produced as his own, by right of ownership over the slaves themselves. What the slave owner did not return to the slave, he kept, and this was the basis of his wealth.

Likewise, feudal kings and other nobility drew their wealth from the work of the serfs and other producers who were forced to give up a share of what they made. The specific mechanisms that accomplished this transfer of wealth from those who created it to those who took it as their right were different under feudalism than under slavery. But the two systems shared a common fundamental fact: the wealth of the property owners was the fruit of the labor of others.

Although slave owners and feudal lords developed different arguments to justify their right to take the wealth created by others, their justifications shared a common theme. They routinely asserted the moral weakness and personal and intellectual inferiority of the producer, whether slave or serf, and, by contrast, the moral superiority and natural goodness and intelligence of the owners and rulers themselves.

This is not to say that the slave owner and the feudal aristocrat didn't occasionally do a full day's work. They could be busy organizing and enforcing the everyday operations of their societies and dealing with the many levels of intrigue and conflict that challenged their power. But, looking back, the work that occupied them was not like the work of those from whom they took their wealth. The self-righteous claims to moral authority advanced by the slaveholding and aristocratic elites of earlier times look quaint, hypocritical, and ignorant by modern, capitalist standards.

Now capitalism dominates the world economy and has established the new standards of political and economic life. Since the end of the Cold War, the capitalist way has been virtually unchallenged. It appears natural, and its standards and justifications are conventional wisdom widely accepted as self-evident. But if we look more closely we can see remarkable similarities between capitalism and earlier societies.

Adam Smith, the first person to take a serious look at wealth in capitalist society, had this to say about where wealth comes from when it is capitalist profit:

> The value which the workmen add to the materials, therefore, resolves itself…into two parts, of which the one pays their wages, the other the profits of their employer.…He would have no interest to employ them unless he expected from the sale of their work something more than what was sufficient to replace his stock.[5]

In other words, profits come from the value workers add when they make new products. Not only do the workers' wages come from what they have produced; all that the capitalist claims as his own as the profit of his enterprise also comes from what the workers have produced. These words of wisdom are from the man whose face decorated neckties proudly worn by the free market economists of the Reagan administration. In fact, Adam Smith tells us, the only reason a capitalist employs anyone at all is the expectation that the employee will generate a profit for the owner through his labor. In short, you are employed to make your employer rich, which comes as no surprise to employers and employees alike, even today.

Most executives of the capitalist class put in full days at work. But, as with the slaveholders and feudal lords before them, the work of modern executives is different from the work of those engaged in production. It is the work of control, of strategic planning, the work of managing intrigue and challenges to their control, whether from their workforce or from other businesses, or the government, or foreign competition. It is the work necessary to organize and maintain the structures that allow them to become and remain rich through the taking Adam Smith described.

Capitalists work hard at what they do. Theirs is not a life of leisure. But it isn't true, as the popular wisdom so often holds, that workers have an easy life by comparison. We often hear that the lucky worker goes home at five o'clock to an evening of beer and television, while the boss stays back to worry about all the details required to keep the business running. Even when the worker doesn't go off to a second job and the boss does work longer hours, the popular wisdom misses the fact that work stress comes less from the number of hours worked than from lack of control on the job. For all the pressures and tough decisions managers and executives face, workers experience more stress and, as a result, have a much higher incidence of ulcers, high blood pressure, heart disease, and other stress-related disorders compared with the managers, professionals, and executives above them.[6]

Capitalists like to say they are the risk takers in society, and this is why they should be richly rewarded. But workers are at constant risk for their jobs and livelihood. Workers risk their health and safety at work and in their neighborhoods to a far greater extent than their employers do. And, in every aspect of life, workers face their risks with far less cushion in case of hard times or bad breaks than do the capitalists. In the aftermath of the financial crisis of 2008, executives in the financial industry who took big risks emerged with their wealth and power intact while millions of working people who took none of those risks ended up losing their homes and jobs. Bank chief executives received a 36 percent increase in pay in 2010 (to an average $9.7 million, or about $38,800 a day), while foreclosure aid to homeowners faded away and financial corporations mobilized lobbyists in an effective campaign to weaken or stall altogether government regulation of the activities that generated the crisis in the first place.[7] In the commercial real estate market, what appeared to be risky investments by real estate moguls went bad, but to no adverse effects on the moguls. Despite having lost tens of millions of dollars, they continued to get credit and operate their businesses, while ordinary people who lost their jobs were forced into bankruptcy and years of bad credit ratings.[8]

In capitalism, as in slavery and feudalism before it, the wealth of the owners comes from the labor of those they control. The specific mechanisms and institutions the capitalists use to take this wealth differ from the ones used by slave owners and feudal kings, and are more complicated. The justifications for this taking are also different. But these differences should not obscure the basic fact that the wealth of the capitalist is not of his own making. His wealth was made by someone else, workers working together.

This fact of economic life in capitalist society has moral consequences. It helps explain why the raw individualism beloved by the champions of the free market is out of touch with reality, and leads to unacceptable social outcomes. What are we to make of the words of Willie Farah, who said of the workers striking his garment factories in Las Cruces, New Mexico, and El Paso, Texas, in 1972: "We have 'em whipped, and we're going to keep 'em whipped"?[9] It was a bitter strike for union recognition that pitted Farah against two thousand workers, mostly Mexican American women, who led a national boycott of Farah clothes as part of their strategy. One of the women reported to a rally of supporters I attended in New York City that Farah had told the striking women to go back to work, declaring: "Without me, you are nothing." Twenty-two months later, Willie Farah apparently concluded that without his workers, *he* was nothing: he signed the first collective bargaining agreement in the history of the company with the Amalgamated Clothing and Textile Workers Union.

Not every capitalist openly belittles his employees as contemptuously as Willie Farah did. But the mentality is widespread. It explains how capitalists can tell their workers that they are lucky to have a job at all, and that asking for better pay or working conditions or trying to organize a union will only cause the company to move away. It explains how capitalists can tell city governments that they must pay hundreds of millions of dollars in subsidies to attract a business to a particular location. It explains how capitalists can tell people that they must accept severe environmental damage as the inevitable consequence of modern production. These matter-of-fact, everyday demands come from the same attitude: that every worker and every community is nothing without the willing presence of the capitalist. The capitalist demands his due as a leader of society because he has had the wit, foresight, and energy to make a lot of money with a successful business.

In discussions of American social policy, "entitlement," meaning social programs to which people have a right, has become a dirty word. Conservatives regularly denounce people on welfare, and even those who get Social Security, for their reliance on these programs. Entitlement is supposed to be the opposite of self-reliance: bad social policy based on bad moral values.

But who is more insistent about entitlement than the capitalists? They want everything: every tax break, every Congressional bailout, every wage concession, every regulatory loophole, every chance to buy candidates, every military intervention into other countries to support their business ventures. They claim these entitlements because their businesses provide jobs to communities, and because they are successful individuals who should keep the rewards of success for themselves. The mother thrown off the welfare rolls could well ask of the capitalist, "Just who is it who's getting something for nothing?"

Here we come back to the reality of individual success and failure. In some important ways, success comes from the work of the individual, of course. But there are limits to what an individual can claim as his or her own accomplishment (or failure). As we saw earlier in this chapter, each of us is not just an individual, isolated from others, making it, or not, on our own. Each of us is also a set of relationships with others, near and far, who help create us and shape what we can and cannot accomplish as individuals, to whom we owe much that cannot be repaid directly in the market. The capitalist, even more than the rest of us, is a social creation. The capitalists' sense of entitlement is out of touch with reality because it denies the social foundation of their wealth. Poor and working people's claims to society's help with the provision of basic needs, or to common courtesy and respect, are more in tune with the realities of our mutual responsibilities. But typically the poor are not militantly insistent about these claims, and workers are on the defensive. Too often they are meek. It is the capitalists who adamantly demand respect, power, deference, a right to their wealth untouched. Whatever excessive claims to entitlement some poor and working people may make, it is a weak echo of the hubristic demands of the wealthy.

The Rise of "Family Values"

In the 1980s and 1990s, as the living standards of the working class steadily deteriorated, "values" came to increasing prominence as a political issue. But values were separated from economic questions. Instead of considering economic justice and social responsibility, values came to mean what some called "family values." As right-wing political forces came to prominence, they redirected the focus of moral debate by asserting conservative responses to such vital questions as abortion, the rights of women, and homosexuality. The energy of these assertions, backed by grassroots mobilizations through many right-wing Christian churches, created a climate in which the moral character of political candidates and party platforms seemed to rest on their stands on these "family values" issues—not on policies to deal with poverty, inequality, military budgets, or the rights of workers to organize unions.

Liberal and pro-labor politicians have answered these attacks in policy terms. But these leaders have too often been on the defensive in the moral debate. They have not expressed a coherent moral code of their own to answer the right's claims of moral leadership. They have not articulated an ethical system to justify their policies, integrate their views on family values with workers' needs, and motivate broad political participation by people who seek moral leadership as well as improvements in their everyday lives.

The rise of the "family values" agenda was the work of Jerry Falwell's Moral Majority, Pat Robertson and Ralph Reed's Christian Coalition, the Family Research Council, and other organizations of the Christian right. Their rise to a central spot in American politics coincided with the increased power of corporate interests to set the country's economic policies.

The Christian right has not limited its program to abortion and school prayer. Their leaders have consistently supported the same limited government, tax cut, privatization, and welfare reform agenda championed by the traditional corporate base of the Republican Party. With the merger of corporate and Christian right agendas, the conservative, pro-business agenda came to be associated with a moral agenda of sorts. The corporate elite and their allies have succeeded in redefining more than the country's economic priorities to support business interests. They have redefined what we mean by values as well.

The New Deal of the 1930s was based on values of mutual responsibility organized through government action, in programs like Social Security, government protection of unions, and laws establishing minimum wages and overtime pay for millions of workers in private corporations. Supporters justified these policies with moral appeals to economic justice and economic democracy. But in recent decades, only "efficiency" has been associated with the word "economic." Justice and democracy are gone. Corporate ideologues, with the assistance of the Christian right, have emptied all economic content from moral debates, and substituted "family values" in their place, making it possible to talk about morality while ignoring the systematic attacks on the working class that I have documented throughout this book.

This change in the meaning of values in public life has been an important part of the attack on working people. It has robbed us of an essential part of what we need to evaluate social policy—an adequate moral compass. To reverse these trends, we will need to address values and morality directly, to construct a politics that finds the right balance between self-interest and community.

The moral claims of the business community are not limited to the political wedge issues of the Christian right. Many traditional business leaders and lobbyists are quite uncomfortable with Christian social conservatism and prefer a direct defense of the "free market" based on appeals to individualism and human freedom. These themes are also welcomed by the religious right, if not put at the center of their particular agenda.

Individualism has a powerful appeal to the American psyche, open as Americans are to the mythic history of struggling immigrants and pioneers surviving by their own wits and growing rich through initiative, hard work, and true grit. The notion resonates with the early history of this country, a time of small farmers, merchants, and individual artisans, before advanced capitalism and its vast, impersonal social networks and institutions came into existence. Appeals to individualism are especially attractive to modern workers, who so often feel fenced in, without power, independence, and apparent future prospects in their daily lives. No one wants to be told they can't do what they want, especially after a long day at work; no one wants to believe that a better future is closed off to them, especially those for whom it is most likely true.

"Individual responsibility" and "family values" combine to form the core of what passes for the ethical foundation of American politics at the start of the twenty-first century. The troubles our families face, we are told, come from the decline in family values and disregard for individual responsibility, the supposed legacy of the amoral liberals and hedonists of the 1960s. Taking its place with poor people, foreigners, and the government, the erosion of family values has become one of the main targets in American politics, used to channel the frustration and anger that working people feel. But "the decline in family values" is a false target. Pursuing it is a one-two punch that only intensifies the alienation that working people experience, while reducing their power to do anything about it.

The stark individualism of the "family values" lobby and the business community has other perverse results. It denies that society has responsibility for anyone except those obviously incapable of helping themselves, the so-called "truly needy." At the same time, it denies that the individual has any responsibility to society. Social programs and the "safety net" are then dismantled, exposing millions to hardship. And those left on their own must act on their own, without regard for social consequences or moral niceties. What can we say about business leaders who champion individualism while supporting ten- and twenty-year jail terms for poor people when they participate in the drug trade in ghettos where there are no regular jobs? Their sanctimony is outdone only by the leaders of the religious right who preach on behalf of families while countenancing the destruction of the material foundation of stable family life.

Linking "family values" politically with the business agenda of the right wing of the Republican Party, as the Christian right has done, has promoted economic policies that have done far more to attack the stability of working class families than anything one might imagine could result from tolerance of abortion or homosexuality. How have deep cuts in medical care, education, housing, and collective bargaining rights served family values? What family values were strengthened when workplace and environmental health and safety enforcement is reduced?

These policies have contributed tangibly to the decline in living standards and life prospects among working class families, yet they have been part of the larger agenda of those promoting "family values." The outright meanness and intolerance that is characteristic of the conservative business and "family values" moral agenda is both striking and repulsive because of this hypocrisy.

In recent decades, the ideology of raw individual power has taken hold even in the realm of charity. The wealthy have come to regard their charitable contributions as platforms to exert direct control over the projects and organizations they fund. The phenomenon has a name, "philanthrocapitalism," suggestive of the entrepreneurial element that has invaded the charitable impulse.[10] Perhaps nowhere has this taken hold more fully than in the charter school movement, in which Bill Gates and other billionaires provide tens of millions of dollars to schools to implement policies they take an active hand in shaping.

The alliance between the Christian right and corporate power has its strains, however, from both sides of the relationship. Leaders and members of some evangelical churches have come to challenge corporate demands for lax environmental regulation. These religious voices have joined secular and scientific communities who raise alarms about global warming, endangered species, mountaintop removal to reach coal deposits, and other business practices that threaten the stability and hospitality of the planet's environment. Together they ask what values are served by economic practices that spoil the earth, the seas, and the air we breathe in the pursuit of private gain.

From the other side, many corporate leaders are uncomfortable with the antiscience declarations coming from religious leaders hostile to the teaching of evolution. To advance the technical knowledge necessary to compete economically, let alone genuinely improve lives, we must be able to distinguish between an opinion and a theory. An opinion may be based on nothing more than prejudice and superstition, or derived from ideological first principles without reference to reality. A theory is based on careful observation, adjusted and refined through empirical tests, and further observation in the process that defines science.

These tensions—concerning the environment, evolution, sexuality, and other elements of the religious right agenda—may yet undermine the coalition that has so effectively served to provide apparent ethical cover to corporate political power. We will return to this question in the next chapter.

Ethical Limits on Capitalism

Raw capitalism is an ugly thing. It is especially shocking when it first looms on the historical stage, when greed becomes the norm and older values succumb to the new ways of the market. In Europe, the human misery and degradation of the early years of capitalism, when farmers found themselves thrown off their land and working in the capitalists' factories, generated strong opposition from early socialist movements as well as from social critics like Robert Owen and novelists like Charles Dickens. In the 1990s, after the collapse of the Soviet system, Russia's plunge into capitalism was no less shocking. The Russian government was weak, unable to exert control over the lawlessness of ruthless and utterly corrupt private businesspeople. Western analysts stressed the importance of establishing strong government institutions in Russia, to shape the market and limit the mafias that had sprung up, although the subsequent consolidation of government power by Vladimir Putin raised alarms in the West. Everyone agrees that private action in totally unregulated markets guarantees chaos and widespread hardship. Yet the problem isn't solved only by creating government regulations and a strong police force. China has both but is not free from the shocks that capitalism brings. One critic of China's conversion to the market sees in her country what could just as well be said of Russia. The growth of private enterprise and markets in China, He Qinglian writes, has been

> a process in which power holders and their hangers-on plundered public wealth. The primary target of their plunder was state property that had been accumulated from forty years of the people's sweat, and their primary means of plunder was political power....
>
> The complaints of most people about inequality [in China] are not about inequality per se but about the sordid methods by which wealth is achieved.... The championing of money as a value has never before reached the point of holding all moral rules in such contempt.... [The challenge of the new capitalism in China is] how to avoid living in an utterly valueless condition.[11]

The moral challenge that capitalism poses operates in practical ways at every level of society. It is most obvious when the rigors of capitalist life first come to a community, before people come to accept capitalist norms as "human nature." But even in an advanced capitalist country like the United States we can see the moral corrosion capitalism entails, and find it appalling.

We see it when a rural community finds itself assaulted by waves of development radiating out from nearby cities. Small merchants are driven out of business by national retail chains in new malls. Farmland and beautiful vistas are destroyed when building advances with no regard for community character or traditions, when property values dominate community values. The pace of life changes, becomes more intense. Everyone notices. It's a new way of life.

This is what happens when HMOs push doctors to sacrifice patient care to protect the bottom line. It is what happens when university professors must find corporate support for their scholarship in the new, entrepreneurial university. In particular, it is what shocked photographers working for *National Geographic,* when the venerable nonprofit magazine opened for-profit outlets for their photographers' work and demanded to keep all the proceeds from use of the photos, after years of respectful working relations with this vital part of their workforce.[12]

In matters great and small, most people think of these developments as wrong, not just unfortunate. We tend to see the naked workings of capitalism as morally degrading. "The love of money is the root of all evil" is not about money, it's about putting money at the forefront. It's about allowing the drive for money to be all-consuming, as it becomes when society puts no restrictions on the drive to maximize profit, and self-interest turns to greed.

Market activity needs institutions and rules to guide it. The social institutions that the Russians and the Chinese must now create to protect themselves from raw market power, we in the United States must also protect *and strengthen* in our own way, as was painfully driven home by the corporate recklessness that led to the financial collapse of 2008. The institutions and policies we create to limit capitalist behavior must be based on some ethical values. These values cannot be rooted in individualism, since it is exactly the excesses of individualism that need to be curbed.

The moral authority to limit individualism comes from the reality that the individual is also social. The individual has obligations to the social network that helps create, shape, and sustain individuals, and also has the power to destroy them. Society can make claims on individuals to be responsible to that social reality, while the individual has a claim to fair and respectful treatment in the social network.

We cannot outlaw greed, any more than we can outlaw any other feeling or attitude. But we can outlaw some of the practical effects of greed, by requiring that the effects of pursuing self-interest do not undermine the rights of others. The debate about values needs to be refocused, to articulate values and morality that can help limit capitalist power. This means product standards, labor standards, environmental standards, standards that have bite, enforced with real consequences for those who violate them. It also means some form of social control on investment and other strategic business decisions. These are not easy things to do, technically or politically. They require concentrated will and careful thought. Looking at the problems with class in mind will help develop the moral compass we need to get it right.

Being against greed is not being against business. Many small, family-run businesses operate in socially responsible ways. Their owners want to make a living, but they also take pride in skilled work, treat their employees well, and respect the community and natural environments in which they do business. The same is true for some big business as well. But too often individual good intentions are overwhelmed by market imperatives, driving owners to socially irresponsible action out of the need to survive. Some of my friends who own small businesses talk about this pressure with the pain and resentment typical of middle class experience. When market imperatives drive business to antisocial action—eat or be eaten, kill or be killed, do what is necessary or go broke—we have a moral problem with far-reaching consequences.

The fact that the capitalists' wealth is social means that the claim that working people make on that wealth is not a request for charity. It is a claim for what they themselves have already created. And, if it is true that it is better to teach a person how to fish than to give that person a bucket of fish, it is also true that workers' demand for wealth need not be put in terms of redistributing existing wealth. Rather, workers' need for wealth is better served by a claim for power over the process and machinery of wealth creation itself.

Because capitalists have a hard time accepting limits, they must be imposed by an opposing power. As the majority in society, the working class can have that power. Unlike capitalists, workers have an interest in understanding and acting upon values that challenge individualism. Working class politics can be bound up with these values. And a working class person, so much more attuned to direct mutual aid on the job and in daily survival than the capitalist, has a greater potential for understanding the interdependent nature of social reality.

Looking at "family values" from a class perspective shows us that families need the values of economic justice, values that give their due to mutual obligations, values that put limits on capitalism and create institutions that promote the material and spiritual well-being of working class families and all people.

Twenty-first century politics, to improve the lives of working class people, will need to challenge the rule of the marketplace. It will take the working class as an organized political force to assert the values of economic justice and muster the power needed to implement policies that flow from them. From the point of view of working people, the task now is to make class issues the wedge issues of the new century. As education scholar Jonathan Kozol said to an audience of teachers concerned about the fate of children in many public schools, "There needs to be moral grandeur in your resistance."[13] Economic justice must become the new moral litmus test, the basic ethical standard against which we measure candidates, public officials, and our social institutions. In the concluding chapters of this book, I turn to the prospects for such a working class politics, already beginning to bubble up in the United States at the start of the twenty-first century.

THE WORKING CLASS AND POWER

The Target of Working Class Power

The reason working people need power is to answer the power arrayed against them. Power needs a target; effective power needs an appropriate target. So, as negative and divisive as it may seem to some, one essential element for working class power is a clear idea of who the enemy is, whose power working class power is arrayed against.

A class understanding of power points to the capitalist class as that target. One of the great weaknesses of the standard view of class—one that sees a vast middle class with a few rich above and the poor below—is that it confuses the target of political conflict. As we saw when we looked at the distributions of income and wealth, when the working class disappears into the middle class, the capitalist class disappears into "the rich." And when the capitalist class disappears from view, it cannot be a target.

Working class people cannot assert their interests without challenging the demands capitalists make on society. Since the beginning of capitalism, capitalists have been challenged by all sections of society, each in its own way trying to limit the power capitalists wield in the market and in the broader society. In the United States in the nineteenth century, pushed by a populist movement of workers, farmers, and small business owners, the government enacted antitrust legislation and railroad and utility rate regulations. In the early twentieth century the Progressive Era increased the power of the government to control corporate actions with such new instruments as the Food and Drug Administration. The

Great Depression of the 1930s brought restrictions on banking and investment practices. Since the 1970s, capitalists have been restrained by a growing number of environmental regulations.

In this long history, the working class has only infrequently brought enough power to bear, with enough vision, to seriously challenge capital. But it has happened, and the results of those contests have brought long-lasting benefits for working people. We see them in Social Security and minimum wage legislation, in government protection for collective bargaining, in occupational health and safety regulations, and in progressive taxation, which takes a higher percentage of a well-off person's income than a low-paid worker's.

Yet all of these limits on capitalists, and many more, are under attack as the twenty-first century unfolds. In the post–Cold War era of capitalism triumphant, few dare to challenge the capitalists' claim that they are the engine of progress, that progress for all of us depends upon their freedom to be capitalists, and that, in the words of the Borg of *Star Trek,* "resistance is futile." Ronald Reagan's buddy, Prime Minister Margaret Thatcher of Britain, summed up this view when she said, "There is no alternative." Even in the years following the 2008 financial crisis there has been no serious challenge to corporate interests and the supposed beneficial power of market competition in all economic matters.

But resistance arises anyway, and it need not be futile. Capitalists are powerful, but not all-powerful. In the remainder of this book, we will look at what it takes to restrain capitalist power, especially by looking at what it takes to bring the power of the working class to bear.

Power in Labor-Management Cooperation?

Beginning in the 1980s, many capitalists made a surprising offer: to give workers more power in running the business, through labor-management cooperation. Corporate executives, academic specialists in labor-management relations, and union leaders promoted the idea of team production, quality circles, and other ways of bringing workers and managers together in a shared responsibility to get the work of the company done, and done well.[1]

The idea was taken from Japanese labor practices at a time when many American business leaders regarded Japan as a model of economic success (the Japanese in turn had taken the idea from IBM and a few other American firms in the 1950s, when Japan was struggling to establish its postwar economy and the United States was the successful one). American managers were looking for improvements in production efficiency and product quality and wanted to tap the ideas and experiences of the workforce. Businesses implemented the techniques in a wide variety of industries, from auto production to municipal transit systems, mining, and hospitals.

Management had another goal for these cooperation programs: to smooth the way for the concessions capitalists were demanding from unions at the time. Management used the offer of cooperation, including putting union representatives on the corporate boards of directors, to sweeten their demands for wage cuts, changes in work rules that weakened worker protections, stepped-up subcontracting, and other policies that reversed decades of union gains.

Labor-management cooperation seems the exact opposite of capitalist domination of the working class. Far from lording it over the workers, management seeks the workers as partners in the production process, fellow "stakeholders" (as people with an interest in the company's success are sometimes called) coming together for the common purpose of making the company profitable, healthy, and a source of stable employment. Workers are to be valued sources of productivity, respected rather than bullied.

During the years of the George W. Bush administration, management attitudes toward labor became more harsh and confrontational, but as the inequalities and massive hardships of the 2009–2011 economic recovery intensify for working people, we may see a revival of efforts at labor-management cooperation. These would be driven by an understanding that workers actually have something to offer in designing work processes for greater productivity, and by corporate recognition that the system's legitimacy requires a more respectful treatment of workers on the job.

Understandably, many workers find something attractive in the prospect of being treated as valued stakeholders. They are drawn to the chance to be treated with respect by their supervisors, as equals in the common effort to turn out a good product in an efficient way. What would it take to make this the social norm, the expectation rather than the exception?

Individual employers may be decent men and women. Many small business owners and major corporate executives respect their workforces and seek means to give their employees a fair shake. But unfortunately, time and time again, the logic of the marketplace overwhelms their best intentions. When times get tough for a business, something has to give. A decent-minded executive may say, "This hurts me more than it hurts you" when passing out the pink slips or raising the workers' share of insurance premiums. He or she may even mean it. But the workers continue to be the canary in the mine shaft: the worker dies before the business does, every time.

During the first term of the Clinton administration, I attended a conference on labor-management cooperation sponsored by the Federal Mediation and Conciliation Service (FMCS). At lunch, I sat with a delegation of workers and senior managers from Hoechst-Celanese, a large plant in Virginia that produced synthetic fiber. It was one of eight factories the company ran in the United States, and the only one whose workers were in a union. Workers and managers sat together at lunch, reviewing the sessions they had attended. They were among the most advanced practitioners of labor-management cooperation in the country, at the conference to share their experiences and to learn from others who had gotten support from the FMCS to set up structures for cooperation.

I asked my tablemates if the company's commitment to cooperation with its workforce meant that the company would soon be negotiating contracts with the union at its seven other facilities. The senior manager at the table was quick to say "no." Some of the workers rolled their eyes a bit. It became clear to me (as it had become clear to them some time before) that to their managers independent organization and power for employees was not part of their idea of cooperation.

Labor-management cooperation was central to saving Harley-Davidson from bankruptcy in the 1990s and at the time became another shining example of the benefits of this approach to all involved. But once the company stabilized, management turned on the workforce and demanded a series of deep concessions despite healthy profits. The company laid off a fifth of the workforce in 2009–2010 and froze wages for existing workers while imposing lower wages and benefits for new hires, as profits rose 40 percent through the recession of 2009.[2]

For workers to be treated as equals in a factory or in society, they must really be equals. This doesn't mean that workers must do the same work as management. It means that workers must be equal in status and in influence over the outcome, despite doing different work. How can this be? It cannot come simply from workers trusting their employers. Whatever labor-management cooperation is appropriate can only come to the degree that workers enter the process with their own independent power.

The Need for Independent Unions

The need for workers to have an independent power base in their relations with employers is recognized and guaranteed in American labor law. The National Labor Relations Act, passed by Congress in 1935 (usually called the Wagner Act, after its sponsor, New York Senator Robert Wagner), is the legal framework for collective bargaining in the private sector.[3] Section 8(a)(2) of the act makes it illegal for an employer to organize a union for its workers, and even prohibits employers from giving any aid to workers if they try to organize a union themselves. This provision is one of the few parts of the Wagner Act that has never been amended. The debate leading to passage of the Wagner Act took place many decades ago, but the issues raised at the time continue to be a guide for us now, when workers are on the defensive and we are thrown back to basic questions like why workers should have any power at all.

The arguments advanced during the Depression for the legal right of workers to organize fell into two broad categories: 1) technical economic arguments about how to escape the grip of the Depression, and 2) moral and ethical support for working people.[4] A look at each reveals lessons for the present.

During the Depression, political leaders widely believed that economic recovery required increased purchasing power among working people. Collective bargaining was seen as the vehicle through which workers could win higher wages. A defense of unions against management attacks came to be an accepted part of the strategy for national economic recovery. This was a sharp reversal from attitudes that had prevailed before the Depression. During the 1920s, following World War I and the Russian Revolution, American business leaders continued their long history of strong opposition to unions by raising the notion of welfare capitalism. Workers had no need for unions, they said, because employers would look after their employees with paternalistic care. Employers promised to increase income and benefits in the context of general prosperity. The strategy was a shield against unionism, the thinking went, since union organizers would find no audience as long as the capitalists provided for their workers. But, as labor historian David Brody has said, "Therein lay the fatal weakness of welfare capitalism. Employers confidently undertook responsibility for labor's well-being. That obligation, in the end, they could not fulfill."[5]

More than three years into the Great Depression, in the first days of the Roosevelt administration, government policy shifted toward support for unions. One of the first laws of the New Deal was the 1933 National Industrial Recovery Act (NIRA), which sought to promote unions and collective bargaining. When workers then tried to organize unions, employers could no longer deny them entirely. Instead, employers took to organizing unions *for* their workers, company unions. Employers refused to bargain with any union the workers had organized themselves, but offered to recognize their own company unions instead.

In the two years following passage of the NIRA, millions of labor hours were lost to production because workers were on strike for recognition of their real unions. Even in the deepest years of the Depression, with the highest unemployment and the greatest stress on workers, the demand for independent unions created turmoil in American industry. Political leaders came to the conclusion that economic recovery required an end to these disruptions. This was a second economic argument for the Wagner Act. The act outlawed company unions, sought to guarantee the right of workers to organize their own unions if they wanted to, and required management to negotiate in good faith with any union that employees chose. To enforce these results, the Wagner Act created the National Labor Relations Board (NLRB) to oversee collective bargaining practices in private industry.

Congress passed the Wagner Act not just because of economic calculations having to do with recovery. Some legislators defended this intrusion on corporate rights and power by calling on ethical considerations as well: fairness, dignity, democracy. Growing inequality in the distributions of income and wealth suggested that workers needed more power to be able to share fairly in the wealth of the country. Supporters of the Wagner Act understood that a worker acting alone to confront a large corporate employer could not win; collective strength was essential. Whether dealing with wages, work rules, or arbitrary treatment by management, unions were seen as a means for the worker to approach the employer as an equal. A collective bargaining agreement could provide the dignity of fair treatment in the daily work life of the union member.

Senator Wagner argued for unions as instruments of democracy:

> The struggle for a voice in industry through the process of collective bargaining is the heart of the struggle for the preservation of political as well as economic democracy in America.... Let men know the dignity of freedom and self-expression in their daily lives and they will never bow to tyranny in any quarter of their national life.[6]

Thus unionism was seen as a bulwark against both fascism and communism. While these movements no longer exert significant influence, the basic point remains: political democracy is strengthened when workers' power finds expression in economic democracy.

Following the 2008 economic crisis, attention again returned to the need to strengthen consumer purchasing power. It was no longer possible to encourage deeper consumer debt, which had fueled the economic boom of the 1990s, sustained whatever economic growth occurred in the early 2000s, and helped blow up the massive housing bubble that led to the crisis of 2008. But instead of finding part of the solution again in higher wages through stronger unions and collective bargaining, policy analysts and politicians sympathetic to labor spoke mainly of creating jobs for the unemployed, without any mention of the wages those jobs paid or the benefits they carried. And, more generally, strategies for economic recovery relied on "competitiveness," not purchasing power. The conventional wisdom became: "We must bend every effort to be competitive in the global economy."

Since the last years of the Carter administration, the identification of competitiveness as the principal economic problem in the U.S. economy has put labor on the defensive. Unlike in the New Deal era, when the economic hardships of the time led to pro-labor policies, in the 1970s the pundits began to say that labor was part of the problem. Presidents Reagan and George H. W. Bush promoted direct assaults on labor as part of a national strategy to become competitive. Workers were portrayed as selfish impediments to lower costs and economic vitality. Too-powerful unions were targeted for destruction. These attacks intensified in the new millennium in the presidency of George W. Bush and intensified still more in Wisconsin and many other states following the 2010 elections. Even the Obama administration has pursued a policy of education reform that presents the teachers' unions as major obstacles to progress. In chapters 1 and 3 we saw the results of these attacks: reduced worker incomes and living standards, erosion of professional middle class autonomy, and much more unequal distributions of income and wealth.

In this context, worker advocates have seen a need to justify unions in terms of competitiveness, to argue that unions do contribute to the country's economic strength. Books have appeared that document higher productivity among union workers compared with nonunion workers in the same industry. Researchers have found that unions are not responsible for the growing U.S. trade deficit, and that unions promote rather than hinder technological change.[7]

These findings, important answers to widespread misconceptions about unions, had some influence in the Clinton administration, which was not as hostile to unions as Reagan or either Bush were, although Clinton did nothing to help workers organize either. In its first two years, the Obama administration also took few steps to enhance workers' ability to organize, greatly disappointing the unions and working people who had knocked themselves out for his election in 2008.

But technical arguments about the contributions unions make to the economy, however well they are documented, cannot recapture what David Brody has called "the spirit of legitimacy" that the Wagner Act gave to unions.[8] To do that, it will be necessary once again to emphasize the moral and ethical dimension of worker power, and its tight connection with democracy. Senator Wagner pointed out over seventy years ago that "the right to bargain collectively is at the bottom of social justice for the worker, as well as the sensible conduct of business affairs."[9] The time has come to make the case for social justice again.

Workers' claim to power in society must be, and easily can be, a moral claim, not simply an assertion of "special interests." Worker rights have an ethical foundation that almost all people will appreciate and embrace. Worker demands to put limits on the operation of raw capitalism by applying an ethic of mutual responsibility can elicit a strong positive response. Widespread public opposition in early 2011 to Wisconsin governor Scott Walker's all-out assault on unions in the public sector, and public opposition to similar initiatives in other states, demonstrated this sentiment.

Unions are the most basic and oldest form of worker power. Through unions, workers are able to exert the strength of numbers to offset the power their employer has because he or she owns the business and has property rights. The evidence is abundant that unions do improve the lives of their members,[10] and the decline in all workers' living standards over the last quarter of the twentieth century coincided with a steady decline in the percentage of workers protected by a collective bargaining agreement. Over a third of the labor force belonged to unions in 1955, the high point; by 1997 the percentage had dropped to 14.1. The decline was steeper among industrial workers, where the percentage in unions fell from nearly half to 16 percent.[11] The story of the Diebold Corporation told in chapter 3 was typical—falling wages for workers and big increases in executive salaries, tied directly to the big drop in the union's power at the company.

When John Sweeney was elected president of the AFL-CIO in 1995, the federation put reversing the long decline in union membership at the top of its priorities. In the first three years of the new emphasis on organizing, tens of thousands of workers in health care, airlines, and other industries voted for union representation. Workers joined unions in greater numbers than at any time in the prior twenty-five years. The focus on organizing continued when Richard Trumka followed Sweeney to the AFL-CIO presidency in 2009, and was a central principle of the Change to Win labor federation with the Service Employees International Union (SEIU) at its core.

But the new organizing effort has not kept pace with the hundreds of thousands of workers who have lost union membership each year when their shops have downsized, moved, or closed down. In 2010 alone, union membership dropped by 619,000 people, to a total of 14.7 million. By 2011, union membership had fallen to less than 12 percent of the workforce, and only 6.9 percent in the private sector—the lowest levels since the 1920s. For the first time, more union members worked in the public sector than for private companies.[12]

Union organizing must be done at the shop floor level, of course, but for a wave of organizing to sweep the country in a way that recalls the surge in union power in the thirties much more will be required. Unions will need to recapture the moral high ground, after years of lethargy, corruption, and portrayal in the media as a "special interest." For workers to win gains that cost the capitalists both freedom of action and money, they will have to project their power far beyond the workplace. Class operates at work, where unions focus, but class also operates in every other aspect of society, where worker power needs to be manifest as well. In fact, as the working class finds ways to assert its power in more aspects of society, based on the values of economic justice, its power will be enhanced everywhere. A single firm, the entire economy, politics, culture, government policy: all these things influence one another. A successful strategy for union organizing will have to ignite a broad social movement of the working class, aimed at putting democratic limits on capitalists' power throughout society. We will return to the scope of working class politics later in this chapter.

Making Competition Constructive

A strong and independent union is not enough to do the job working people need done. Even if an employer were to accept worker participation in all aspects of enterprise planning and operations, workers' interests cannot be well served if their power is limited to the enterprise level. This is because each business operates in the context of the entire market, so that the workforce is subject to the force of competitive pressures. As long as the workforce is tied to the fortunes of one company alone, and the company has to survive in the market, the power of workers in one company will be incomplete at best. The logic of corporate survival sooner or later tends to draw workers in one company into whipsaw competition with workers in other companies, in a race to reduce wages and working conditions to keep their company profitable and at least some of their jobs in existence. Sometimes this competition among workers descends to competition among plants owned by a single company, to see which one can outbid its "competitors" for the company's work. Workers' apparent ability to negotiate a share of the gains of labor-management cooperation within the individual plant or office tends to be overwhelmed by the erosion of those gains in the fierce competition among companies or between subunits of a single company.

The challenge, then, is to channel competition. We hear over and over that competition is the key to social progress, the cornerstone of our economic system and therefore of democracy. There is no question that competition can improve productivity, stimulate better quality products, and promote the efficient use of resources. But nothing about competition automatically leads to these positive results, or distributes their benefits to working people. Workers' task is to make competition constructive and to exercise their power to benefit from their own productivity.

Competition is constructive when the firm improves the quality of its product to attract new customers. Competition is constructive when new technology improves worker productivity so the product can be produced more cheaply. Competition is constructive when worker skills and productivity are improved through training, which can result in higher wages as well as lower costs of production and a competitive advantage in the marketplace.

But competition often takes other forms with negative consequences. A company can lower its costs by reducing wages and benefits. The company can demand that the workers simply work harder through longer hours or old-fashioned speedup. (How many people have heard management challenge them to "do more with less"?) It can lower costs by cutting corners on quality or on health and safety standards. The company can get a competitive advantage by shifting its costs of production to the public, demanding subsidies or tax breaks. Sometimes the company saves money by spending less on pollution control, forcing the surrounding community to suffer the consequences or pay to correct them. Somehow workers must apply enough power to prohibit destructive forms of competition.

The advantages of limiting competition can be seen if we look at the years following World War II, when many industrial unions were able to stop employers from competing by cutting wages. The key to "taking wages out of competition" was forcing all the major employers in an industry to pay the same wage through a common agreement. Sometimes the union signed a single agreement with a trade group representing the employers. Master agreements in trucking, mining, and apparel set wages and conditions across entire industries. In other industries (auto, steel, rubber, and meatpacking), the union would negotiate an agreement with one company and use that agreement as a pattern for other settlements.

Industry-wide and pattern bargaining fell apart beginning in the late 1970s. Perhaps the most important breach came in 1979, when the United Auto Workers agreed to allow Chrysler to pay lower wages than other U.S. auto makers as part of a package to save Chrysler from bankruptcy. The company's argument was the need to preserve nearly two hundred thousand jobs. The concessions the UAW gave Chrysler on wages and working conditions broke the pattern, based on Chrysler's special needs, but General Motors and Ford immediately began to demand concessions of their own, even though they were still profitable. The pressure to take cuts at the profitable firms, to match the competition within the industry that the UAW itself had helped set in motion, became irresistible. The race to the bottom had begun.

At about the same time, Congress deregulated the trucking and airline industries. Most people associate deregulation and the promotion of market competition with the pro-business agenda of the Republican Party. But the process began during the Carter administration, championed by no less a liberal figure than Ted Kennedy. The result for workers in these industries was not good. Without rules regulating the terms of competition, such as standards mandating certain levels of airline service to small cities, individual companies were free to—and forced to—compete more fiercely. Naturally they sought concessions from their workers to gain cost advantages, while ending service to dozens of cities across the country. Nonunion carriers emerged in the new open markets, adding to the pressure on wages and conditions. The Teamsters' National Master Freight

Agreement shrank to a fraction of its former coverage, as companies opted to deal with the union individually. Wages came back into competition, and they fell.

The easier it is for management to respond to competitive pressure in destructive ways, the less likely it is to take the more difficult path of technical innovation or quality improvements. If a business can lower its costs by paying women less for the same work as men, or by paying substandard wages to blacks, Hispanics, or immigrants, management will take that easy but pernicious path rather than do the right thing by treating everyone equally and finding another way to compete. If wages are out of competition, on the other hand, companies are forced to find other ways to improve their finances. Health and safety standards or product quality should not be open to deterioration to improve the bottom line. Watering down environmental protections may be tempting when the company cries "Competition!" but, from society's point of view, what good is a company that violates its responsibilities to the community? Closing off these alternatives will drive out of business only those companies that cannot compete by constructive means.

To take basic worker and community needs out of competition is to apply the values that challenge the unrestricted workings of capitalism. We saw in chapter 5 that self-interest turns to greed when self-interest disrespects the relationships and mutual obligations we have with one another. Enforcing prohibitions on discrimination and taking wages, product standards, health and safety, and environmental effects out of competition simply recognizes the responsibilities any business has to the social network of which it is part.

But who will design and impose these limits? Who will enforce them, and with what means? The capitalist class is powerful, and capitalists resist restrictions on profit-making opportunities. We may realize what has to be done to protect ourselves from capitalists in power, as the mice in the old parable understood very well that they needed to put a bell around the cat's neck to warn of its approach. We, like the mice, must ask, "Who will bell the cat?"

Obviously, working class people will have to organize and apply their power to put restraints on capitalist power. Workers have the motive, the means, and the opportunity to confront capitalist power, and workers are the majority of the population. But without a clear moral basis for action, and without organization and a platform, working class power is only a potential.

Ethics and Working Class Power

The moral foundations of working class power are respect for mutual aid and the recognition of social relationships for which each of us is responsible. These were the themes of chapter 5, where we explored the ethical limits of capitalist values. To challenge capitalist power, working class power will have to assert a different set of values, one more in tune with the reality of people's interconnected lives, more respectful of the limits of individualism but without denying individuality.

Samuel Gompers, a founder of the American Federation of Labor and its leader from 1886 to 1924, was once asked, "What do workers want?" His response has been handed down through generations: "More." This is the single most famous statement attributed to an American labor leader to explain workers' goals. In fact, AFL unions did win more money for their members. But from the beginning they also fought for more than material improvements. Despite the fact that AFL unions were often racist and exclusionary, they nonetheless championed some social reform movements of the day, such as free and compulsory public education. When the CIO industrial unions were formed in the 1930s, they took on a wide range of social functions, from housing and public health to theater.

Reducing labor's program simply to "more" tends to rob the labor movement of its ethical power and imply that workers are simply greedy, the moral equivalent of the capitalists. But Gompers had more to say than "more." In his annual report to the AFL national convention in 1898, he told the worker delegates:

> The toilers of our country look to you to devise ways and means by which a more thorough organization of the wage-earners may be accomplished, and to save our children in their infancy from being forced into the maelstrom of wage slavery. Let us see to it that they are not dwarfed in body and mind, or brought to a premature death by early drudgery; give them the sunshine of the school-room and playground, instead of the factory and the workshop. To protect the workers in their inalienable rights to a higher and better life; to protect them, not only as equals before the law, but also in their rights to the product of their labor; to protect their lives, their limbs, their health, their homes, their firesides, their liberties as men, as workers, and as citizens; to overcome prejudice and antagonism; to secure to them the right to life, and the opportunity to maintain that life; the right to be full sharers in the abundance which is the result of their brain and brawn, and the civilization of which they are the founders and the mainstay; to this the workers are entitled beyond the cavil of a doubt. With nothing less ought they, or will they, be satisfied. The attainment of these is the glorious mission of the trade unions. No higher or nobler mission ever fell to the lot of a people than that committed to the working class—a class of which we have the honor to be members.[13]

Even with these ringing words, Gompers championed a particularly conservative approach to union building.[14] But he was hardly an advocate of capitalist individualism. His words in 1916 are as true and important today as they were then: "The question propounded centuries ago, 'Am I my brother's keeper?' is being answered by the labor movement and the social conscience it arouses. Yes; you are your brother's keeper, and unless you help to lighten his burden yours will be made so much the heavier."[15]

Of course, given the limited incomes of working families and the enormous inequalities between workers and capitalists, the worker demand for more is amply justified. It was featured in the title of the book published by John Sweeney as he set out his basic agenda as the new AFL-CIO president: *America Needs a Raise.*[16] After a decade at the start of the twenty-first century during which inequality continued to increase, real wages continued to fall, and benefits were cut for tens of millions of workers, the desire for more only increased in intensity and legitimacy. But to get more, working people need to reassert their demands not just for more but for different: Different values. Different ways of treating people. Different ways of using power. Different ways of competing. Otherwise workers may occasionally get more, but in too many ways it will just be more of the same.

The different approach required must be guided by the working class values we explored in the last chapter, which emphasize mutual aid and responsibility for one another in addition to oneself. These values suggest certain social norms to guide the actual policies that would embody and implement the values. While the details of appropriate policies will depend on the specific conditions in which they are implemented, which cannot be known in the abstract, we can identify some important guiding norms.

A society that gave priority to the values and interests of working people would assert the central importance of a job for all who want one. It would share the wealth created by labor with those who do the work, by providing its people with the resources they need for adequate food, shelter, health care, and education, either through wages paid or available social programs. It would provide dignity at work and in retirement. It would protect the rights of working people to unions and collective bargaining, and guarantee a democratic political process not dominated by the corrupting influences of corporate money. It would defend itself without dominating other countries and peoples.

Creating such a society will require a long, conscious process. Meanwhile, in the everyday struggle for a job and a living wage in the capitalist marketplace, workers must compete with one another. The logic of this competition for immediate survival makes the question of "more" a daily concern that too often divides workers when they would do better united—further reason why the very terms of competition have to change.

Workers are not the only people hoping for different, not just more. Much of the middle class and some individual capitalists too want a society with fairness, dignity, and democracy, not just for themselves but for others. These issues come up in many aspects of our lives, not just at work or having to do with economic power. The civil rights movements among immigrants, blacks, Hispanics, and other nationalities, the movements for women's equality and for gay and lesbian rights, all these have pointed to systematic ethical failures in American society. To the degree that they have been successful, the country has moved closer to the goals of economic and social justice. A workers' movement seeking the moral high ground will need to join with and reinforce these and all other social movements that speak to us from that same high ground.

Although class is by no means the only aspect of our social identity that is important, a person interested in being treated fairly in any aspect of life needs to address the power of capitalists in the economy. In the 1960s, after black people won the right to eat a hamburger at the same lunch counter with whites, it didn't take long before people started to ask: What good does it do to have the right to eat a hamburger if you can't afford to pay for one? Many believe that our commitment to democracy is discharged if everyone has the same formal opportunity for success, in that it is illegal to stop a person from succeeding by discriminating because of race, gender, sexual orientation, or religious belief. But this formal equality before the law is often undermined by a gross inequality of resources needed to take advantage of the opportunities that are formally available. As Lyndon Johnson once remarked in defense of affirmative action, it's fine and good to say that everyone is equal in a race when they all start at the same line, but what if some of the runners start there with shackles on their legs? With the 2009 U.S. Supreme Court decision in *Citizens United,* giving corporations (and their much weaker and less wealthy union counterparts) unlimited freedom to pour money into the electoral process in support of corporate-friendly candidates, the practical imbalance of class political power became all the greater.

Working Class and Other Identities

In recent decades, these complex issues have been raised by social movements associated with a number of different identities that people have regarding race, gender, sexual orientation, nationality, and religion. "Identity politics" in its many forms has often led to conflicts that have put white men on the defensive. But these identity movements have also positively reinforced one another, each contributing to the others' ability to improve the treatment of particular slices of society and thus to extend the bounds of freedom and equality throughout society, including for white men.

Since the 1950s upsurge of African American activism, followed by the second wave of feminism and many other strands of identity politics, the basic legal forms of justice have been extended to tens of millions of women and minorities. Anyone who values fairness, dignity, and democracy must count these developments as important successes, even if they are not yet complete.

But, as we saw in chapter 2, the rise of identity politics coincided with the decline in class politics, in the context of the unwillingness of most unions to address racism and sexism in society, even as suffered by their own members. This has had important consequences for everyone, not just for workers. We saw when we looked at the composition of the working class in the United States that it is made up of men and women of all nationalities and races. The middle class too is a broad mix and increasingly women and minorities are among the capitalists as well. This means that there are class differences *within* other identities, differences that are not always acknowledged. We see evidence of these class divisions in the many tensions related to affirmative action programs.

When President George H. W. Bush appointed Clarence Thomas to the Supreme Court, the ironies were unmistakable. To replace the liberal African American Thurgood Marshall, whose entire career as a lawyer and Supreme Court justice had been devoted to finding ways to advance the interests of working people as well as minorities, Bush found a highly conservative African American whose decisions have favored property interests and the needs of corporate America. Many people have noted the irony that Justice Thomas is a strong opponent of affirmative action, even though he went to Yale Law School on an affirmative action program, was hired into the U.S. government as an attorney to deal with civil rights and affirmative action issues, and would surely not have been appointed to the Supreme Court if he were not black. Among the many black lawyers, judges, and legal scholars qualified for the job, President Bush chose one of the few who is pro-business and antilabor.

It is a sign of progress in the United States and a fact that can encourage aspirations among black children and serve as an example to all children that an African American sits on the Supreme Court. Thomas's appointment was nonetheless a blow to those who look to government to limit capitalist power, as well as a taunt to liberal defenders of affirmative action. Justice Thomas does nothing to advance the interests of working class people, no matter what race or gender they are.

Similar contradictions arise among feminists. In 1998, the National Organization for Women began a long-term national campaign called "Put a Woman in the White House." The idea was to create conditions that would make it possible for a woman to be elected president by the year 2008. NOW conducted a national survey of women asking their preferences among a number of possible women candidates for the job. To the dismay of many feminists, Elizabeth Dole emerged as a leading choice.[17]

The problem was that Dole was already running for the Republican Party nomination for president, but on a conservative platform of tax cuts for the well-off, restricted government, and limited access to abortion. Her pro-business agenda held out no hope for improving the lives of millions of working class women in need of better child care, health insurance, and union representation. To many feminists, these issues are an essential part of a pro-woman agenda. Elizabeth Dole was a reminder that just having a woman as a candidate is no guarantee that most women's interests will be well represented.

Throughout the history of movements for the emancipation of women and African Americans, the interests, needs, experiences, and sensibilities of the middle class or capitalist members of the group have clashed with those of the working class members of the group. The solidarity of race or gender has never been complete because class differences have been, and continue to be, real and important among people of any identity.

Some of these tensions appeared in the politics of the 1990s as the "gender gap" and the overwhelming loyalty of African American voters to the Democratic Party. The Republicans have tried to win women and African Americans to their pro-business ranks, and to some extent they have found a sympathetic audience. But their success has been quite limited, because the actual experiences of most women and African Americans make them suspicious of go-it-alone individualism.

Because of racism and sexism, the lives of most women, blacks, and other minorities, even middle class and some capitalist members of these groups, have quite a lot in common with the experience of the working class, including white workers. Of course, most women and minorities are in the working class. But their experiences are not just those of all workers. They experience the particular discrimination of gender, race, and nationality. Even though these workers experience discrimination in different specific ways compared with women and minorities in other classes, they share with all women and minorities a basic interest in ending discrimination. Many women and minorities in every class live with a basic insecurity that brings the same kinds of tensions to their lives that workers feel. We saw this in the stark statistics about poverty in chapter 4. Even middle class women often murmur "there but for the grace of God go I" when they encounter a bag lady on the streets, fearing that they may be just a divorce away from the streets themselves.

Members of a group under attack, whether the attack comes about because of race, gender, or class, learn the importance of mutual aid. They gain an appreciation for the place of luck in their lives, and come to grips early with the many limits that social structures place on their ability to rise on their individual merits. These common experiences, although different in their particular forms, give rise to a common openness to values that promote cooperation. This is one reason why any party openly representing the capitalist class has trouble attracting the allegiance of women and minorities.

When Clarence Thomas embraced the Republican Party and turned his back on the needs and experience of the black community, he didn't become white or an "Oreo," black on the outside but white on the inside. Somewhere in his journey from working class poverty to the Supreme Court, he lined up with the capitalists and took on their values and beliefs. That is what has estranged him from most of the African American population, although class is rarely mentioned as a consideration in the story. When Elizabeth Dole disappointed feminist leaders, it was not because she acted like a man. More to the point, she acted like a capitalist, promoting a set of values and policies that were good for business, but bad for most women. Most women knew that, even if class is not often a conscious part of their thinking.[18]

The values that underlie working class politics also speak to the life experiences and aspirations of most women and minorities. But it does not follow that advancing the interests of working people automatically helps women and minorities. American political and social history is full of examples of workers and their unions acting in racist, sexist, mean-spirited ways. (Of course, workers are no more racist or sexist than others in society. For every racist union there is a racist country club. For every fire department that has trouble accepting women firefighters there is a law firm that won't promote women to managing partner.) Working class politics cannot be a substitute for identity politics based on race, gender, or sexual orientation. To be most effective, working class politics needs to complement and incorporate these other movements.

The affirmative action question is a case in point. Opponents of affirmative action say that race and gender are no longer proper categories for special treatment. After all, why give special preferences to the children of black professionals or to middle class young women who have had every advantage their brothers have had? Why continue to pay attention to race and gender when we have elected an African American president and women have held high cabinet positions and made credible runs for president? Their argument is that we have made so much progress toward racial and gender equality, especially in the middle class, that affirmative action is inappropriate, even if it was once justified.

The more sophisticated opponents of race- and gender-based affirmative action propose a different set of preferences, based on economic status. In this view, special consideration should be given to students from poor neighborhoods when they apply to college or seek employment or an apprenticeship. They argue that this would open up opportunities for some white men, true, but only for those who really need the help. "Reverse discrimination" against white men would end. And, because women and minorities are concentrated among the poor, any program that helps poor people would also help the very women and minorities who need it, without extending privileges to those who have already escaped the disadvantages of poverty.

An affirmative action program for people from economically disadvantaged homes would bring real improvements to the working class. Debate on this issue is part of today's climate of renewed interest in the existence and life circumstances of the working class. But any realistic appraisal of those circumstances would have to include recognition that *within* the working class, and even within the poorer sections of the working class, not all workers are equal.

Racism, sexism, and homophobia remain active ingredients in the life experiences of the working class. This is not just because some workers are racist, sexist, and homophobic. It is mainly because employers, housing managers, police, and college admissions committees continue to carry out such practices. The fact that racism and sexism are still alive in the lives of the working class means that class-based affirmative action cannot be a substitute for race- and gender-based affirmative action. Within class-based affirmative action, race and gender preferences need to continue, extending also to the middle and even capitalist classes, as in "set-asides" for minority business owners. These preferences should work together.

We have complicated identities. People experience unjust treatment because they are workers, or because they are black or Asian or of some other ethnic group, or because they are female or gay or lesbian. In one way or another, the suffering that people experience because of having one or more of these identities is wrong. It is unfair. It violates their dignity. It betrays the promise of democracy. This suffering needs to be eliminated.

Thus a working class movement that focuses only on the injuries of class will ignore the injuries people suffer in other aspects of their lives. There are two problems with this. First and foremost, it is simply wrong for workers to ignore the injuries of racism, sexism, and homophobia: they violate the same values that workers promote for themselves when they try to put limits on capitalist behavior.

The second problem is a practical result of the moral failure that is the first problem. If working class organizations neglect the insults of racism and sexism, women and minorities who insist upon justice for themselves may build identity movements that disregard the working class standing of most women and minorities. Those movements will then be less effective in winning anything for working women or working class minorities, and less useful as allies to workers' organizations.

In the fight against capitalist priorities, workers need every ally they can muster. It is especially stupid to alienate people who are trying to fight for the same values. A proper respect for *all* claims to fair treatment will increase the power workers exercise as workers, by drawing more closely together all parts of the working class: men and women, whites and blacks, people of all nationalities. And movements for civil rights in turn gain strength if they can ally with the labor movement.

What unites these movements is the values each is based upon, their common aspiration for social and economic justice. We teach our children to share and to take turns. We need to adopt those ethics in our political behavior as well. In doing so we not only act morally. We increase our strength in the long run by drawing more people to us as allies.

We saw earlier that the practical urgency of our immediate needs and the emphasis on competition push us in the opposite direction, away from cooperation. The old union slogan "An injury to one is an injury to all" has become a quaint abstraction. Everyone seems to want to corner the suffering market, claiming it all and then claiming for themselves first access to relief. But what is the gain in finding relief from our own indignity if we pile indignity on others? In the longer run, it backfires. It is another example of how legitimate concern for self-interest goes over into destructive greed when the interests of others are ignored.

The 1963 March on Washington, at which the Rev. Martin Luther King, Jr., gave his famous "I have a dream" speech, is one among many historical examples of worker support for other social movements. That march, rightly known as one of the central moments of the modern civil rights movement, was sponsored and organized by many unions as well as civil rights organizations. The mostly white United Auto Workers, United Electrical Workers, and International Ladies' Garment Workers' Union were among the several unions that joined with the black Brotherhood of Sleeping Car Porters to put up money and organize hundreds of buses to take their members, white and black, to Washington. The event was called the March on Washington for Jobs and Freedom, in recognition of the close connection between economic opportunity and political and civil rights.

Religion and Working Class Politics

Organized religion in U.S. politics at the beginning of the twenty-first century is largely a right-wing presence. But there is nothing inherent in religious faith that takes it necessarily to that side of social issues. In fact, over much of the late twentieth century, religious belief has motivated progressive, pro-labor activity. The role of many black churches in the civil rights movement of the 1950s and 1960s is an example. The political work of the Rev. Jesse Jackson has also provided a powerful lesson in the possibilities for religiously based politics in sharp opposition to the religious right.[19] By the 1988 presidential primaries, Jackson's direct and clear appeal to working class interests brought him over seven million votes, including millions from white workers.

Many religious denominations have put forward statements supporting economic justice.[20] The specific content varies but they share common themes. All stress that human dignity must be protected in any economic arrangement, recognize the central importance of work for human beings, call for policies to secure full employment, and express moral concern for the great disparities of income and wealth that arise in capitalism. All call for the empowerment of the poor. All agree that the exercise of private property rights should be ethically limited by standards of social justice to which the business community must be held accountable. In the words of the United States Conference of Catholic Bishops:

> The freedom of entrepreneurship, business, and finance should be protected, but the accountability of this freedom to the common good and the norms of justice must be assured.[21]

How is this accountability to be achieved? In addition to moral arguments, which are important but have limited force, several important religious documents strongly endorse the right of workers to organize unions and strike. In an influential encyclical issued in 1981, Pope John Paul II taught that "there is a need for ever new movements of solidarity of the workers and with the workers. This solidarity must be present whenever it is called for by the social degrading of the subject of work [the workers themselves], by exploitation of the workers....The Church is fully committed to this cause."[22]

Despite such pronouncements, labor advocates have not, of course, found steadfast support from organized religion. Pro-labor ethical views are opposed by other religious leaders who cite teachings in defense of private property and managerial authority. Some Christians even dismiss claims to social and economic justice as "envy legitimized."[23] These kinds of statements intensify the distrust many feel for religious activism in social affairs, especially in light of the practice of the Christian right in the 1980s and 1990s.

Yet, as the working class takes up the tasks of developing its power in the new millennium, religious leaders and organizations can make important contributions. Their call for "social justice for the worker" has already laid the basis for labor-religion coalitions that have taken up many pro-worker issues in the 1990s and 2000s, from the right to organize unions to "living wage" campaigns, from strike support to calls for enforcement of health and safety standards.[24] Conversations within labor-religion coalitions can make important contributions to the public presentation of labor's case in ethical terms, which must be the basis of any successful labor strategy. This will have the added benefit of challenging the religious right for the ethical high ground in political debate, rather than leaving the moral agenda to the enemies of labor.

Within religious communities, as within every institution in society, differences of opinion exist that reflect differences in class interests. Tens of millions of people in the United States, including many union members, reflect on life's circumstances in religious terms and seek guidance toward ethical conduct through their faith. With the end of the Cold War, the old fears of communist influence that were exploited by religious conservatives are slipping away. Even some Christian fundamentalists are open to a pro-labor economic justice agenda.[25] It can only be good for working class politics when religious people come to understand that their religious commitments can be expressed with a pro-labor voice. That knowledge can spread only if worker interests are actively defended in churches, synagogues, and mosques.

But the fundamentals of economic justice can also be explained and defended in secular terms. Today, as in the Great Depression and all other times in the history of capitalism, the ethical foundation for labor's agenda lies in the outrages of daily life that millions of working people experience. You don't need to be religious to see them and respond.

Independent Organization

To exercise power in the broadest reaches of society, working people need independent organizations. At work, these are the unions. But the same principles that require unions to be under the control of workers, free from sponsorship by management, also require that working class organizations in other parts of society be in the hands of workers themselves. In cultural affairs, in education, in the media, in politics, working people need to develop their own independent base of power.

At various times in the past the working class did have some of these instruments. For example, in the 1950s the UAW had a twice-daily radio program, "Shift Break," that broadcast news about the union, the auto companies, the larger economy, and social issues from the point of view of working people. One indication of its meaning to the community was that no U.S. radio station would carry it. The program was broadcast on CKLW, a Canadian station across the

Detroit River. By the mid-1960s the UAW had stopped producing the program. But with corporate control of the mass media becoming ever more concentrated, it is time for the labor movement to carve out a presence in broadcasting again. This could be done with radio and television at the local level, produced by individual unions or central labor councils, as well as at the national level through the AFL-CIO. Labor access to mainstream media outlets is not going to be easier now than it was in the 1950s, but working people can muster the creative energy to make high-quality programs and fight to get them out to the public, even if it takes setting up a labor broadcast network. The enormous power of the Internet and social media provide alternative means to a wide audience, which may yet come to marginalize traditional print and broadcast outlets.

Another essential ingredient of working class power is independent political organizations under worker control. Politics is much broader than electing people to office, although electoral politics is certainly an important part of the mix. Some working class advocacy will come from community-based organizations. But most worker politics will be done in activity organized by unions or by central labor councils, because, despite their dwindling numbers, unions have the money and the organizational structures in place to carry out political work. Voter registration campaigns and work on ballot initiatives such as living wage campaigns, as well as backing candidates and lobbying, are high on labor's agenda.

Still, less than 12 percent of the labor force is in unions. A powerful labor movement will have to be much more than a strong union movement. Working people will need to assert their presence and interests directly within movements that do not obviously connect with class or work, like those for universal health care, affordable housing, representative media, affirmative action, environmental protection, immigrant rights, and other concerns that mobilize people together across class boundaries. Unions need to support these movements even though they extend far beyond collective bargaining and will be led by many activists who are not union members. The stronger such movements are and the greater their capacity to change the political and ethical balance in the country, the better the social climate will be for day-to-day, shop-based organizing. The more vehicles that exist to promote worker interests, the more each aspect of the movement can concentrate on its own area of work without feeling the pull of so many things to do at once.

This approach would carry unions beyond their current conception of "associate membership," which allows workers who are not union members to apply for union-based credit cards and auto insurance at favorable terms. If unions also offered associate membership for participation in broad social movements, a more expansive view of labor politics would emerge. If the AFL-CIO's Working

America would go beyond being a get-out-the-vote apparatus that occasionally asks people to lobby local city councils and become an organization of social activists meeting regularly to design and implement political mobilizations *between* elections, the basis of independent labor politics would be strengthened.

Traditionally the Democratic Party has been the "party of the working man." Unions have had a long and sometimes difficult relationship with the Democratic Party, and today the AFL-CIO is again trying to exert power through that channel. Unions exerted enormous effort to elect Barack Obama in 2008, but it remains to be seen whether this strategy can turn the Democratic Party into a real force of the working class rather than, at best, a party dominated by corporate interests that is sometimes willing to listen to the needs workers express, and occasionally willing to do something about them.

The best potential instrument, but the most difficult to build, would be an independent Labor Party, engaging the entire working class, union and nonunion alike. Third party politics has a marginal history in the United States. The last third party to become fully established was the Republican Party, formed before the Civil War; it consolidated its power only in the context of that profound political conflict. In 1996, union leaders and rank-and-file activists founded a Labor Party that mobilized people through campaigns on health care, international trade, Social Security, and the right to organize. Despite an initial burst of energy, within five years it petered out. In New York State, the Working Families Party, dominated by the Communications Workers of America and other unions, was instrumental in securing increases in the minimum wage and other pro-worker measures in the first years of the twenty-first century. Its success depends on the opportunities created by fusion politics, in which a candidate for office can appear on the lines of more than one political party.

Fusion politics has sharp limits. New York is one of only nine states that allow this practice. More important, fusion politics depends on alliance with one of the principal political parties, typically the Democratic Party for a labor agenda. But the Democratic Party has long since ceased to be the party of working people. Its candidates and party apparatus depend crucially on large amounts of funding from wealthy supporters whose interests advance workers' needs only incidentally. One indication of the limitations of fusion politics arose in New York in the 2010 governor's race, in which the Working Families Party felt compelled to support the Democratic Party candidate, Andrew Cuomo, despite Cuomo's explicit commitment to attacking public sector unions, and his explicit invitation to the business community to help shape his policy agenda.

If workers are to exert real political power in the twenty-first century, they will need to develop political power in a social movement for new priorities that extends well beyond electoral seasons. And if unions are to play a role in such a movement, they will have to attract a new generation of young people who have no experience with them. In 1997 just over 5 percent of workers aged 16–24 were union members.[26] By 2010 the proportion had fallen to 4.3 percent, a nearly 20 percent decline.[27] Having grown up in a time when union power was in decline, many young people have heard only about corruption and top-down authority in the labor movement, if they have any knowledge of unions at all. Too often these stories are true. Too often an entrenched union leadership uses the union as a dues-collecting machine, taking resources from the rank and file but giving workers no authority over union policies or bargaining demands.

Unions are not automatically instruments of worker power. There can be no working class power unless the institutions workers use to exercise power are democratically worker-run themselves. Top-down, bureaucratic unions will ultimately fail. Union leaders in suits who sit down to negotiate with the boss as equals are not equal because of what they wear to the table. They are equal to the degree that they can bring power to the table, and in the end that power rests only in the active and organized rank and file who make the union their own. This is as true in politics as it is in collective bargaining. When workers do not feel they are in charge in their union, they pay little heed to its political work or endorsements.[28]

The importance of democratic institutions of control in the labor movement cannot be underestimated. Both unions and working class political organizations, whether the Democratic Party (if it can achieve that status) or a Labor Party, must be in the hands of a mobilized rank and file that grapples with the real issues of the day and sets policy for their organizations. Beyond these organizational concerns, to vie for power on a national scale the working class will need institutions through which to develop long-term strategic thinking and related policy proposals on the entire range of issues confronting the country, challenging the institutions already available to the corporate ruling class. We will return to this point in chapter 9.

For the working class to consolidate independent power, working people need to address the issues of the day, not just those that come up at work. Again, the *labor* movement must be bigger than the *union* movement, and organize beyond it. Unions as they have survived out of the twentieth century may not endure, and as currently constituted will almost certainly not lead the resurgence of working class organization required to change the direction of U.S. society. New and more vibrant organizations may emerge to lead the drive, drawing the established organizations along in their wake, as happened in the civil rights movement of the 1950s and 1960s.[29]

To challenge capitalists, workers need to think big, boldly, and creatively. Working people need to take on and seek to influence all aspects of society, to find ways to implement the values that sustain us as individuals in community. Working people deserve to be, and need to be, brave in the scope of their assertion of power, voracious in their desire to learn, and consistent in their attempts to achieve social justice. Not every individual will want to participate, but the working class needs leaders committed to these tasks, leaders who are able to energize as broad a section of working people as possible to take part.

7

POWER AND GLOBALIZATION

Trade Is Trade, Foreign and Domestic

Working class power sometimes seems impossible in the "global economy." The fact that a capitalist can pick up shop and move overseas is a formidable challenge and a common threat when workers start to organize. But we sometimes forget that the global economy is just the capitalist economy operating across national boundaries. There is hardly any difference between international and interstate trade, between domestic and international competition.

Often people think of the U.S. economy as somehow separate from the global economy: our domestic economy is here, globalization is "out there" in China, India, Honduras, and other countries now producing goods and services we used to produce here. But global supply chains exist in which parts are made all over the world and assembled somewhere into final products. Finance flows freely across borders. People cross borders all over the world to find work, not just into the United States. Trillions of dollars of goods and services are traded every year beyond their countries of origin. With all this going on worldwide, we will be better served to understand the global economy as an increasingly integrated structure of markets in which people in the United States and in most other countries engage in economic activity that draws us all into a common global capitalist process.

All too often, critics of this global system divide the world into two broad camps: the "global north," representing the advanced capitalist countries, and the "global south," representing the developing countries of Asia, Africa, and Latin

143

America. These critics see the global south as victim of the raw self-interest asserted in world politics by the powers of the global north. But this way of looking at the world confuses countries with classes. It conceals the fact that developing countries have elites within them that support global capitalism because they benefit from it, sharing interests and aspirations with their counterparts in the industrial countries. At the same time, the countries of the global north have working classes whose interests challenge those of capitalists in all countries, and who might ally with their counterparts in developing countries. On the global stage, as well as within single countries, understanding class clarifies a political question: Who are our friends and who are our enemies?[1]

One feature of globalization is the ability of capital to move across borders to find cheap labor. Within the United States, workers have been dealing with the problem of "runaway shops" as long as owners have moved business from one city to another. Long before business moved from the United States to Mexico, business moved from Massachusetts to South Carolina. From the point of view of the worker whose job is leaving town, it hardly matters if it goes to a different state or to a different country. Despite the power advantage that capitalists have in their ability to move, workers have historically been able to make gains even with capital moving between states. Today they are beginning to find the ways to make gains in the global economy as well.

Media and financial analysts usually discuss international trade as though it is a separate world from the domestic economy, but it is not. The same capitalist principles and values that operate domestically operate globally, although the fact that different countries are involved, with different currencies and economic policies, creates complications. As we deal with globalization, it will be helpful to keep careful track of what is similar and what is different about international trade compared with the domestic economy. Although the differences tend to get the attention, the similarities are more important.

The most important similarity is that trade can generally improve our lives, including the lives of working class people. The first lesson of economics, going all the way back to Adam Smith and still true, is that trade allows for specialization and the division of labor, which allow us to create more with limited resources. This is a reason to welcome opportunities to trade. But two questions arise about the benefits of trade: Who gets the added wealth made possible by trade? And how can workers survive the instability caused by trading competition, which destroys some jobs as it creates others?

These problems appear in domestic trade just as much as in global trade. Jobs cannot be saved from international competition any more or less than they can be saved from domestic competition and economic change. The problem in each case is how to deal with the transitions and the risks of trade, and how to use some of the gains from trade to pay for the costs. The techniques we can use to do this domestically are available to handle international trade as well. But thus far we haven't solved these problems domestically any better than we have in global trade, because the principal winners in both arenas, the capitalists, are reluctant to give up their gains, and have done so only when push has come to political and economic shove.

It makes no more sense to solve the problems created by international trade by stopping that trade than it does to save jobs by stopping all trade between Oregon and Nebraska. Pat Buchanan draws support for limiting international trade by appealing to U.S. super-nationalism, and the militarism and racism that go with it. For him, international trade is bad while domestic capitalism is good.[2] But why would a beef packer in Oregon feel better about losing her job to a worker in Nebraska than to a worker in Argentina, except that one is North American and the other is not?

International trade and capital flows present the same problems as domestic trade and capital mobility, except that nationalism complicates the understanding people have of what is happening. Workers lose their jobs; that's a problem. It doesn't matter who got the job or why. Make new jobs and train the workers for them. That is part of a solution. When there are problems caused by international trade, the focus needs to be on fixing the problems, not stopping the trade.

In 1980, I spoke with a group of workers in Minneapolis. International trade was just coming into focus as a problem for American workers because of the Japanese economy's rising strength at the time. The workers from a local Ford plant argued for high tariffs or import quotas or some other means to limit Japanese car imports, to save their jobs. Other workers in the room built thermostats for Honeywell. They were sympathetic to the UAW people, listened carefully, and wanted to find an answer. But they also pointed out that two-thirds of what they made went to Germany. They wondered if saving auto workers' jobs through a quota would cost them their own jobs if the German government somehow decided to restrict imports of Honeywell thermostats.

For a moment we counted jobs, comparing those that might be saved at the Ford plant with those that might be lost at Honeywell, but it soon became clear that the problem couldn't be solved with that calculation. Why should one group of workers be asked to sacrifice their jobs to save the jobs of another group? No one thought that made sense.

The same issues come up in the continuing debate about the North American Free Trade Agreement (NAFTA) that links the United States with Canada and Mexico. Both advocates and opponents have spent a great deal of time comparing the number of jobs lost to imports to the number of jobs created to supply new export markets. But that comparison isn't the point. Trade creates some jobs and wipes out others. Some winners will be U.S. workers, some Mexican and Canadian. The same is true for the losers. The point is to help those who lose their jobs, not to complain about those who get them.

The problem that U.S. workers face isn't caused by Mexican or Canadian workers, any more than it is caused by workers in another state or city in the United States. The problem comes from the capitalists who take the gains from trade and then put workers into competition with one another, instead of using some of those gains to smooth the difficult transitions that any change in trade will cause. NAFTA is grossly unfair to workers. But the measure of that unfairness is not the number of jobs created or lost. It lies in the greater power NAFTA gives to capitalists, while undermining the power workers have to join in the gains from trade.

One indication of this inequality is the different way NAFTA treats capitalists on the one hand and workers and the environment on the other, when disputes arise. If a capitalist feels his or her business interests have been violated under the terms of the treaty, enforcement mechanisms can result in fines and punitive tariffs against the offending party. But worker interests and environmental protections are not part of the treaty. They are discussed in "side agreements" that the Clinton administration negotiated on top of the basic agreement, which it had inherited from the first Bush administration in a form that was completely silent about labor and the environment. The side agreements state good intentions, but offer no enforcement mechanism. Violations go unpunished if workers or the environment are injured.

We saw a vivid indication of this power difference in the days just before NAFTA went to a vote in Congress in November 1993. Many industries jockeyed for favors in the final package, lobbying intensely through their trade associations to have their products made exempt from the treaty. Unions strongly opposed the whole deal because of the weakness of the side agreements. Even though the Clinton administration and treaty advocates bitterly criticized labor's opposition as the pursuit of narrow special interest, at the last minute Clinton gave special assurances to sugarcane and citrus growers. Their products would continue to have specific protections and not be subject to more intense competition from Mexico. Why did President Clinton insist on these last-minute changes in the agreement and win them from Mexican negotiators? Because he needed the votes of the Louisiana (sugar) and Florida (citrus and sugar) congressional delegations, and he got them.[3] Sometimes, it seems, special interests are not called "special interests."

When NAFTA passed, an academic economist I know who is a strong supporter of free trade muttered, "If it's really free trade, why is the bill over two thousand pages long?" NAFTA and other trade treaties contain hundreds of

provisions and exceptions that favor interests powerful enough to gain protection. "Free trade" isn't free, any more than tax time means it's time for everyone
to pay taxes. With both trade and taxes, class differences in power play the dominant role.

In 1993, the labor movement was largely powerless to shape trade arrangements. By 1997, with new leadership and better organization, the story had
begun to change. The AFL-CIO successfully lobbied to block Congress from giving "fast track" approval to future trade agreements, thus leaving proposed treaties open to amendments that could win concessions for workers. The business
community was alarmed, and newspaper editorials worried about the prospect
of trade being "held hostage" to union demands. But from the point of view of
the working class, what happened was that trade, for a change, was not entirely
hostage to corporate demands. These disputes continued through the George W.
Bush administration into the early Obama years, where standoffs between
labor and capital have until 2011 blocked passage of free trade agreements with
Colombia, Panama, and Korea.

Just as workers need to take wages and safety standards out of competition
in the domestic economy, they need to do the same in international trade. The
problem with NAFTA is that it encourages the kind of competition that takes
advantage of low wages and weak labor and environmental protections in Mexico. Trade is not the problem. The problem is trade without standards to block
the effects of greed.

NAFTA has had significant effects on immigration as well. According to
authors of an Institute for Policy Studies report, it "almost certainly contributed to the sharp increase in the number of Mexicans living in the U.S. without
authorization, from 2 million in 1990 to an estimated 6.2 million in 2005. With
barriers to agricultural imports lifted [by NAFTA], Mexican farmers have found
themselves competing with an influx of cheap, heavily subsidized U.S. agricultural commodities. Facing dire poverty in the Mexican countryside, millions
have made the wrenching decision to leave behind families and communities
and head northward."[4]

Immigration, the movement of workers across borders, is inseparable from
the more general movement of capital across borders, and international trade in
goods and services. Capitalism has been an international system since the earliest days of European exploration and conquest that coincided with the development of markets, from the sixteenth century onward. New immigrants to
the United States from Ireland and central, eastern, and southern Europe were
treated harshly by native-born whites descended from earlier waves of English
immigrants, but there were no legal restrictions on entry to the United States
(except for people from China, and for reasons of disease) until 1924. After the

Russian revolution of 1917, fear of radicals, communists, and anarchists entering the country led Congress to create strict immigration quotas and impose political tests to keep new people out. These restrictions, as amended in major immigration reform legislation in 1965 and 1986, generate seemingly insoluble social and personal problems.

We saw in chapter 4 that immigrants are subject to a variety of attacks based on myths and faulty stereotypes. But international movements of working people are a natural part of global capitalism. Corporate executives generally support immigration to have the largest available pool of workers. But the corporate preference for various "guest worker" programs, in which workers enter the country legally for a limited period on condition that they work for specific employers, creates a three-tier labor force: native-born and permanent-resident workers, guest workers, and undocumented workers, each tier with different rights and degrees of economic and social vulnerability. These divisions weaken working people's ability to join together for common standards and rights of employment—wages, working conditions, ability to limit the power of the employer—and common political action.

Increasingly the capitalist class constitutes itself on a global scale.[5] The capitalists remain powerful within their own countries, but, as Chrystia Freeland writes, "the real community life of the 21st century plutocracy occurs on the international conference circuit."[6] Major capitalists from around the world and the senior managers, academics, and media personalities who operate in those circles come together at such places as the World Economic Forum in Davos, Switzerland, the Aspen Ideas Festival, the Clinton Global Initiative, the Bilderberg Group, and the Boao Forum for Asia. They form the networks and common understandings that play a central part in drawing individuals of like circumstance into a coherent economic and social class. "They are becoming a transglobal community of peers who have more in common with each other than with their countrymen back home," Freeland writes. In 2010, the CEOs of two of the five largest U.S. banks (Citigroup and Morgan Stanley) were immigrants, as were the CEOs of Pepsico and Pimco, the largest bond-trading company in the United States.[7]

Capitalists want the greatest freedom they can win for themselves. They tend to think they are entitled to go anywhere and do anything that makes a profit. Their demand to be able to invest internationally without restriction just expands their demand to be freed from burdensome labor and environmental restrictions in the United States. The same motive, to get rich by any means available, at any cost to others, drives them at home and abroad. That is why, in international trade as well as in the domestic economy, we need enforceable standards to keep the drive for profit from going over into greed. The problem for working people is to find ways to limit the power of capital and to promote competition through better productivity and quality, not through a cross-border hunt for the lowest wages. With limits in place, working people could more easily capture some of the gains from trade and higher productivity, in higher income, cheaper products, or a shorter work week. To secure those limits, workers need to overcome the three-tier labor system that business seeks to impose through immigration policies that divide the workforce according to immigration status. And workers need to form global networks that can enforce these limits on an international scale.

Enforcing International Standards

We are back to the question of who will bell the cat. Just how are these standards going to be drafted and applied? How will they be enforced? At the international level, solving these problems will involve three things: asserting the standards of the International Labour Organization (ILO) and the UN's Universal Declaration of Human Rights, enforcing these standards through government action, and bringing to bear the power of a labor movement organized across international boundaries.

In 1948, following the catastrophes of world war, the United Nations adopted a statement of universal human rights, to assert an international moral standard. Workers are human beings and remain human when they go to work. No employer and no government has the right to take human rights away. Property rights do not include the authority to violate the human rights of those without property, anywhere.

The ILO has adopted four standards, or "conventions," asserting the human rights that working people have. They are a prohibition against slavery, a prohibition against child labor, a prohibition against discrimination based on race, gender, nationality, and religion, and the right to organize unions and bargain collectively to seek improvements in working conditions.

We can evaluate the labor relations practices of any country and any corporation against these standards. We can say that the products of any country or any company violating these standards are not welcome for sale in the United States. We can say that any corporation chartered in the United States that violates these standards, anywhere in the world, will lose its charter and so lose the right to do business in the United States.

These labor standards carry the moral force of basic human rights recognized by the international community for over sixty years. The fact that they have gone unenforced because corporations have the power to ignore them is no reason to treat them only as abstract good intentions. These standards belong high on the banners of a working class movement in the era of globalization, serious and literal demands in a struggle for power and moral authority.

The standard that proclaims the right of workers to organize is particularly important because that right is what makes working class power possible. In countries as diverse and as important to U.S. trade relations as China, Mexico, Saudi Arabia, and Indonesia, leaders of independent union organizing efforts are routinely arrested and put in prison if not simply killed. In Iraq in 2011, the government still kept in force the 1987 law promulgated by Saddam Hussein that prohibited unions and collective bargaining in the public sector, which in Iraq includes over 80 percent of the workforce, in the oil fields, ports, electric utilities, heavy manufacturing, transport system, and education. This was one of the few laws the United States kept in force after deposing the Saddam Hussein regime, as it sought to create a free-market haven for business. Long after Saddam Hussein disappeared from power, the law has been the basis of severe repression of Iraqi trade unions.[8] These practices are unacceptable in a trading or political partner. The ILO standards should be a basic guide for U.S. trade and foreign policy.

But even in the United States it is not easy to organize unions in the business climate of the early twenty-first century. As in Baghdad and Basra, public sector unions have no legal protection in North Carolina and Indiana. The state governments in Wisconsin and Ohio were quick to destroy collective bargaining rights for public employees once militant pro-business majorities were elected in 2010. As Joe Alvarez, eastern regional director of the AFL-CIO in 1999, put it to a gathering of academic friends of labor: "Organizing a union is one of the very few rights Americans exercise in fear."[9] This is still the case. Businesses regularly fire union organizers and intimidate workers who might show an interest in the union's message, in violation of Wagner Act protections workers are supposed to have.[10] Companies pursue aggressive union-busting strategies, hiring consultants who specialize in keeping the workplace "union-free." After NAFTA passed, businesses increased their threats to move to Mexico to thwart union organizing campaigns.[11]

The fact that many U.S. corporations routinely fire and otherwise harass and intimidate their employees who try to organize unions is further evidence that the issues raised in international trade are no different from those involved in the domestic economy. When U.S. workers make demands for better treatment of workers in Mexico, Iraq, and China, they are also making demands on corporations in the United States.

To be effective, these demands must come from a labor movement no longer limited to national boundaries. The U.S. working class must organize together with workers in other countries. One reason they must is that often a single employer operates across countries. To take wages and working conditions out of competition, workers producing the same product for the same company using the same technology need to win the same treatment through bargaining coordinated internationally, just as they must do when dealing with a large company or industry-wide bargaining domestically. But workers have a common interest in the enforcement of international labor standards no matter who the employer. When U.S. workers insist that workers in other countries have the right to organize, they make it easier to call upon those other workers for help in solving their own problems.

International organizing of this kind can be done, as three examples from the mid to late 1990s show. Beginning in 1994, the Union of Needletrades, Industrial, and Textile Employees (UNITE, which then represented nearly a million workers in the United States) began organizing among the eight hundred thousand workers in the apparel industry in Mexico, Central America, and the Caribbean. Union representation was weak or nonexistent for these workers, most of whom worked for subcontractors to major U.S. apparel firms. UNITE helped organize unions that bargained contracts for five thousand workers in the Dominican Republic by 1999, and scattered contracts elsewhere.

Organizing in these countries is difficult and dangerous because unions are routinely and ruthlessly suppressed. Even successful efforts can be undone, as when Phillips–Van Heusen closed its facility in Guatemala a year and a half after workers there won the first union contract with a textile subcontractor in that country.

In the 1920s, subcontractors in New Jersey were considered foreign labor to the unions who had agreements with apparel makers in New York City. Today it is Honduras and Indonesia. But the same response applies: "The union has to follow the work."[12]

Sometimes workers in the United States must go overseas to get to their employer. When workers at Bridgestone-Firestone tire factories in Tennessee and Oklahoma went on strike over the company's union-busting strategy, the corporate decision makers were in Japan. Led by the United Steelworkers (which had merged with the rubber workers' union earlier in the 1990s), the workers took their dispute to the international arena. They traveled to Japan and to Bridgestone plants in Europe and South America to enlist the support of workers there. In 1996, after twenty-two months of intense international pressure on Bridgestone and its bankers and directors, the U.S. workers won. A local campaign would surely have been unsuccessful.

Workers in the United States can build on campaigns that have already shown the possibility of international labor cooperation, possibly working through the international trade secretariats that already exist. For example, the International Textile, Garment and Leather Workers Federation, based in Brussels, Belgium, includes union affiliates that represent over nine million workers in over a hundred countries.

We are some distance from effective international union organizing, but initial experience and organizational structures already exist.[13] Just as it has taken decades for international capitalism to develop rules and procedures, it will take some time for labor to mount the international stage. In the process, U.S. workers will have to become more active in support of workers organizing overseas, and not simply look abroad for others to support labor here.

Unions are not the only instrument that can challenge globalization through international action. The campaign to defeat the Multilateral Agreement on Investment (MAI) in 1997 and 1998 showed the power of environmental groups and other nongovernmental organizations (NGOs). The MAI was a treaty negotiated quietly by the major capitalist countries of the world, beginning in 1996. The idea was to bring down barriers to the flow of capital across borders, just as NAFTA and GATT had reduced barriers to trade in goods and services. The proposal would have voided any country's legal restrictions on international capital investment and given capitalists complete authority to conduct their business however they liked in any signatory country. For two years, the weekly negotiation sessions were held without public notice, but in 1997, as a draft treaty took shape, word of it began to leak out. Led by labor, environmental, and grassroots citizen groups, and joined by politicians defending national autonomy, an international firestorm of organized opposition arose, first on the Internet, then in politicians' offices. The radical demand by business to escape regulation was defeated and MAI was shelved.[14]

The battle over MAI is a reminder that our focus on globalization shouldn't be limited to trade in goods and services. Investment flows are also critically important. People often forget that NAFTA was only partly about freeing trade by lowering tariffs. It was more about opening up the Mexican economy to U.S. investment in banking, insurance, and business services, as well as in other sectors of the economy that Mexico had long closed to foreign capital. The point was to allow *capital* to move more freely, as well as goods and services.

Capital investment takes two forms, each with its own problems. First, investment can buy or build productive assets, factories and office buildings in which real work will be done. This kind of overseas investment should be subject to the same kinds of standards—labor laws, environmental rules, prohibitions on child labor—that regulate competition in domestic situations. Those were the limits the MAI tried to wipe out.

The second form of investment, called portfolio investment, involves buying and selling securities (stocks and bonds) rather than productive assets. Portfolio investment lends itself to short-term speculation, gambling on price changes in securities and currencies rather than relying on the long-term growth in output and profit that can come from the productive assets of direct investment. Portfolio investment has become much larger relative to direct investment.

In 1980, U.S. portfolio investment abroad was 18 percent of direct investment. By 1997, U.S. direct investment abroad had increased by more than 600 percent, but portfolio investment had increased nearly 2,500 percent, and reached 72 percent of direct investment flows.[15] In 1975, cross-border investments in stocks and bonds by U.S. investors were 4 percent of the GDP (Gross Domestic Product, the value of all goods and services produced in the country that year). By 1980, they had more than doubled, to 9 percent. By 1997, these U.S. portfolio investments abroad exploded to 213 percent of the GDP.[16] Between 1997 and 2009, U.S. direct investment abroad grew nearly fourfold, but portfolio investments grew more than fivefold.[17]

Meanwhile, international currency transactions—in which people in one country buy the currencies of other countries—also went through the roof. In 1986, the average daily value of currencies traded worldwide (total, not just by Americans) was $200 billion. By 1998, it had risen to $1.5 trillion, *every day.*[18] This 750 percent increase in currency trading came at a time when the volume of world trade in goods and services was growing by only about 5 percent per year.[19] By 2010, currency trades had risen another 267 percent to $4 trillion per day while the volume of trade grew only about 75 percent in the same period.[20] More than 95 percent of currency trades in 2010 were speculative, with less than 5 percent required to pay for trade in goods and services.[21]

Growth in trade is one reason for an increasing need for foreign currency. If Americans buy 5 percent more wine and other products from France, say, we will need about 5 percent more euros to pay for them. But the recent explosion in currency transactions has far outstripped the growth in actual trade. The bulk of the increase reflects a huge amount of speculation on the currency values themselves.

One problem with this development is that exchange rates have sometimes come to be determined by speculative flows of money rather than the real conditions of production in a country. Since exchange rates are the price of a country's money, they have a direct and profound effect on the economic conditions of that country. Speculative flows are by their nature volatile, so the domination of exchange rates by speculation leads to instability. The economic crises that shook Asia and Latin America in the late 1990s are a case in point.

The financial crisis beginning in 2008 was a profound shock to those in the United States, but also to Europeans. It too was caused by wild speculation, mainly in newly invented obscure financial instruments unchecked by any regulator, public or private. Whole economies, from Iceland to Greece to the United States, were thrown into crisis, and existing global institutions were unable to meet the challenge. Seeking a coordinated international response early in the crisis, the major industrialized countries in the Group of Seven (G7) invited thirteen less developed but rising economic powers into the inner circle in late 2008, creating the G20 that included Brazil, Russia, India, China, Indonesia, South Africa, Turkey, and other national elites new to the world stage. But international economic and political arrangements were still in disarray as late as 2011, as European economic and political leaders struggled to maintain the euro and preserve the economic health of their national banks while responding to the Greek debt crisis, and political and economic elites disagreed on the best responses.[22]

There is no single world government that can subordinate individual countries to a single global policy or set of institutions, as a national government can regulate states and other internal jurisdictions. But economic elites from the industrial countries, joined by India, South Africa, Peru, and many other countries, formed the World Trade Organization (WTO) in 1995 to set and enforce economic rules that promoted "free trade" and unrestricted capital flows. By 2008 the WTO involved 153 member countries, each pledged to apply the doctrine of free markets in their own economic policies.

Despite this commitment in principle, the nations of the WTO have had a hard time extending it into policies that challenge powerful interests at home. Among the most difficult conflicts to resolve have been agricultural subsidies and the protection (or not) of intellectual property. As I write these words, the Doha Round of negotiations has been paralyzed for ten years. An early meeting of the WTO nations in Seattle in November 1999, made famous by the massive demonstrations of anti-globalization activists from around the world, also had failed to come to agreement. The Seattle failure is often ascribed to the demonstrations, but the WTO director-general at the time, New Zealander Mike Moore, had been warning for months before the meeting that disagreements threatened to result in failure, disagreements that had not been resolved by the time WTO leaders came to Seattle.

Instability in a world dominated by capitalist power means misery for working class people. Some capitalists do go down in any crisis, but overall the response of the international economic authorities of the World Bank, the International Monetary Fund, and the U.S. Treasury is to bail out the banks and the major corporate players, while imposing harsh discipline and austerity on workers, reflecting the relative power of the two sides.

A working class response to instability would be to demand that its underlying causes be controlled. This means putting limits on speculative flows of money, which is not easy to do either politically or technically, because business has a way of finding creative ways to get around regulations, but minimum time periods can be imposed between buying and selling securities and currencies. It also means imposing binding limits on the risky behavior of financial institutions, and forcing their shareholders and executives to bear the burden of failure. More broadly, it means constructing and enforcing policies that force all businesses to compete in constructive ways, without degrading workers, the environment, or the culture. A country can refuse a business the right to operate in its borders if it violates regulations.

Not every capitalist welcomes the explosion in speculative activity. Many business leaders understand that instability is dangerous to their power, and that derivatives and other bizarre and arcane financial instruments designed to limit risk only expose investors to greater risk after all. After World War II the United States and Britain put into place a set of international rules that limited speculation, but those rules fell apart in the 1970s. More recently we are again hearing from business and academic leaders that steps need to be taken to rein in speculation and return the markets to investment in real productive assets.[23]

Enforcing limits on capital flows and speculation requires the third force that workers need in the global economy, the government. There is a limit to the scope of ILO standards and to what unions and NGOs can do in collective bargaining and social campaigns across national borders. As important as these two elements are, government power as the third element in the workers' arsenal will be essential. Workers' relationship to government power is the subject of the next chapter.

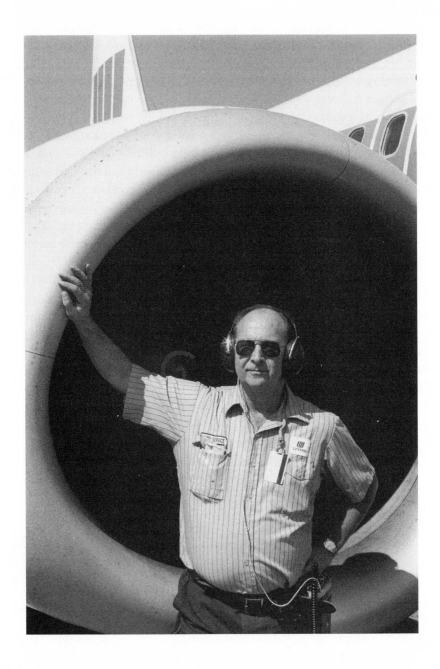

POWER AND THE GOVERNMENT

Just who shapes government activity, and what interests and values guide it, is a basic question of democracy. When the working class contests for power, it has to enter the political arena and seek to shape public policy.

I have friends who are sympathetic with worker needs but who feel it is hopeless to take on the government and try to use it to limit capitalist behavior. They look at all the money going into political campaigns from corporate interests, and all the money big corporations spend on lobbying, and the steady back-and-forth flow of corporate leaders between government and the private sector, and conclude that big business has a lock on government. In their view, if working people are to find relief from their problems, it will be through individual solutions, and by getting the government as far out of their lives as possible.

I have other friends who have concluded that corporations are a government unto themselves. Instead of seeing the connection between corporate power and government as extremely tight, bought and paid for, they see the government as essentially irrelevant in the era of globalization and huge multinational corporations. In their view, corporations have so much power and so much flexibility to move their operations from country to country to escape regulation that no national governmental power can limit them. The same practical conclusion follows from this view as from the first: we are on our own; the government cannot help us.

Both of these views, the government as the private property of the corporations, and the corporation as escape artist from government power, share an exaggerated sense of corporate power and a despair about the possibility of challenging it. Neither premise is true, it turns out. Corporations are not in a world by themselves, without need of government support. That's why they spend hundreds of millions of dollars each year to influence what the government does. Nor are corporations all-powerful in what they get from government. Even in the 1980s and 1990s, and again in the Obama administration, with the labor movement relatively weak, workers have managed to win some battles over government policy. The capitalists have certainly not given up on government. Neither should the working class.

The Reagan Revolution

It wasn't so long ago that even within the capitalist class, some believed that the government should restrict business activity and help to provide for working people. Franklin Roosevelt organized the New Deal with considerable support from the business class (although Roosevelt also earned the undying hatred of others in the business community who forever viewed him as a traitor for supporting unions and putting some government restrictions on business practices).

Roosevelt was a Democrat, but after World War II some Republican leaders also moved in a liberal direction. Nelson Rockefeller, governor of New York from 1959 to 1973, tried to take this element of the Republican Party into the White House, but the 1964 convention nominated conservative Barry Goldwater instead. The most pro-business and antilabor contingents gained strength in the Republican Party over time—as they would soon in the Democratic Party also. However, the idea that government had a role to play in limiting business continued on, even within the Republican Party. Richard Nixon, perhaps the twentieth-century Republican politician most hated by liberal and pro-labor people, responded favorably to the demands of popular movements for the Clean Air Act, the Clean Water Act, the law that established the Occupational Safety and Health Administration (OSHA), an increase in the minimum wage, and a variety of other liberal measures. While the corporate community was not as a whole happy about these laws, many capitalists did support them as proper steps for government to take in the public interest.

This tradition in the Republican Party was finally reversed by Ronald Reagan. It was Reagan who made popular the slogan that government is part of the problem, not the solution. Reagan found a large audience, one including many workers, although he represented the most pro-business, antilabor parts of the capitalist class. He was a personable, consummate politician, which allowed him to tap into the frustrations many workers were feeling by 1980. But the reality of the Reagan revolution was that business asked us to give up on the government even as they moved to consolidate their grip on it for their own purposes. Reagan's assault on government was part of a period of intense class warfare by capital against labor.

Let's look at Reagan's actions on the environment as an example. His first secretary of the interior, James Watt, well represented the corporate attitude toward government regulation that the Reagan revolution brought to power. Watt's agenda was to wipe out rules that protected the environment, national parks, and national forests from destructive corporate behavior. But this was not a policy that tried to cut *all* ties between business and government. Regulations had to go, but government subsidies to timber, ranching, and mining interests continued right along, giving capitalists essentially free access to public lands and resources for their own private use and profit.[1]

Reagan did much more that was tremendously harmful to working people and wildly beneficial to capitalists. The tax burden on workers in the bottom 60 percent of the income distribution actually went up with the first Reagan tax cuts, while the share of income paid by the richest 1 percent went down by almost half.[2] Reagan hadn't been in office half a year before he destroyed PATCO, the air traffic controllers' union, crushing their strike with an unprecedented mass firing of over eleven thousand government workers. Ironically, PATCO had supported him in the 1980 election.

Reagan's action was a clear signal for open season on unions, which many corporations eagerly picked up. By mid-1982, Reagan's early economic policy had created a national unemployment rate of 14 percent, and the country fell into its deepest recession since the Great Depression. During Reagan's second term, beginning in 1985, a reaction to the bald selfishness and destructiveness of the first term's policies began to set in. Beginning with the 1986 tax revisions, Congress began to close some loopholes for the rich, and the working class finally got some modest tax relief. There was no greater sympathy for unions, but Reagan's vice president, George H. W. Bush, tried to convey a softer touch when he ran for president in 1988 with references to "a thousand points of light," evoking the generosity Americans display in helping one another out.

As destructive as Reagan was for working people, it was actually during the prior administration, the Democratic administration of Jimmy Carter, that the first real steps toward the deregulation of business were taken. It was liberal Ted Kennedy who sponsored deregulation of the airline industry. In fact, over the last thirty-five years Democrats and Republicans have competed with each other and copied from one another in withdrawing the government from the market, except to facilitate business profits. The rise of this brand of politics has been sharply contested within each party, and President Clinton had to defeat the traditional labor base of the Democratic Party to take control of the party's agenda. Clinton and Obama have been less harsh on labor compared with Reagan and Bush father and son. In the Democrats' version of society, we should have capitalism with a human face. But if they have felt our pain, they too often gave free rein to those who inflicted the pain upon us.

During the Clinton administration, while welfare to poor women and children was cut, corporate welfare continued: subsidies, tax breaks, and other financial favors continued to pour into corporate treasuries. This cost the taxpayers anywhere from $50 to $300 billion a year, depending on which subsidies you count.[3] The close connection between business and government through lobbying meant that almost every piece of legislation included some provision granting a favor to some business or industry. As I was writing the first edition of this book, a small news story appeared that documented "favors" in the law that benefited cruise line companies.[4] Most of us probably don't think too often about cruise line companies, but those companies are in legislators' offices making sure that legislators and government agency personnel think about them favorably when laws are written and applied.

The doors were as wide open during the Clinton administration as in any other. Big commercial and investment banks won the right to expand in new and risky ways when the 1933 Glass-Steagall Act was repealed, returning us to the unregulated banking environment that led to the Great Depression. Meanwhile, the budget-cutting agenda meant less oversight of business practices by a weaker Securities and Exchange Commission and billions of dollars in lost revenue as a much-reduced IRS staff was unable to pursue tax cheats.[5]

During the financial crisis of 2008 we saw the results of the weakening of government regulatory power that began with Clinton and continued into the George W. Bush administration. As Bush put it to a charity fundraising dinner in 2000, "This is an impressive crowd—the haves and the have-mores. Some people call you the elites; I call you my base."[6] Bush-era policies delivered to this base. But even in the Obama administration that followed, corporate interests continued to dominate, as Wall Street profited while Main Street remained mired in foreclosures and unemployment, in what was known as the economic recovery. The financial sector fought off stringent regulation, and top-earning people continued to keep their low tax rates. Rates were reduced further for corporations. Health-care reform legislation passed only after corporate interests in the insurance and pharmaceutical industries were secured as a condition for any deal to extend benefits to the broader public.

Describing the ultimately unsuccessful attempt to enact federal environmental legislation in 2010 to cap carbon emissions, Ryan Lizza reported on the intense lobbying undertaken by corporate interests, and the negotiations that leading senators entered into with the business community when trying to reach an agreement. As Al Gore described the process that frustrated the legislation, "It's to the point where it's virtually impossible for participants in the current political system to enact any significant change without first seeking and gaining permission from the largest commercial interests affected by the proposed change."[7] The nonpartisan Government Accountability Office of the U.S. Congress came to a similar conclusion in reviewing the actions of the Nuclear Regulatory Commission (NRC) in its formulation of safety rules for the nuclear power industry. It found that the NRC appeared to have based its decisions about rules to protect nuclear power plants from terrorist attacks after 9/11 "on whatever the industry considered reasonable and feasible to defend against rather than on an assessment of the terrorist threat itself."[8]

The Third Way

Out of all the conflict over the proper role of government, the Clinton Democrats formulated a "third way" between the laissez-faire of the Republican right and the liberal interventionism of the traditional pro-labor Democrats. In the Third Way (also championed by British Prime Minister Tony Blair through his New Labour Party and Gerhard Schroeder in the German Social Democratic Party), the government has a legitimate role to play in facilitating individual initiative and personal success. The government should provide the basic tools everyone needs to be competitive: education, the physical infrastructure of roads and water systems, and public health and safety. In this view, the government is here to help us all, workers as well as small and big business, to each in our own way be best positioned to take advantage of the opportunities the market provides. Obama administration policies extend this approach into the second decade of the twenty-first century.

This is a view that does challenge the Republican right. Not only does it assert a legitimate role for government in the economy, it also extends government responsibility to help working people. In the Clinton years, working people saw some real improvements. Beginning in 1993, Congress passed the Family Leave Act, an increase in the minimum wage, and an extension of the Earned Income Tax Credit, which greatly reduced the tax burden on the poorest 20 percent of the population. In a similar vein, the first law President Obama signed upon taking office in 2009 was the Lilly Ledbetter Fair Pay Act, improving women's standing to sue against pay discrimination, reversing a Supreme Court decision that had severely restricted those rights. But these gains did nothing to change basic power relations in the economy. In fact, during the Clinton years economic power tilted more toward capital, because of NAFTA, repeal of regulation of the financial industry, and vigorous imposition of corporate interests in the global economy. Corporate power was hardly less dominant in the early Obama years.

Proponents of the Third Way seek to win corporate support, and so repudiate the supposedly bankrupt doctrine of government intervention into the economy. Thus it downplays the role of government regulation to constrain the workings of the market and promotes instead the government as facilitator. The Third Way essentially gives up on the state as a source of power in the economy. The capitalists tell us we are on our own. Seeking to soothe business interests, the Third Way tells us the same thing, once the government secures our initial stake in the form of education and equal opportunity.

The Social Wage

Before coming back to the topic of government power to intervene in the market, let's look at the role of the government as service provider. One useful way to analyze government spending is to consider the "social wage." The social wage consists of government-provided services that people need to live and to develop their ability to work, paid for out of tax revenues. The social wage supplements the private wage people receive from their employers. The public education our children receive is part of the social wage, as are food stamps and public spending for higher education, housing, and health care.

A good example of the social wage was higher education at the public City University of New York, provided for over a hundred years tuition-free. This public benefit enabled many tens of thousands of young working class people to have access to higher education. New York City and the entire country have benefited from the success of these graduates. But recently right-wing budget cutters have mounted an attack on CUNY, imposing tuition and then raising it repeatedly, cutting financial aid, and wiping out remedial programs for students ill-prepared at the high school level. They have made it harder for working class kids to get the college education they often eagerly pursue.

A young university professor I know, from a working class family, tells this story to confirm the point:

> If not for the low tuition available at Queens College [CUNY] back when I was an undergrad, I probably wouldn't have gone to college. If [then New York governor Mario] Cuomo had implemented the tuition hikes that he did soon after I left, that alone might've driven me out of

college. I got out of the working class, but I had to really work hard to do it, and I was able to do it because of the more generous policies of the time, and lots of luck. Financial aid was also still available for me at the time. Now think about someone at the lower end of the working class. You take away the affirmative action laws, you take away financial aid, tuitions are increasing. What happens? Those policies made the working class able to compete with the middle class for skills and jobs. You take them away, and the middle class is still the middle class. But the working class takes a hit.[9]

The attacks on CUNY provide another example of the interconnections between class and race. Opponents of CUNY began to impose tuition and to end remedial help when more and more of the student body had become black, Hispanic, and Asian. But making it harder for these students inevitably made it harder for *all* students from working class families.

When government provides resources through the social wage, two important things happen. People have access to basic services independent of their incomes or even of having a job. And private employers don't need to pay their employees a wage big enough to buy those services in the market. Both are consequences of the social nature of our economy.

Most people work for several employers in the course of their lives. The social wage recognizes that capitalists owe responsibility to more than just their own workers at the moment they employ them. Years before they enter the job market, when future workers are getting the education and the basic health care they will ultimately rely upon at work, employers have no idea which particular workers they will hire. They have a responsibility and an interest to make sure that any workers they may ultimately depend upon are well-educated, healthy, productive people. Simply paying a private wage at the time of employment is not enough, because the productive capacity of working people is determined long before they are hired by any particular employer, in a process that society is responsible for collectively.

The social wage also rests on the belief that every person is entitled to a basic level of support, independent of his or her economic condition. It reflects the ethic of mutual aid I described in chapter 5. Rich or poor, capitalist or worker or middle class professional, we participate in a social process that overall creates tremendous wealth. It is hardly a radical call for equality to insist that every child have equal access to basic education, health, and shelter in a society that can afford it.

Social services are paid for through taxes, of course. Just as the capitalist pays the private wage, taxes to pay the social wage should also come from capital. Here is where "Third Way" advocates of the social wage run afoul of the corporate interests they seek to serve. With few exceptions, business leaders demand lower corporate taxes and a smaller tax burden for the rich.

Antitax rhetoric sometimes sounds good to working people when they need more money to make ends meet. But the small tax cuts workers receive are far less than the benefits that go to the very rich. More than that, the small tax cuts certainly can't pay to replace the government services that are cut as a result of the attacks on "tax-and-spend liberalism." What is the advantage to a working family in paying $120 less a year in taxes if tuition goes up a thousand dollars and the public hospital closes down?

Privatization

The United States has had a long tradition of libertarian free market thinking that calls for the end of government and its replacement by private corporations that would provide everything from schools and postal service to the functions of the police and courts. People with such views were on the fringes of the Republican Party in the Goldwater era, but have lately come much closer to center stage. Privatization is now the mantra of a wide range of politicians and much of business.

One consequence of the Third Way's emphasis on government as service provider is that it leads directly to the corporate demand for privatization of government services. If the government is a service provider, it is in direct competition with the private sector. Corporate leaders claim this is inappropriate in principle and inefficient in practice. In their view, it is only right for private business to provide government services, as another way to make money. Having won the battle against government regulation of business practices, even with the New Democrats of the Clinton variety, all that is left for the antigovernment, pro-business agenda is to get rid of even that part of government that provides services.

The schools are a prime target. Reviewing the status of efforts to privatize education, New York Times reporter Edward Wyatt explained the underlying motivation: "As in health care, entrepreneurs assume that they will be able to solve the intractable problems that have baffled government and non-profit institutions."[10] But what intractable problems have been solved by greater penetration of for-profit HMOs and market competition into the health-care industry? Costs continue to rise for employers and workers alike. Health insurance is available to a smaller fraction of the population. Doctors are organizing unions. And the industry spends tens of millions of dollars to lobby Congress against a patient bill of rights.

Many public schools do have grave problems that demand solution, especially in working class communities. Parents understandably seek alternatives in private schools, including religious ones. Capitalists, eager to make a profit, want to meet this demand, and stimulate it with a constant barrage of "information" about the inefficiencies of government and the virtues of the market. Debate over school vouchers takes place in this context, another example of teamwork between the religious right and corporate interests.

The problems in public education have many sources. But there is something perverse about capitalists and the religious right coming to the rescue when for decades they have been at the forefront of efforts to strip public schools of the resources needed to educate children, resources which they now offer from the private sector, for a profit. These are the same people who have tried everything to hold down local property taxes, opposed every effort to equalize the financing of public schools through state revenues, and tried to dismantle the U.S. Department of Education. Not surprisingly they have also been relentless critics of teachers' unions.

Wyatt found, contrary to capitalist claims, that "where for-profit enterprises have been introduced in education, there is little evidence so far that students are performing better, that high school graduates are getting better jobs or that corporations are teaching skills that benefit the individual as well as the company." What's more, the leading private education company, Edison Schools, Inc., has consistently lost money—an astonishing $50 million on revenues of $132 million in the 1998–1999 school year.[11] But hope springs eternal: capitalists continue to undermine the public schools, dreaming of cashing in someday, somehow.

The argument against privatization of public services has many elements.[12] Let's consider a few of the main points here. The core of the capitalists' claim is that competition promotes efficiency, so private businesses will deliver better products at lower cost than a government monopoly. Yet the U.S. Social Security Administration, for example, manages its funds at a cost of less than 1 percent in overhead. The private insurance industry averages 10 percent. The privatized social security system in Chile, often held up as a model, runs at a cost of 30 percent.[13] Reports from Britain are that privatizing social security there has been a "financial flop."[14]

Sometimes private firms enter into competition with the government by taking only the most potentially profitable segments of the market, leaving the rest behind. This "cherry picking" helps explain why the first experience with HMOs was profitable. HMOs, Wyatt writes, "were initially able to cut costs by offering services to groups of relatively healthy people—employees of big corporations, for example. But as HMOs began supplementing their growth by recruiting less healthy individuals, costs rose, profitability sank and investors faced big losses."[15]

Voucher plans in education would lead to the same result. Henry M. Levin, a professor of economics and education who heads the Columbia University Teachers College National Center for the Study of Privatization in Education, explained that "private schools and those public schools that are run by for-profit management typically seek students that are not costly to educate. That's not cheating. They are playing by the rules of the game. They want to do a good job, but they also want to make a profit. But the result is that you can't really compare them with public schools."[16]

Private schools can screen out problem kids who require a lot of attention and resources (i.e., cost more money). But what can work in a few select schools cannot work for an entire school system that must educate the general population of children. This is why private schools that champion vouchers insist on being allowed to take only the most motivated students, consigning the rest to what would remain of the underfunded public schools. Private schools are thus what marketing people call a "niche item"; they are not a panacea. Vouchers will allow some children to go to better schools, which is why many working class parents support them. But better education for *all* children cannot come through a plan that simply increases the response of school managers to the market without increasing the total resources devoted to the children.[17]

Prison privatization is another example of disastrous results despite big promises. When the Wackenhut Corporation took over the New Mexico state prison system, the guards got fewer resources while inmates murdered one another in unprecedented numbers as internal security deteriorated. The state canceled the contract only after one of the guards was killed.[18] In New York City jails, private provision of health care led to such a deterioration of service, including four inmate deaths, that the district attorney initiated an investigation and the contract was ended.[19] These experiences in the United States are repeated all over the world, wherever prison privatization spreads.[20]

The claim that private enterprise is more efficient than the public sector goes against experience as recent as 2011, when this book went to press. A study of private prisons in Arizona found that "privately operated prisons can cost more to operate than state-run prisons—even though they often steer clear of the sickest, costliest inmates."[21] The Texas state comptroller, Republican Carole Keeton Strayhorn, found that the private corporation Accenture, which had taken over the state's Child Health Insurance Program in 2005, dropped thirty thousand children from their rolls and concluded, "The Accenture contract appears to be the perfect storm of wasted tax dollars, reduced access to services for our most vulnerable Texans, and profiteering at the expense of our Texas taxpayers."[22]

Why should it be that corporate managers are more effective than their public counterparts? Presumably because of the pressures and enticements of the profit motive. But is it really true that the profit motive brings with it public service? When Wall Street clamors for the opportunity to invest Social Security money, isn't the dominant purpose the chance for profit, not the security of the elderly? Is it really true that most of our teachers and school boards lack dedication to their students, or that public managers motivated by feelings of a job well done are necessarily inferior to their money-motivated private counterparts?

It may seem reasonable to expect that the private sector, which pays its managers so much more than the public sector, would attract the best talent. But is it really true that the smart people automatically follow the money? Or is it that the people most interested in money follow the money? This is especially a problem where the purpose is supposed to be public service, by definition.

The market answers to people with money. No private business claims to serve everyone, nor should it, because it would be unprofitable to do so. Yet the purpose of government *is* to serve everyone, not just those who can pay the freight. That is why privatization is fundamentally hostile to the interests of those with relatively little money, which is to say the working class.

As to the claim that the private sector will provide more upright and public-spirited leadership than turf-protecting government bureaucrats, we need only look at the "Law" section of the *Wall Street Journal*. Nearly every day another story appears about a corporate executive found guilty of fraud, a major company fined for unethical practices. Corporations are regularly found guilty of criminal offenses, and in the 1990s were subject to criminal penalties (as opposed to civil judgments) that ranged as high as half a billion dollars.[23]

Big money can lead to big fraud. Corporate swindles often involve hundreds of millions of dollars and tremendous skill; they are not penny-ante schemes. In 1996, companies in the travel business, for example, defrauded their customers of over $12 billion.[24] That was nearly as much as the entire federal budget for Aid to Families with Dependent Children (AFDC) that year. One study of 103 top brands of privately sold bottled water found that 23 of them "violated California's strict limits for some contaminants, usually arsenic or one of several cancer-causing man-made organic chemicals." Serious bacterial contamination was found in eighteen brands. By contrast, only a tenth of the public water systems in the country failed to meet these standards, less than half the rate for private companies.[25] So why should we think that private executives charged with the responsibility of making the maximum possible amount of money for their shareholders will be as public-spirited as government officials? The scale of private-sector fraud by management at Enron, WorldCom, and the banks and investment firms leading up to the 2008 crisis, and the extent of public damage that arose from these practices, dwarf any historical example of wrongdoing or inefficiency by public officials.

When public school teachers oppose vouchers, the privatizers claim it as evidence that the teachers are only out for themselves, willing to condemn their students to bleak futures in selfish pursuit of their special interests. Leaving aside the hypocrisy involved when the business community complains about anyone pursuing self-interest, it is the teachers who are defending the long-term interests of their working class students by calling for increased resources to all public schools. Teachers, parent groups, community organizations, unions, and other worker organizations need to form strong coalitions to defend and improve public education.

Government Power in the Market

The government is not simply a service provider. It does exercise power toward certain social ends, on behalf of some people, limiting others. In an economy that includes conflicting interests, and where the raw market power of the capitalists tends to be far greater than the power workers have, it is not enough simply to say that the government is here to "level the playing field" of equal opportunity and then let the market go. To serve the needs of working people, the government has to take on more than the role of facilitator that characterizes the Third Way. It must exercise its power to put limits on capitalists and their property rights, even as it tries to facilitate the opportunity of workers, middle class professionals, and small business owners. Only the government can put uniform restrictions on capitalist behavior, to prohibit destructive forms of competition. This is what the working class needs to address as it contests for power.

For example, corporations often enlist workers to fight against government environmental regulations, in the name of saving jobs. In the coal and logging industries, unions and other workers' organizations have been especially militant and hostile to environmental limits. In coal, the problem is protecting the atmosphere from excessive carbon dioxide. In logging, the issue is clear-cutting versus the preservation of endangered species and old-growth forests.

People need jobs. But sustaining the environment is essential to the long-term survival of human society on this earth. The conflict between these two needs is made worse when capitalists cannot be made to take environmental costs into account in the normal workings of the market. The conflict becomes acute for workers when no other jobs are available. Just as a business violates human rights when it demands that workers accept degrading conditions for the privilege of having a job, it is wrong when the corporate world demands that workers, and all of us, accept environmental degradation in exchange for a company's willingness simply to create jobs. Just as competition alone is not enough—we have to ask "what kind?"—it is not enough that a company creates jobs. There too we have to ask "what kind?" Laws that cause job loss when protecting the environment should include assistance for workers in moving into other work.

Even constructive types of competition disrupt jobs and workers' lives. Businesses come and go. Some win, some lose. In the transitions that inevitably occur in this healthy process, people need help that government can provide. Workers need training for new jobs, or the opportunity to take time off with pay for renewal, just as university professors take sabbaticals. Business owners need help starting new businesses. We already have a "trade adjustment" policy that helps workers and business owners recover from losses caused by international competition. These programs were enacted to cushion the impact of free trade. The same principle should apply to domestic trade, to smooth out the burdens of the marketplace.

As the market answers to money, the political process can be made to answer to people with votes and the political organization to mobilize their voting power. The greed of the marketplace can be limited, in practice if not in motive, through the imposition of public restraints. We often forget an important fact: corporations are publicly chartered. No corporation can exist without public permission, and the public can set the terms by which it will grant that approval. We can propose a series of measures that amount to "reverse privatization." Instead of giving up government functions, we can reinforce the application of legitimate government power over the affairs of private business. This power would steer corporate behavior away from destructive acts as a condition of continued permission to operate. It could also influence prices people pay, for example if government could secure the ability to negotiate drug prices in the Medicare program, a power which the pharmaceutical industry successfully blocked when the program was first created in the George W. Bush administration in 2006.

Working Class Politics

After the U.S. Supreme Court halted the Florida vote recount in 2000 and gave the presidency to George W. Bush, most Democrats roundly condemned Ralph Nader, the independent presidential candidate whom many blamed for costing Al Gore the votes he needed to win. Early in 2001, Paul Wellstone, the liberal senator from Minnesota, reflected on the Nader candidacy.

"I disagree with Nader when he says the differences between Democrats and Republicans make no difference—it really does make a big difference on issues like the environment or Roe v. Wade or Supreme Court appointments. On the other hand, when you get to what was once upon a time called 'class issues,' or major issues of wealth and power, the differences do narrow considerably."[26]

More than a decade into the new millennium, one of the most important questions we face is the proper role of government. Contrary to the antigovernment rhetoric flowing from many pro-business politicians, leaders of the capitalist class have not abandoned the field, thinking that the government is irrelevant. They are actively looking for government policies that serve their needs. Working people too must get organized to use their weight in the debate and tilt the outcome toward working class interests. Otherwise there will long continue to be similarities between the two major parties "on what was once upon a time called 'class issues.'"

Great as the need for working class participation in politics is, it is not easy to get. Many people distrust government and have stopped looking to it for help. Those who gain from worker apathy and passivity like to encourage hatred of government with stories about the inefficiencies of state departments of motor vehicles. Everyone does have a story to tell about an outrageous clerk in a government office—but then everyone also has a story to tell about a giant corporation that has treated them like dirt. For all the stories of inept government bureaucrats, much of the country was outraged and threatened when the federal government shut down in late 1995. When Republicans retook control of the House of Representatives in 2011, they did not use their power to repeat that shutdown.

People's distrust of government stems not so much from government ineptitude as from their correct perception of corporate influence in government, or in some cases the treatment they receive from the police. For all the stories people like to tell about civil servants, most would base their distrust of government in the far graver sentiment expressed by Manuel Gonzales, a worker in the Bronx, when he told a reporter why he didn't vote in the 1998 elections: "[Voting] doesn't count anyway. The politicians do what they like. It's not a people country. It's a money country."[27]

People do not like to waste their time. They tend to be practical and want results, or at least the prospect of results, before putting time into any activity, time that is stretched far too thin with the complications of daily life. Working class withdrawal from politics, as reflected in the statistics on who votes and who doesn't, comes not from selfishness or unconcern about the larger world. It comes from a sense that politics is a waste of energy.

Every year universities across the country take a survey to assess the attitudes of students graduating from college. I looked closely at the results, particularly among the students I teach at the State University of New York at Stony Brook, who are often from working class backgrounds. The survey results confirmed what I had heard in many conversations: students want to make a lot of money, but they care about other people and want to help them. The best way to help others, students think, is to be a good person and help on an individual level, through charity or by volunteering in a fire department or as a Big Brother or Big Sister. They do not believe in the effectiveness of collective political action, and have very little interest in politics.[28] The 2008 Obama campaign reignited student interest in politics, but in 2011 it remained to be seen if this enthusiasm would be sustained through the frustrations and compromises of the early Obama administration.

In general, working class people do not have to learn the importance of cooperation and mutual aid. They do not need lectures about altruism. In this relatively quiescent era, the problem is how to convey a sense of possibility in *collective* action, to show that working in a union or in a political movement will produce a payoff. Partly this involves confronting the limits of a philosophy of individualism, since in truth individual acts of charity and volunteer aid cannot rescue the working class from its condition, however good and helpful the individual actions may be. Mainly workers need to build the kind of unions and political organizations that people can have confidence in, and that do show results because they are in the hands of workers themselves.

Working class politics will grow out of the necessity to respond to capitalist power. It will reflect the experience working people gain in building their own organizations through victories and defeats. Whatever the specific forms and content this new politics will invent, one thing seems certain: the ability of working people to contest for power depends in large part upon their knowledge of class and their ability to use that knowledge to build the broadest possible social movement for economic justice.

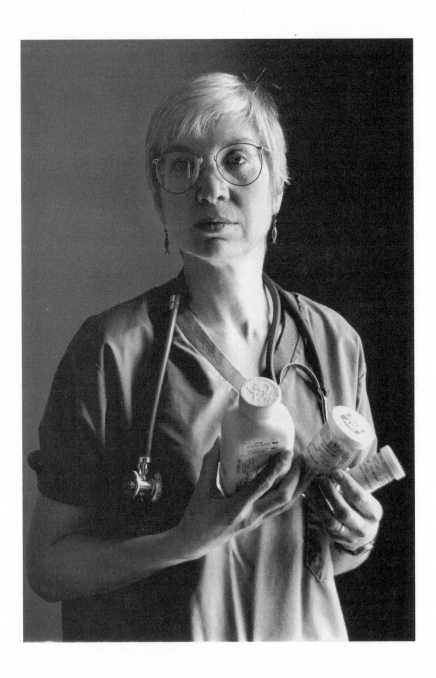

INTO THE MILLENNIUM

We can get a sense of the speed at which the ordinary course of life is changing if we recall the world as it was not so long ago, in 1995. With that year in mind, go back thirty-five years, to 1960, and compare the two worlds. In 1960, the Cold War was raging. African Americans couldn't vote in much of the country. Only Ghana had achieved independence from colonial rule in Africa. The Beatles had just gotten together in Liverpool. My father used a slide rule to do his engineering calculations. It was a totally different world.

Now go back another thirty-five years, and think about 1925. Henry Ford had invented the assembly line just ten years earlier. Only a handful of people had radios. Mao Zedong was a schoolteacher observing with interest spontaneous peasant uprisings in a chaotic rural China. Hitler was a blip on the political screen. Economists and business leaders were certain that the Great Depression, still four years away, was impossible. It was a totally different world.

Thirty-five years before that, it was 1890, and no one could foresee World War One. Queen Victoria was on the throne of England, and the Qing Dynasty still ruled in China. Only dreamers thought of revolution in Russia. Thirty-five years before that, it was 1855, and slavery still existed in the United States. Much more than half the population lived on farms. Germany and Italy didn't yet exist. And so on.

Thirty-five years is not much time, often less than a person's working lifetime. But it is more than enough time for profound changes in social organization, politics, technology, culture, and economic life. One influential conservative writer suggested that the triumph of capitalism in the Cold War had brought the "end of history."[1] But this was certainly a pipe dream (or a nightmare for those on the wrong side of the power relations that capitalism triumphant has tried to consolidate).

When the first edition of this book was published in 2000, we were five years into another thirty-five-year period of history. Since 1995 we had seen the rise of the Internet, the economic crisis in Asia, nearly full employment in the United States, and new leadership elected in the AFL-CIO. As the new millennium opened, workers and academics were beginning to show an increased interest in class. But, as I wrote at the time, we could not know which of these phenomena would be transitory, even within the coming thirty years, and which would cause profound changes in our world. And we still cannot know what the world will be like in 2030, any more than someone living in 1960 could know what it would be like to live in 1995.

In the years since the first edition of *The Working Class Majority,* dramatic changes have come to the United States and to the world. We have gone from economic growth with federal government budget surpluses, declining poverty, and rising real wages, to traumatic financial crisis on a global scale and an official "recovery" in the United States that sustains persistent unemployment at levels not seen since the Great Depression of the 1930s, declining real wages, and massive federal budget deficits. Inequality of income and wealth continue to expand, now as then.

The development of China into a world economic power, seemingly on the distant horizon just a decade ago, is now an obvious reality—joined by India, Brazil, and other developing countries that have muscled into the center of world affairs by forcing the expansion of the G7 to the G20 after 2003. The euro replaced national currencies across Europe in 2002, yet by 2011 its continued existence was in doubt because of strains caused by the debt crises in Greece and other euro-zone countries. The attacks of September 11, 2001, and subsequent wars in Iraq and Afghanistan have also transformed the international scene, and reshaped concerns and priorities within the United States. Developments in the Internet, still quite new in 1999, have revolutionized methods of communications and political activity, with whole new worlds of social networking and information gathering and delivery. The policies of No Child Left Behind and the Race to the Top have transformed schools, teaching, and the entire world of education.

But far from having arrived at some new resting place, we are headed into uncharted territory with big changes still to come in the aftermath of the financial crisis of 2008 and the many other changes already underway since 2000. The start of the second decade of the twenty-first century comes with great uncertainly about the future direction of the United States, its place in the world, and the prospects of its people. Whatever the changes will be—their content, how they will be decided and by whom, and what effects the changes will have on ordinary people and the nation's corporate and financial elite—how they will work out is necessarily unclear.

This book argues that the many changes we have seen, and that we will continue to experience, arise from an underlying continuity: class dynamics that are central in shaping the present and the future, as they have been central to the changes we have seen since the first edition of this book appeared, and far further back into history. Yet even as evidence of class divisions is stronger than at any time in living memory, the existence of class in the United States continues to be one of the great secrets.

In the popular media, the most common representations of the political and economic antagonists that arose in the 2008 economic crisis were "Wall Street" and "Main Street." This way of speaking does recognize the profound differences of interest across sections of society, instead of continuing the fiction that we are all one, with common interests as Americans. But it tells us almost nothing helpful about those differences—what exactly they are based on, who is specifically affected, and what might be done to resolve the conflicts in the interests of Main Street.

References to "Wall Street" point to the big banks, investment houses, and other parts of the financial sector that received hundreds of billions of dollars in federal funds for bailouts in 2008 and 2009. Occasionally the term also includes the auto companies that received bailouts, and other big corporations that behaved irresponsibly in the years leading to the crisis. "Main Street," on the other hand, refers to average people, those who have lost their jobs, their homes, their plans and hopes for the future, those who are struggling to operate small businesses without the government help that corporate giants have arranged for themselves. Populist cries that in one way or another denounce Wall Street and champion Main Street recognize the difference in treatment these two parts of society have experienced.

When this division is expressed in terms of class, however, it is typically only Main Street that gets class standing, and then only as the "middle class." Wall Street in the popular conception is not a class but only some companies and their senior executives who have behaved badly and perhaps deserve the punishment of bankruptcy and limits on bonuses. In the 2010 debates on the extension of the Bush-era tax cuts, discussion focused on two pieces of the policy: tax rates for the "millionaires and billionaires," referring to people in the top 2 percent of incomes, making over $250,000 a year, and tax rates for the "middle class," or everyone else. As is so common, the working class didn't enter into the discussion.

In the first decade of the twenty-first century, newspaper articles sometimes included references to "working class," using it as an adjective to describe a neighborhood, a family, or a working person, but the working class as a noun, a social reality, remained largely unmentioned. During the 2008 presidential primary and general election campaigns, analysts did refer to the working class when questioning whether candidate Barack Obama could win over the working class from Hillary Clinton, and then John McCain. But what they meant was the *white*, usually male, members of the working class, leaving aside the presence in the working class of millions of African Americans, Hispanics, other minority groups, and often women. To these analysts, the fact that Obama won overwhelming support in the black working class and strong support among Hispanic workers meant nothing about his draw in the working class. Instead, the black working class was subsumed into the black race, Hispanic workers into the Latino ethnic category. "The working class" was limited to white people (mostly men) in blue-collar occupations, suffering job losses in the swing states of the Rust Belt.

White working class people are a specific demographic who tend to vote differently from black and Hispanic working class voters, so there is good reason to consider white workers as a separate category for electoral analysis.[2] But there is more to life than voting, and there is more to politics than elections. Racial differences in the United States continue to be significant in the economy and broader society, but we make a mistake if we use those differences to eradicate class as a central part of life.

In fact, the election of Barack Obama to the presidency heightens the significance of class, as does the fact that Hillary Clinton nearly made it, and that women and African Americans are now in some of the highest positions of government administration, Congress, and the courts. The election of an African American president was a watershed moment in U.S. history. Many people, white as well as black and Hispanic, voted for Obama with great pride in helping the country to take that step. But, having taken that step, we have come more fully to the point where class issues rise in priority in the political process.

Politically, the next African American candidate for president will not carry the historic freight that Barack Obama carried. Race will no longer carry quite the same meaning, although it will not dissolve as fully or quickly as anti-Catholic sentiment did after the election of John F. Kennedy as president in 1960. Meanwhile, in society, class differences are becoming ever more obvious and important. Wall Street—the capitalist class, the corporate elite—has increasingly consolidated power and ability to shape policy in their interests, while Main Street—the working class and much of the middle class—has seen its capacity and life chances dramatically deteriorate. Candidates' positions on these class differences may gain importance relative to race and gender in the decade or two following Obama's 2008 election, particularly if working people organize forcefully for their economic needs in ways we haven't seen since the 1940s.

Since the first edition of this book, for the first time in generations a decade went by in which incomes for working class families, not just individuals, and parts of the middle class stayed flat or declined. At the same time, as we saw in chapter 3, the incomes of top earners in the corporate hierarchy went up spectacularly. Poverty has risen to the highest levels in nearly twenty years. Millions of families have been thrown out of their homes in foreclosure proceedings in which banks have often followed fraudulent procedures to secure property to which they have no demonstrable legal claim.[3] At the start of 2011, more than one in six workers was unemployed, working part time involuntarily, or so discouraged at the prospect of finding work that they had stopped looking for work altogether. Long-term unemployment (more than six months) affects a far greater percent of unemployed than at any time in decades.[4]

In the tax debate of December 2010, however, business interests in Congress refused to extend unemployment compensation payments to millions of these workers until they could force Congress to accept the extension of tax cuts for the 2 percent of households earning more than $250,000 a year in taxable income—the corporate elite and high-earning professionals. Despite rhetoric to the contrary, less than 3 percent of small business owners benefited from this provision. The same tax package structured changes in a way that *increased* taxes for households making $40,000 or less and filing joint returns, or individuals making less than $20,000 a year—together over a quarter of the population, almost all of them working class people.[5] What began as a tax proposal that benefited all (but limited the benefit for high-income people to the first $250,000 of their income) turned into another way to increase the burden on lower-income people while aiding the rich to the fullest extent possible. The tax package also included more generous treatment of estate taxes, allowing the wealthy to avoid taxes on additional millions of dollars.

On one side of the tracks, economic insecurity and great suffering spread throughout the country. On the other, the U.S. edition of the *Financial Times* was publishing every weekend a special supplement titled *How to Spend It,* showcasing fabulously expensive and luxurious clothes, resort retreats, home decorations, and personal accessories for the pleasure of top earners who didn't know what to do with their money.

These developments simply continue a long history of increasing corporate power at the expense of working people. Back in 1978, then-president of the United Auto Workers union Doug Fraser resigned from a national joint labor-management group, explaining that he could not serve with business leaders as if they were all equal partners in a reasonable conversation seeking common solutions to common problems. In his letter of resignation, Fraser wrote:

> I believe leaders of the business community, with few exceptions, have chosen to wage a one-sided class war today in this country—a war against working people, the unemployed, the poor, the minorities, the very young and the very old, and even many in the middle class of our society. The leaders of industry, commerce and finance in the United States have broken and discarded the fragile, unwritten compact previously existing during a past period of growth and progress.[6]

Fraser went on to describe battles over health care, employment, and Social Security. The same conflicts are at play more than thirty years later. Yet, writing at the end of 2010, one national political analyst reflected on the willingness of the Obama administration to agree to extend tax cuts for incomes above $250,000: "The operatives brooded that the politics could turn against them, despite polling showing little public appetite for the upper-income cuts. 'They view it through the class warfare stuff—Kerry in 2004, Gore in 2000,' says one administration official. 'They worry they'll get painted as lefties.'"[7]

When Al Gore or John Kerry raised issues of poverty, worker rights, or excessive corporate power in their presidential campaigns, they were regularly attacked for waging "class warfare," dismissed as ideologues of the left, and presented as divisive figures unfit to lead the United States. Yet, as Doug Fraser pointed out in 1978, there *is* class warfare going on in the United States, a judgment even more obviously true in the second decade of the twenty-first century.

Doug Fraser called it a "one-sided" class war because the working class at the time was not organizing broadly to resist the assaults coming from corporate halls of power. Since then, class warfare has intensified but remains just as one-sided. Since the 1970s, unions, including the UAW, have accepted concession after concession. Wages have stagnated and declined. Workers have lost health insurance coverage. Private pensions have shrunk or disappeared altogether. "Two-tier" agreements bring newly hired workers onto the job at wages often half of those earned by workers hired in earlier years, and with fewer benefits. In practice, the promise of saved jobs in compensation for these cuts did not materialize. Union membership has dwindled to 12 percent of the workforce, less than half what it was when Fraser raised the alarm in 1978, and lower than any time since the 1920s.

Class warfare has a long and violent history in the United States. But after the acceptance and protection of unions and collective bargaining in federal law during the Great Depression in 1935, direct police and military suppression of strikes and union organizing has been largely replaced by legal limits that increasingly favor corporate interests over those of working people. While the end of bloody labor battles may suggest the end of class warfare, in fact it has continued, now through greater and greater restrictions on the legal channels of working class power available to limit the exercise of corporate power.

These limits, imposed by federal and state legislation, court judgments, and administrative rulings concerning the procedures of union organizing and collective bargaining, developed as part of a coordinated and well-planned corporate campaign to reverse the gains working people made in the New Deal and in the two decades following World War II. The business community never accepted New Deal assertions of government authority into private market activity as legitimate. The all-out conservative assault came to dominate the Republican Party in the Barry Goldwater presidential candidacy in 1964, which explicitly called for the end of Social Security and union rights while championing the free market and opposing civil rights for African Americans. In that first national challenge, Lyndon Johnson trounced Goldwater, who won only his native state of Arizona and five Deep South states that were in rebellion against the Civil Rights Act of 1964.

As President Johnson's War on Poverty and Great Society programs came into force and the civil rights, Black Power, and anti–Vietnam War movements grew on campuses and in communities across the country, the conservative reaction intensified. When the election of Richard Nixon in 1968 was not enough to stop those progressive movements, and when Nixon himself signed environmental protection legislation and the Occupational Safety and Health Act, which imposed new restrictions and regulations on business, the corporate community again stepped up its resistance.

In the summer of 1971, Lewis Powell (soon to be appointed to the U.S. Supreme Court by President Nixon) wrote a long memo to the director of education at the U.S. Chamber of Commerce. Titled "Attack on America's Free Enterprise System," the memo reviewed the breadth and depth of hostility to corporate interests that a worried Powell saw throughout U.S. society at that time. The problem, he judged, went far beyond the few socialists and communists who had been traditional adversaries. "The most disquieting voices joining the chorus of criticism come from perfectly respectable elements of society: from the college campus, the pulpit, the media, the intellectual and literary journals, the arts and sciences, and from politicians."[8]

As we look back forty years later, it seems hard to recall or imagine an environment of public opinion so widely critical of business. Changes from Powell's time, still unfolding in the direction of business interests, are a testament to the power, thoughtfulness, and thoroughness of the corporate response that followed.

The 1971 Powell memo proposed that the Chamber of Commerce and business community more broadly "confront this problem as a primary responsibility of corporate management." He proposed a mobilization of financial and intellectual resources that "would be designed to enlighten public thinking—not so much about the businessman and his individual role as about the system which he administers." This task, Powell wrote, "involves far more than an increased emphasis on 'public relations' or 'governmental affairs'—two areas in which corporations long have invested substantial sums. . . . It is essential that spokesmen for the enterprise system—at all levels and at every opportunity—be far more aggressive than in the past." To accomplish this mission, to reach into the academic world, the mass media, politics, and policy development with views that promote corporate interests in the free enterprise system, Powell wrote, "The first essential is to establish the staffs of eminent scholars, writers and speakers, who will do the thinking, the analysis, the writing and the speaking."

Powell was not alone in these sentiments and ideas. His memo was just one indication of the gathering for serious battle that the business community undertook. During the 1970s, institutions came into existence that promoted the activities Powell thought essential—among them the Cato Institute, the Heritage Foundation, and the Manhattan Institute—while others that already existed, like the American Enterprise Institute, greatly expanded their work. New magazines and journals appeared to debate and disseminate analysis and policy-related ideas friendly to corporate interests. All this was paid for with hundreds of millions of dollars provided by the foundations of wealthy business leaders like David and Charles Koch, William Simon, Richard Mellon Scaife, John M. Olin, and others convinced of the necessity and wisdom of creating the corporate intellectual and political infrastructure that Lewis Powell and others had prescribed.[9]

Within a few years, Doug Fraser identified this newly aggressive assertion of corporate interests and power as "one-sided class war." But neither he nor anyone else in labor leadership knew what to do to mount an effective response, nor did the traditional centers of support for working people in mainstream American politics respond forcefully.

These weak responses on behalf of working people continue today, when it appears that corporate power will only increase further relative to working people. In one striking example, the U.S. Supreme Court opened the floodgates for unlimited corporate money to enter the electoral process in the 2010 *Citizens United* case.[10] In this and other cases, the Supreme Court has shown a much greater acceptance of business interests in their decisions compared with earlier decades. Between 1968 and the first five years of the Roberts court, the rate of business-friendly rulings by the court more than doubled.[11]

The Tea Party movement that sprang up immediately after Barack Obama entered the White House as president proved to be a significant force shaping the political agenda in the 2010 election season. While its publicists portrayed the Tea Party as an expression of ordinary people from Main Street, sick and tired of the "elites" who raise taxes and use government to bail out Wall Street, the reality was different. While some working class people were certainly involved in Tea Party activity, they did not characterize the movement. Its members were generally wealthier and more educated than average, overwhelmingly white, and self-identified with the Republican Party. [12]

As became clear through the 2010 primary campaign season, the Tea Party was essentially a movement wholly within the Republican Party, mounting a bid for power and influence in that arena. Not surprisingly, the principal organizational and financial backing came from long-time experienced Republican Party leaders on the far right edge of the party, including former U.S. congressional leader Dick Armey and his FreedomWorks organization, and multibillionaire energy executives David and Charles Koch.[13] The movement and its political spokespeople got powerful megaphones and amplifiers from the Fox cable news channel and dozens of right-wing radio personalities, Rush Limbaugh being the most notorious.

The deep economic crisis gripping most people and regions of the country in 2010 provided enough frustration and anger to make the Tea Party message attractive to some working class voters, especially in the absence of a clear alternative message speaking to their needs. But the Tea Party was hardly a populist movement in the American tradition, which has almost always challenged the power of banks and big business by demanding government intervention to control corporate power on behalf of workers, farmers, and small business owners.[14] Directly contradicting this tradition, the Tea Party instead called for less regulation of corporate power, smaller and weaker government, and direct attacks on labor unions. The Tea Party movement championed the reversal of gains made by earlier populist movements in the United States: regulation of food and drug manufacture, the progressive income tax, regulation of banks, protection of unions and union organizers, civil rights, access to health care, environmental protection, occupational health and safety protections, and mass access to quality public education.

The Tea Party agenda proposed to champion ordinary people by stripping government of resources and power, opening the path to greater corporate power. It was a starkly *corporate* agenda, remarkably similar to the program Barry Goldwater unsuccessfully presented to the American people in 1964, and to the vision Lewis Powell created for the U.S. Chamber of Commerce in 1971. With electoral victories for Tea Party candidates in many races in 2010, what seemed marginal, even crazy, in the sixties and seventies was now within the mainstream of American politics, if not yet fully dominant in policy making.

The Tea Party appears to promote personal freedom by calling for reduced government. But personal freedom requires individuals to have health, education, and economic stability. Without these basic conditions the promise of individual freedom is empty in reality. Yet they are unavailable to individuals with little money or social standing when acting on their own. Far from indications of tyranny, government programs that provide these essentials are central to individual liberty, which cannot be real for working people left defenseless before corporate power. Too often, liberals defend social programs in terms of altruism or charity, treating people in need of them essentially as passive wards of a benevolent state, as we saw in the discussion of poverty in chapter 4. This approach unfortunately cedes the language of individual liberty to the Tea Party and others who seek to dismantle government programs. Understanding the relationship of individual freedom to government programs for health, education, and economic security can help people to assert working class values of mutual aid while affirming the aspirations all people have for individual growth and fulfillment.[15]

As the third year of President Obama's presidency got under way, the balance continued to weigh increasingly in the direction of corporate power. Obama's appointment of William Daley as his chief of staff at the start of 2011 was announced on the *New York Times* website in a report that attributed to Daley a "well-rounded résumé," described as follows:

> Mr. Daley, 62, who is not close friends with Mr. Obama, even though both share a Chicago base, has a well-rounded résumé. It includes work as "a lawyer in private practice, a bank president, a telecommunications company executive, a political strategist, a fund-raiser and campaign chief, a lobbyist for foreign corporations (he advocated on tax matters for Nestlé and a Canadian petroleum company)" and a three-year stint as commerce secretary in the Clinton administration. His brother, Richard M. Daley, is departing after six terms as mayor of Chicago, where his family has an almost royal status.... [Daley joined the JPMorgan Chase] senior leadership team as head of its new Office of Corporate Social Responsibility, whose most important function was to oversee Chase's global lobbying efforts.... Mr. Daley was never registered as a lobbyist for Chase, but he ... was the direct supervisor of Peter L. Scher, another former Clinton administration official, who runs the bank's lobbying shop in Washington.[16]

Such a background can only be considered well-rounded if you look no further than the top levels of American corporate and political power for points of reference. In this circle, the same news report noted, the U.S. Chamber of Commerce was more than satisfied by the appointment, which was meant in part to be a signal to the business community that President Obama was open to their concerns. Meanwhile, more traditional elements of the Democratic Party base, associated with workers' interests and who in recent years were derided as "liberals," were unhappy.

Whatever the fate of the Tea Party phenomenon as such, the dynamic it represents and advances—increasing power for corporate interests, declining prospects for working people and much of the middle class—will certainly continue to operate forcefully in American society in coming years.

The main arena for the extension of class war in the United States in this period has become the public sector. The conflict involves several separate but related issues concerning the proper role and scope of government, and raises profound questions about democracy.

In its main features, the corporate agenda calls for the end of many public services, either through privatization or outright cancelation. It calls for dismantling most, if not all, government regulations of business practices. In their place, corporations volunteer self-regulation through a particular form of privatization in which businesses replace governments to privately monitor their own facilities for health and safety standards. Corporations propose to guarantee on their own say-so the safety of medicines and eggs, of mining and offshore oil-rig operations. In the wake of the 2008–2009 financial crisis, the finance industry lobbied hard, and to a large degree successfully, to escape strict regulation. But self-regulation in finance didn't work any better than it had in the food and pharmaceutical industries where private corporate abuse led to Congress establishing the Food and Drug Administration.

In the 2008 financial crisis and its aftermath, the big banks and investment houses got Congress to implement a common practice: let the taxpayers bear the burden of paying off the losses private businesses suffer from bad decisions they've made, but let the private businesses keep the profits they accrue during and after the bailouts. The same pattern applied to the auto industry in 2009, and has applied to the nuclear power utilities since the 1950s. In Iceland and Ireland, public finances were completely undermined when their governments took over the debts the banks had piled up in reckless speculation.

In addition to relaxed regulation, the corporate agenda calls for the reduction of taxes, especially on businesses and the income and wealth of the wealthy. It calls for the weakening or abolition of unions for public sector workers and for cuts in their current pay, pensions, and health benefits. It calls for stripping government of its capacity to protect the economic and environmental standards of workers in the private sector as well. Taken all together, it is an agenda designed to increase greatly the power and profit making of corporations at the expense of working people.

This agenda is not new, but it has gained broader support than at any time since the 1920s. Those who promote it justify it on several grounds. There are the twin claims that small government is essential to personal liberty while big government corrodes individual responsibility. There are the related claims that jobs, economic growth, and the creation of wealth require unrestricted business practices led by entrepreneurs who must be allowed to get as rich as possible, and a labor force disciplined to work hard by the fear of poverty and deprivation. For those who are still not persuaded, advocates of the corporate agenda have asserted a new element of the argument, apparently more clearly based in fact: the danger of large deficits in the federal government budget, and the fiscal crises gripping state governments across the country. The large budget deficits arising after the 2008 financial crisis appeared as "undeniable conditions" that required cuts in public services and reduced living standards for public sector workers.*

At the beginning of 2011, Joe Scarborough, principal host of the MSNBC talk show *Morning Joe*, addressed the upcoming year's political agenda for shrinking

---

*Federal government deficits and resulting debt are usually not a problem. The government is not like a family that must balance its budget. The government is more like a corporation that lives longer than its individual shareholders or citizens. If it borrows to support productive activity that will generate greater future wealth, from which the debt with interest can be repaid (as for education, public health, roads, ports, and rail transportation), the debt is benign.

Large deficits over an extended period can sometimes be a problem. If there is full employment and a booming economy, government borrowing may increase interest rates and make it more difficult for private businesses to borrow to expand their operations. But in a period of widespread unemployment and businesses not investing (as was the case in 2009–2011), government deficits do not create this problem. Instead they help to prevent deeper unemployment and more widespread bankruptcies. They save taxpayers money over time by securing and improving the economic activity that generates more wealth, growth, and taxes in the future.

The idea that the deficits burden our children and grandchildren who must repay it misses two important points: first, current borrowing may create a better world in which our children and grandchildren will live; second, the interest that our grandchildren will pay will go to other of our grandchildren who will own government bonds—through their private pension funds, in the Social Security Trust Fund, or directly. Future interest payments are not a net burden on future generations, but a transfer of wealth from those who then pay taxes, but own few or no bonds, to those who own government bonds and may also pay taxes from which the interest is paid.

Interest paid to foreign businesses and governments who own U.S. government bonds does leave the U.S. economy (in 2010 amounting to 30 percent of total interest payments, up from 19 percent in 2000—see "Ownership of Federal Securities," *Treasury Bulletin*, December 2010, http://www.fms .treas.gov/bulletin/index.html), but foreign ownership of U.S. government bonds reflects the strength of the dollar as a reserve currency others wish to hold—a plus for the United States—and the large deficit in the U.S. balance of trade, which must be addressed with tools other than adjusting the levels of government debt.

All in all, government deficits in the early years of the Obama administration were not a real concern, but were used to scare people into believing that public services and living standards for public workers must be reduced.

the public sector and attacking public sector unions. Observing that this agenda was front and center for conservative governors like John Kasich of Ohio and Scott Walker of Wisconsin, as well as liberals like Jerry Brown in California and Andrew Cuomo in New York, Scarborough informed his viewers: "This is not a question of ideology. It's just simple arithmetic."[17]

The claim that state and federal budget deficits are a matter of simple arithmetic, the difference between revenues and expenditures, which explains why "there's no money," hides the deeply ideological origins of the problem. There is a long history of explicit corporate planning to shrink the government by starving it of revenues, explicitly anticipating and seeking to bring about the fiscal crises that now appear as a matter of arithmetic, apparently driven by greedy public workers and their unions. David Stockman, President Ronald Reagan's budget director in the early 1980s, explained the strategy as the Reagan administration pursued it, using massive tax cuts at the start of his presidency, expecting that the resulting deficits would force large cuts in spending for federal programs. But Congress wouldn't go along, so the deficit ballooned; the strategy failed when Congress raised taxes in 1986 to deal with the deficit problem, rather than cutting deeply into government programs.[18] Grover Norquist, who founded the group Americans for Tax Reform in 1985, when it was clear that the initial steps by Reagan weren't working as planned, explained the strategy in stark terms: to shrink government "down to the size where we can drown it in the bathtub."[19]

By 2011, fiscal crises at the federal and state levels created circumstances for a new run at this agenda. Thirty years of tax cuts, especially for corporations and the wealthy, had drained public treasuries at all levels. For decades, state and local governments had simply not paid into public pension funds the money required to meet their pension obligations for public workers, which had been negotiated in collective bargaining agreements secured in signed contracts. In these negotiations, workers had traded current wage increases for retirement security. Not paying into the pension funds has been a practice equivalent to stealing workers' wages, but a hidden means of doing so.

Extraordinary levels of federal government spending for the wars in Iraq and Afghanistan and in response to the deep financial and economic crises of 2008–2009 resulted in extraordinary short-term federal deficits. Deep recession in states across the country limited state and local revenues while requiring increased spending to deal with high levels of poverty and unemployment. Corporate policy specialists portrayed these government deficits as the country's most serious problem, while they sustained the political climate in which tax increases on corporations and wealthy people were politically nearly impossible to implement. All that remained was to drown government services and public sector unions in the bathtub.

The hypocrisy with which corporate representatives pursued the deficit agenda at the end of 2010 and into the start of the 112th Congress gives some clue as to the emptiness of their concern for the deficit and their use of budget issues boldly to advance corporate interests. Two examples illustrate the point. In the debate on extending Bush-era tax cuts for incomes above $250,000 per year in December 2010, corporate representatives in Congress made clear their different approaches to the deficit in relation to the needs of working people compared with the wealthy. In the name of holding down the deficit, they demanded that the $57 billion expense of extending unemployment compensation to millions of long-term unemployed workers, included in the bill, be paid for with equivalent cuts in other programs. But they demanded no such offset for the $801 billion in tax cuts the bill provided. They refused even to consider aid to the unemployed until the interests of the wealthiest Americans were advanced, without the slightest concern for the great increase to the deficit and national debt their approach involved.[20] Continuing this approach, the new rules for the House of Representatives announced by Speaker John Boehner for the 112th Congress required all new programs to be paid for with equivalent cuts, except for tax reductions and the consequences of repealing the 2010 health-care bill that extended insurance coverage to tens of millions of workers while lowering the long-term deficit.[21] (The original health-care bill had been strongly opposed by the U.S. Chamber of Commerce and other corporate groups, in and out of the health-care industry.)

Responding to this broad agenda in ways that protect and advance the interests of working people will not be easy. In 2010, for the first time in history, more people were in public sector unions than in unions representing workers in the private sector. This has made it easier for the corporate agenda of privatization and smaller government to take hold. Private sector workers, whose wages and benefits have shrunk over the past thirty-five years as unions have lost power, have sometimes joined in attacking "bloated" public budgets that continue to pay benefits to teachers, sanitation workers, and police and fire personnel. By the end of 2010, officials in private sector unions in New York and New Jersey, traditional labor strongholds, had lent their public support to legislation and commissions designed to weaken public sector unions and cut wages and benefits for public sector workers.[22] The old trick of divide and conquer had worked once again.

Unions representing the construction trades have taken this path in hopes that improved public finances will allow more public funding of construction projects, leading to more jobs for their members at a time when the unemployment rate for construction trades has exceeded 20 percent in many parts of the country. The short-term logic of this approach is contradicted by the fact that city councils and state legislatures who attack public sector unions are no more sympathetic to unions in the private sector. In the name of the same apparent budget-cutting needs, these same people seek to repeal laws that require public construction projects to use union labor or at least pay union wages.

Attacks on public sector unions quickly extend to attacks on *all* unions. Similarly, by 2010, the long decline of private sector unions had created conditions that would weaken unions in the public sector. The traditional practice by which wages and benefits won by some unions became patterns for others to reach for, in a process that over time spread prosperity more broadly, has been reversed. We have come instead to the point where reductions in living standards for some now draw others into the vortex of decline.

Reversing this balance of class power requires the assertion of working class values, interests, and power at a time when unions and other defenders of working people are weaker than at any time since the 1920s. On the other side of the coin, corporate power in the political process, and related media and educational arenas, is gaining strength and seeking ways to increase its capacity still further in all aspects of society, including in the public sector. As one commentator explained it: "This threat to public employee unions...is aimed to be a body blow to the American labor movement...it takes away the primary organizational force against corporate power and abuses in the country."[23]

The 2011 battle over public sector unions in Wisconsin revealed the antidemocratic nature of Governor Walker's agenda. He presented his antiunion legislative proposal as a budget-related matter, something he said was necessary to close the state's fiscal deficit. But when the unions accepted the cuts in wages and benefits the proposal would enact (almost exactly what the governor and legislature had given corporations in tax cuts in the first days of their power the previous month), the governor persisted. He continued to push for the legislation because it would end collective bargaining for public workers in Wisconsin and greatly restrict working people's ability to engage in collective political activity through their unions.

The purpose was clear. In the 2008 presidential election, Steven Greenhouse noted in the *New York Times,* "while white male non-union workers voted against President Obama by a margin of 16 percentage points, he won among white male union voters by 18 points."[24] Without unions, little would stand between the American people and total corporate control of the country. Not surprisingly, Governor Walker received substantial campaign contributions from the ultra-conservative billionaire Koch brothers.[25]

The equivalence of tax cuts for corporations and benefit cuts for workers in Wisconsin was a trade-off that well expressed the priorities working people need to reverse. Another example arose in the relationship between the budget deficits that states faced in 2011 and the cost of the wars in Iraq and Afghanistan that year. Wisconsin's people, for example, sent $2.7 billion in federal taxes toward the costs of the wars that year, while facing an annual budget deficit of about $1.35 billion. New York residents paid $15.5 billion for the wars in 2011 while suffering from the consequences of an $8.5 billion state deficit.[26]

This connection was taken up by mayors facing severe budget crises as they met in June 2011 and called for an end to the wars and redirection of the funds to meet urgent domestic needs.[27] More broadly, the New Priorities Network formed in 2010 to draw together labor, community, and religious organizations to challenge the claim that "there is no money" and call for the end of the wars and redirection of wasteful military spending to meet a new set of priorities consistent with human needs.[28]

The 2011 Wisconsin legislation sparked one of the most significant labor uprisings in recent decades, as tens of thousands of workers occupied the state capitol for over two weeks, bringing together private sector and public sector workers, students, community groups, farmers—all united to resist this rebalance of power. The police refused to clear the building, some of its officers changing into civilian clothes after their tours and returning to join the protest. The legislation passed, and a state court injunction to keep the law from being enforced failed to hold.

Legislation modeled on Wisconsin was introduced in Maine, Massachusetts, Michigan, Ohio and elsewhere in the early part of 2011. These efforts paralleled other legislation that would restrict voting by poor people through the imposition of various identity requirements and the end of opportunities for easy voter registration. By mid-2011 there had not been a duplication of the Wisconsin uprising in other states.

In this environment, it is essential that workers and their leaders and allies understand and address the power relations driving this history, and organize an effective response. Working people need to establish an intellectual framework, cultural climate, and organizational capacity to reverse direction. Whatever steps will be necessary, a clear understanding of class is an essential foundation for future progress.

The stark changes we have seen since 2000, and the dramatic and growing gap between Wall Street and Main Street, open possibilities for serious reflection and creative action. Immigrant worker centers across the country offer hope and guidance for energetic mobilizations for economic and social justice, as they have shown with mass marches on May Day beginning in 2006. It is also promising that the AFL-CIO has welcomed worker centers into central labor councils, which until the early years of the new millennium had been restricted to official unions only. This followed the historic change in union attitudes toward immigrant labor in 2000, when AFL-CIO leadership turned away from its traditional anti-immigrant stance and embraced the view that immigrant workers are first and foremost workers deserving of union protections.

Successful examples of militant worker resistance to corporate demands, such as the factory takeover by union workers fighting the closing of Republic Windows and Doors in Chicago in 2008, can provide inspiration and guidance for other worker actions. At the U.S. Social Forum in Detroit in June 2010, hundreds of immigrants from worker centers across the country and vibrant organizations like the Restaurant Opportunities Centers, Domestic Workers United, and New York Taxi Workers Alliance formed the Excluded Workers Congress to coordinate and expand organizing.[29] Despite the presence of over fifteen thousand progressive activists with deep roots in labor and community organizations meeting for six days, the U.S. Social Forum drew no notice in the mainstream media.

Various independent media outlets already exist upon which extensive information and communication networks might be built. While not a substitute for in-person encounters, social networking sites and other Internet platforms offer organizing tools. National news sources, among them *Democracy Now!* and *Worker's Independent News,* can be expanded and used as models for the many more radio, television, and web-based resources working people will need to overcome the limitations of the mainstream media. Scholars, activists, and artists have formed the Working Class Studies Association to encourage the deeper understanding of class dynamics in all aspects of society. Progressive think tanks like the Economic Policy Institute, the Center for Economic and Policy Research, and the Fiscal Policy Institute could expand their work and adopt more clearly the language of class in presenting the context for their social analyses and policy proposals.

These and other resources are already available to working people at the start of the second decade of the twenty-first century, but their scope is severely limited in comparison with the need. Partly this is a question of limited financial resources. The main obstacle to the development of class-based movements, however, has been the limited scope of understanding and vision brought to the tasks by union leadership and their allies in the political and academic worlds. The organized labor movement devotes hundreds of millions of dollars to presidential and congressional electoral campaigns, but virtually nothing to the media, cultural, and intellectual resources working people must develop to vie for power.

Despite dedicated efforts by John Sweeney, Richard Trumka, and other labor leaders to stir effective union organizing drives from 1995 onward, union membership has declined. Despite hundreds of millions of dollars and uncounted millions of hours of volunteer campaign work poured into Democratic Party electoral efforts, workers are on the short end of the policy stick even when

Democrats dominate governments. Despite frequent acknowledgment in media and scholarly circles that inequality has increased and that working people have suffered greatly, inequality and suffering continue to spread. These failures arise in large measure from the intensely applied corporate agenda I have outlined above, but we must also look at labor's leadership to assess weaknesses and find ways to improve workers' chances.

In my experience, senior labor leaders understand very well that there are classes in the United States, that there is a working class and a capitalist class, and that class warfare is going on. But they are generally not willing to acknowledge these things publicly, or to organize accordingly. Union leaders prefer to speak of their current goals and past accomplishments in terms of bringing their members and all working people into the middle class, which obscures social reality. Unions are tied to the Democratic Party, unwilling to develop centers of independent working class political power. Union leaders are typically unwilling to fund groups or initiatives they cannot fully control, which dampens creativity and initiative. They rarely take cultural expression seriously as a vital part of everyone's personal well-being and morale, as essential ingredients of any social movement.

If unions are to reverse their declines in membership and organize millions into action at workplaces and in the political process, they cannot be content simply to organize shop by shop, employer by employer. To be effective, organizing drives have to unfold in the context of a broader social movement that brings working people into bold challenges for power at all levels and presents the cause of working people in the broadest moral and social contexts. Perhaps traditional unions will not be able to change enough to play a strong role in this process. It may be that new organizations will arise, as was the case in the civil rights movement of the 1950s and 1960s, when traditional civil rights organizations, despite important past contributions, were not able to generate the energy that the newly formed Southern Christian Leadership Conference and Student Non-Violent Coordinating Committee brought to the tasks.[30] We cannot know when or specifically how such a movement will emerge, or who will lead it, but history shows that no suffering extends forever without people rising up to redress the grievances.

The corporate world brings far more money to their cause than working people will ever be able to muster. But money isn't everything. In the 1930s the CIO organized millions of workers with very little money, but nearly unlimited amounts of energy, courage, and vision. The Montgomery (Alabama) Improvement Association, Southern Christian Leadership Conference, and Student Non-Violent Coordinating Committee galvanized a huge civil rights movement that transformed the country. They did this not with large sums of money but with energy, courage, and vision. In more recent times, Domestic Workers United successfully organized to win legislation to provide basic rights and protections for the tens of thousands of nannies, housekeepers, and other domestic workers routinely abused by their personal employers.[31] These mostly immigrant women won with very little money but a great deal of energy, courage, and vision.

Ralph Nader addressed the question of money in a 2009 fantasy novel titled *Only the Super-Rich Can Save Us.* Nader first estimated the cost of fielding a political operation that could win the presidency and enough seats in Congress and state offices to insure that a progressive agenda would become law, guaranteeing worker rights, environmental protection, and true universal health care in a single-payer Medicare-for-All system. It came to seventeen billion dollars. He then wrote a book in which seventeen billionaires of liberal persuasion—like George Soros, Oprah Winfrey, Bill Gates, Warren Buffett—came up with the money to sustain the organizing over the years it would take to succeed. Fun as it may be contemplate, it's a fantasy that takes us in the wrong imaginative direction. Only we can save us.

Just as, in 1971, Lewis Powell understood and articulated an agenda *for a class* rather than for a particular company or industry, so must working people forty years later respond with assertions of their own class interests, going beyond the ready divisions of public and private, building trades and services, native-born and immigrant. Powell, stretching his point for effect, asserted that the challenge corporations faced at that time was a challenge to the very system, explaining to the Chamber of Commerce, "If our system is to survive, top management must be equally concerned with protecting and preserving the system itself."[32] It is no stretch to say that if working people are to survive in an environment of economic security and well-being, then they too must include but also go beyond attention to their own workplace, industry, race, gender, or ethnicity, and come together to challenge the system itself.

The future is not arbitrary. Its seeds are in the present, in the tensions that exist within society. In part, the events that will shape our future are happening now—guided by people who, in their attempts to resolve social conflicts, make crucial decisions. The power to make these decisions, the power to make history, is closely tied to the power of class.

The capitalist class has a wide variety of institutions through which to understand change and to work out and implement policies that shape change in ways that advance the interests of that class. Capitalists have think tanks. They have political parties and trade associations and university scholars working on their problems. They have media at their disposal to help shape public opinion. As history unfolds, capitalists cannot control everything, but they do try to see to it that whatever happens, their interests are preserved as much as possible.

If the working class is to advance its own interests in the process that makes history, working people will have to challenge the power of the capitalists in every aspect of society. In the turmoil of change sure to come, in the economy, in technology, politics, and culture, the working class must be present with its own independent organizations. These organizations need to be democratically run, in the hands of working people themselves, if they are to reflect the interests of the majority.

What values will guide us as a society as change unfolds? How will the working class define its interests and design policies that help improve workers' lives? What forces can be mustered to implement the values of economic justice? These are fundamental questions for democracy, ones that will be contested in politics, not just of the electoral variety, but politics in the broadest sense of the operation of power relations in all of society.

We cannot know the outcome in advance. We cannot even know very much about the specific policies that will be appropriate to economic justice as time goes on, because policies must correspond to specific conditions, and without knowing future circumstances, detailed policy prescriptions are mostly hot air.

There is a second reason why we cannot know the details of a policy blueprint that will make the world right for the working class majority. Working class people have not had enough chance to discuss the issues and come to any conclusions of their own. This will happen only as the working class organizes itself as an independent force in society. In the course of organizing, workers will learn the conditions they face and debate the ways they propose to deal with them. This broad process is the heart of democracy.

Despite the uncertainties, we have reason for optimism. Consider one example. When the auto workers at Henry Ford's Rouge plant organized a union there in 1940, as many as one out of every three workers among the 78,000 people in the factory was an antiunion spy who reported union activity to management.[33] Ford had goon squads who regularly beat up union organizers and broke up union meetings. Yet the union prevailed. The working class won a measure of power. American labor history is full of dramatic stories like this.[34] We know that we will be surprised by how the future works out. What seems impossible or silly or too strange for words today will not necessarily seem that way in thirty years.

At the start of the American Civil War, the British philosopher and social theorist John Stuart Mill wrote:

> The entire history of social improvement has been a series of transitions by which one custom or institution after another, from being a supposed primary necessity of social existence, has passed into the rank of a universally stigmatized injustice and tyranny. So it has been with

the distinctions of slaves and freemen, nobles and serfs, patricians and plebeians; and so it will be, and in part already is, with the aristocracies of color, race, and sex.[35]

It is now up to us to think and act in ways that will eventually add to this list of past injustice and tyranny the domination of capitalist over worker. This is our greatest challenge and headiest opportunity. This is what is at stake as we go further into the new millennium.

Notes

INTRODUCTION

1. Henry F. Myers, *Wall Street Journal*, November 25, 1991, A1. The others featured in the series of weekly articles were Freud and Einstein.

2. Andrew Levison, *The Working Class Majority* (New York: Coward, McCann, & Geoghegan, 1974; Penguin Books, 1975).

CHAPTER 1

1. *Economic Report of the President, 1999*, Table B-46, 380.

2. *Economic Report of the President, 2010*, Table B-46, 384–85.

3. "Saturn Workers Vote to Authorize Strike," *New York Times*, July 20, 1998, A10; Keith Bradsher, "Labor's Peace with G.M. Unraveling at Saturn," *New York Times*, July 22, 1998, A1; Fara Warner, "UAW Call GM Relations Rocky; Can't Rule Out Possible Walkouts," *Wall Street Journal*, August 26, 1998, A4. For a fuller discussion of the limits of the Saturn experience, see Mike Parker and Jane Slaughter, *Working Smart* (Detroit: Labor Notes, 1994), chapter 9.

4. "Saturn Discontinued by GM," press release, September 30, 2009, http://blogs.inter netautoguide.com/6589884/industry-news/saturn-discontinued-by-gm-penske-automotive-group-doesnt-buy-brand/index.html.

5. ESOP Association, *ESOP Statistics*, http://www.esopassociation.org/media/media_statistics.asp.

6. Adria Scharf and Richard Marens, "ESOPs: The Revolution Hasn't Arrived Yet," *Left Business Observer*, no. 80 (November 17, 1997): 4–5.

7. Steven Greenhouse, "Passenger Service Workers Unionize at United Airlines," *New York Times*, July 18, 1998, A7.

8. U.S. Department of Commerce, *Statistical Abstract of the United States: 2010*, Table 741; and Bureau of Labor Statistics News Release, "New Quarterly Data from BLS on Business Employment Dynamics by Size of Firm Summary," Table B, December 8, 2005, http://www.bls.gov/news.release/cewfs.nr0.htm.

9. U.S. Department of Commerce, *Statistical Abstract of the United States: 2010*, Table 728.

10. Ibid.

11. BLS News Release, December 8, 2005 (see note 8) and *Statistical Abstract of the United States: 2010*, Table 729.

12. BLS News Release, December 8, 2005 (see note 8).

13. *Statistical Abstract of the United States: 2010*, Table 729.

14. "Statistics at a Glance," Federal Deposit Insurance Corporation, http://fdic.gov /bank/statistical/stats/2010jun/industry.html.

15. "Large Commercial Banks," Federal Reserve, http://www.federalreserve.gov/releases /lbr/current/default.htm; "Statistics at a Glance," Federal Deposit Insurance Corporation.

16. *Statistical Abstract of the United States: 2010*, Table 803.

17. Ibid., Table 808.

18. Ibid., Table 746.

19. Ibid., Tables 739, 987.

20. "Another Cola War Brewing?" *Food Processing* 69, no. 6 (2008): 23.

21. Pascal Zachary, "Let's Play Oligopoly!" *Wall Street Journal*, March 8, 1999, B1.

22. "Profits and Balance Sheet Developments at U.S. Commercial Banks in 2008," *Federal Reserve Bulletin* 95 (2009), http://www.federalreserve.gov/pubs/bulletin/2009/articles/bankprofit/dlink/fig04.htm.

23. Interview with Michael Schwartz, sociologist and scholar of interlocking corporate directorships, May 8, 1997.

24. Peter Mariolis, "Interlocking Directorates and Control of Corporations: The Theory of Bank Control," *Social Sciences Quarterly* 56 (1975), quoted in G. William Domhoff, *Who Rules America Now?* (New York: Simon and Schuster, 1983), 71.

25. There is a large literature on the ruling class in the United States. My discussion owes much to the work of G. William Domhoff, *Who Rules America?*, 6th ed., (New York: McGraw-Hill, 2009), and Beth Mintz and Michael Schwartz, *The Power Structure of American Business* (Chicago: University of Chicago Press, 1985).

26. See, among a wide literature, E. P. Thompson, *The Making of the English Working Class* (New York: Vintage, 1966); G. William Domhoff, *Who Rules America?;* Robert Heilbroner, *The Nature and Logic of Capitalism* (New York: W. W. Norton, 1986); and Samuel Bowles and Herbert Gintis, *Schooling in Capitalist America* (Boston: Basic Books, 1977).

27. Pamela Ryckman, "A Club for Women Atop the Ladder," *New York Times*, April 3, 2011, Business 1, describing the Belizean Grove. The Executive Leadership Council, founded in 1986, is an organization of over five hundred senior-level African American executives, men and women, from Fortune 500 corporations; http://www.elcinfo.com. "Black Entrepreneurs and Executives Profiles" http://www.blackentrepreneurprofile.com; "African Americans Lost Ground on Fortune 500 Boards: Blacks Remain Seriously Underrepresented," Executive Leadership Council, press release, July 17, 2009, http://www.elcinfo.com/BoardCensus.php.

28. *NLRB v. Yeshiva University,* 444 U.S. 672 (1980). The court more recently extended its logic to exclude many nurses from union protection in the 2001 Kentucky River case, *NLRB v. Kentucky River Community Care, Inc.,* 532 U.S. 706 (2001).

29. Gardiner Harris, "As Physicians' Jobs Change, So Do Their Politics," *New York Times*, May 30, 2011, A1.

30. Louis Uchitelle and N. R. Kleinfeld, *New York Times,* daily reports, March 3–10, 1996.

31. Steven Hipple, "Worker Displacement in an Expanding Economy," *Monthly Labor Review* 120, no. 12 (December 1997), 26–39.

32. A striking example is the well publicized, much reviewed, and widely distributed film *Waiting for Superman.*

33. Joe Nocera, "Lesson Plan from a Reformer," *New York Times,* November 13, 2010, B1.

34. Ann Rogers et al., "The Working Hours of Hospital Staff Nurses and Patient Safety," *Health Affairs* 23, no. 4 (July/August 2004), 1–11.

35. "Mandatory Overtime," *Nursing World,* American Nurses Association, August 5, 2010, http://www.nursingworld.org/mainmenucategories/ANAPoliticalPower/State/State LegislativeAgenda/MandatoryOvertime.aspx.

36. "National Survey of Part-time Adjunct Faculty," *American Academic* 2 (March 2010), 3.

37. See Karl Marx and Friedrich Engels, *The Communist Manifesto,* in *The Marx-Engels Reader,* 2nd ed., ed. Robert C. Tucker (New York: W. W. Norton, 1978), 476.

38. John Sperling, address to the Conference on Visions for the Future: Academic Collective Bargaining in 2020, National Center for the Study of Collective Bargaining in Higher Education, Baruch College, City University of New York, March 20, 2000, author's notes.

39. "National Survey of Part-time Adjunct Faculty," *American Academic* 2 (March 2010), 8.

40. U.S. Department of Labor, *Employment and Earnings.* January issues each year report numbers of people employed the previous year in over five hundred occupational categories, based on household surveys. These data include the self-employed but for people who hold multiple jobs only the principal source of income is reported.

41. U.S. Department of Labor, *Employment and Earnings,* January 2011, Table 1.

42. "Production and Nonsupervisory Employees on Private Nonfarm Payrolls by Major Industry Sector and Selected Industry Detail, Seasonally Adjusted," U.S. Department of Labor, Bureau of Labor Statistics, Current Employment Statistics, ftp://ftp.bls .gov/pub/suppl/empsit.ceseeb5.txt, and "Employees on nonfarm payrolls by major industry sector and selected industry detail, seasonally adjusted," ftp://ftp.bls.gov/pub/suppl /empsit.ceseeb3.txt.

43. "Employees on Nonfarm Payrolls by Major Industry Sector and Selected Industry Detail, Seasonally Adjusted," U.S. Department of Labor, Bureau of Labor Statistics, Current Employment Statistics, ftp://ftp.bls.gov/pub/suppl/empsit.ceseeb3.txt.

44. Throughout the twentieth century the labor force changed composition as the economy developed, corporations grew and diversified, and as management functions became more complex and were themselves subject to division of labor in which working class jobs were created to accomplish managerial functions, under the supervision of middle layers of management. An excellent description and analysis of this process is in Harry Braverman, *Labor and Monopoly Capital* (New York: Monthly Review Press, 1974).

45. *Economic Report of the President, 1999,* Table B-46.

46. Calculations based on *Employment and Earnings,* January 2011, Table 1.

47. All calculations based on data in *Employment and Earnings,* January 2011, Table 1. Relative pay for different jobs can be found in U.S. Department of Labor, Bureau of Labor Statistics, Occupational Employment Statistics, http://www.bls.gov/oes/current/oes_nat.htm.

48. U.S. Census Bureau, *Survey of Business Owners, 2007,* http://www.census.gov/econ/ sbo.

49. Robert Johnson, "Climbing to the Top of Black Businesses," *Wall Street Journal,* May 10, 1999, B1.

50. Doug Henwood, "Trash-o-nomics," in *White Trash: Race and Class in America,* ed. Matt Wray and Annalee Newitz (New York: Routledge, 1997), 189.

51. Calculated from U.S. Census Bureau, Census 2000, EEO Data Tool, http://www .census.gov/eeo2000/index.html. 2010 data not available at time of publication.

52. See, for example, "The Top 50 Women in World Business—2010," *Financial Times,* http://womenatthetop.ft.com/; for African American chief executives, see "African American CEO's of Fortune 500 Companies," Black Entrepreneur Profile, http://www.blackentre preneurprofile.com/fortune-500-ceos.

53. See, for example, Theodore W. Allen, *The Invention of the White Race,* 2 vols. (New York: Verso, 1994 and 1997); Theodore W. Allen, *Class Struggle and the Origin of Racial Slavery: The Invention of the White Race,* edited and with an introduction by Jeffery B. Perry (Stony Brook: Center for Study of Working Class Life, 2006); Mike Davis, *Prisoners of the American Dream: Politics and Economy in the History of the U.S. Working Class,* 2nd ed. (New York: W. W. Norton, 2000); Noel Ignatiev, *How the Irish Became White* (New York: Routledge, 2008); David Roediger, *The Wages of Whiteness: Race and the Making of the American Working Class* (New York: Verso, 1999); Chip Smith and Malcolm Goff, *The Cost of Privilege: Taking on the System of White Supremacy* (Livermore, Calif.: Camino Press, 2007).

54. "AFL-CIO Secretary-Treasurer Richard Trumka's Remarks to USW Convention, July 1, 2008," United Steelworkers, http://usw.org/media_center/testimony_remarks?id=0003.

55. "Contingent and Alternative Employment Arrangement, February 2005," *News*, Bureau of Labor Statistics, USDL 05–1433, July 27, 2005, http://www.bls.gov/news .release/pdf/conemp.pdf.

56. Kevin P. Lynch, "A Brief Overview of Organizing Employees Wrongly Identified as 'Independent Contractors,' " International Association of Machinists & Aerospace Workers, District 15, no date.

CHAPTER 2

1. Reeve Vanneman and Lynn Weber Cannon, *The American Perception of Class* (Philadelphia: Temple University Press, 1987), 87.

2. *Ragged Dick* and *Phil, the Fiddler* are among four novels reprinted in Horatio Alger, Jr., *Struggling Upward, and Other Works* (New York: Crown Publishers, 1945).

3. U.S. Department of Commerce, *Statistical Abstract of the United States, 2010*, Table 606.

4. Bureau of Labor Statistics, *Occupational Outlook Handbook, 2010–2011*, Table 2, http://www.bls.gov/oco/oco2003.htm#occupation_d.

5. Robert Reich, *The Work of Nations: Preparing Ourselves for 21st Century Capitalism* (New York: Alfred Knopf, 1991), 177–180, 185–195.

6. David B. Grusky, "American Social Mobility in the 19th and 20th Centuries," CDE Working Paper 86–28, University of Wisconsin Center for Demography and Ecology, Madison, 1986.

7. Michael Hout, "More Universalism, Less Structural Mobility: The American Occupational Structure in the 1980s," *American Journal of Sociology* 93, no. 6 (May 1988), 1358–1400.

8. Kurt Schrammel, "Labor Market Success of Young Adults from Two Generations," *Monthly Labor Review* 121, no. 2 (February 1998), 3–9.

9. Samuel Bowles, Herbert Gintis, and Melissa Osborne Groves (eds.), *Unequal Chances* (NY: Russell Sage, 2005), 2, quoted in Benjamin I. Page and Lawrence R. Jacobs, *Class War?* (Chicago: University of Chicago Press, 2009)

10. Hout, 1389.

11. "Educational Attainment in the United States: 2009—Detailed Tables," U.S. Census Bureau, Current Population Survey, *2009 Annual Social and Economic Supplement*, http:// www.census.gov/hhes/socdemo/education/data/cps/2009/tables.html.

12. "Family Income and Educational Attainment, 1970 to 2009," *Postsecondary Education Opportunity*, no. 221 (November 2010), http://www.postsecondary.org/last12/ 221_1110pg1_16.pdf.

13. Lawrence E. Gladieux and Watson Scott Swail, "Financial Aid Is Not Enough: Improving the Odds of College Success," *College Board Review*, no. 185 (Summer 1998), 18, 20, citing U.S. Department of Education data.

14. Daniel P. McMurrer, Mark Condon, and Isabel V. Sawhill, *Intergenerational Mobility in the United States* (Washington, D.C.: Urban Institute, 1997), 8.

15. Peter Gottschalk and Sheldon Danziger, "Family Income Mobility—How Much Is There and Has It Changed?" (unpublished article, July 1997, Table 4).

16. David Segal, "Is Law School a Losing Game?" *New York Times*, January 8, 2011, http://www.nytimes.com/.

17. Henry James, *An International Episode* [1878] (New York: Penguin, 1985), 41.

18. *Economic Report of the President, 2010*, Table B-1.

19. Modeling and promoting consumption extends to the upper reaches of the corporate realm. Every weekend, the American edition of the *Financial Times* includes a glossy supplement titled *How to Spend It*, containing ads for $1,200 wastebaskets, dresses for $10,000, and wristwatches with multiple dials for still more.

20. A good history of the course and impact of anticommunism on the American labor movement can be found in Stanley Aronowitz, *From the Ashes of the Old* (New York: Houghton Mifflin, 1998).

21. The process was complex. In 1962, Students for a Democratic Society (SDS) was formed in opposition to anticommunism but with ties to the UAW and other progressive, anticommunist unions. As the Vietnam War intensified, relations between the academic left and unions deteriorated into mutual distrust. It was only after the election of new leadership in the AFL-CIO in 1995 that ties have been renewed between labor and the academic left.

22. See, for example, Mike Davis, *Prisoners of the American Dream* (London: Verso, 1986), especially chapters 1–3; Stanley Aronowitz, *False Promises: The Shaping of American Working Class Consciousness* (New York: McGraw Hill, 1973), especially chapter 3.

23. Charisse Jones, "Free From Want, but Just Getting By: In the Middle—New York on $38,000 a Year," *New York Times,* February 18, 1995, A1.

24. Andrea Bernstein on the *Brian Lehrer Show,* WNYC, November 4, 2010.

25. Larry Gabriel, "Working Families Are Caught in the Middle Class Squeeze: More and More Families Live Paycheck to Paycheck," *Solidarity* (September/October 2004).

26. William J. Puette, *Through Jaundiced Eyes: How the Media View Organized Labor* (Ithaca: Cornell University/ILR Press, 1992).

27. For a fuller exploration of the role of television in shaping postwar attitudes about the working class, see the film *Class Dismissed,* written by Pepi Leistyna (Northampton, Mass.: Media Education Foundation, 2005); for an assessment of television and the press, see Diana Kendall, *Framing Class: Media Representations of Wealth and Poverty in America,* 2nd ed. (Lanham, Md.: Rowan and Littlefield, 2011).

28. Ben Bagdikian, *The Media Monopoly,* 5th ed. (Boston: Beacon Press, 1997); Danny Schechter, *The More You Watch, the Less You Know* (New York: Seven Stories Press, 1997); *EXTRA!* 11, no. 4 (July/August 1998); James Ledbetter, *Made Possible By...: The Death of Public Broadcasting in the United States* (London: Verso, 1998), excerpted in *EXTRA!* 11, no. 3 (May/June 1998), 25–27.

29. Eric Alterman, "PBS on the Run," *Nation,* February 24, 1997, 4–5; Janine Jackson, "Film Rejection Highlights PBS Bias," *EXTRA!* 11, no. 1 (January–February 1998), 6–8.

30. As one of many examples, Merrill Lynch sponsored a seven-part public television series on personal finance. The host of the series was Stefanie Powers, well-known television star and, at the time of the series, on the board of directors of two multibillion-dollar mutual funds. Geraldine Fabricant, *New York Times,* July 12, 1998, Section 3, 1.

31. Kurt Eichenwald, "Videotapes Take Star Role at Archer Daniels Trial," *New York Times,* August 4, 1998, D1.

32. "The New York Times Poll," *New York Times,* March 5, 1996, A16.

33. Richard Centers, *The Psychology of Social Classes* (Princeton: Princeton University Press, 1949). For a review of the later debate about what influences people's understanding of their class position and recent findings, see Vanneman and Cannon, *The American Perception of Class.*

34. Roper Center for Public Opinion Research, 1998, DIALOG (R) File 468, Question ID: USABCWP.6161 Q912 (survey conducted in August 1996).

35. National Opinion Research Center, http://publicdata.norc.org/.

36. Jennifer L. Hochschild, *Facing Up to the American Dream: Race, Class, and the Soul of the Nation* (Princeton: Princeton University Press, 1995), 215–220.

37. Roper Center for Public Opinion Research, 1998, DIALOG (R) File 468, Question ID: USNYT.042296 R84 (survey conducted in December 1995).

38. Vanneman and Cannon, *The American Perception of Class,* 276–278.

39. Ibid.

CHAPTER 3

1. Michael Winerip, "Canton's Economic Seesaw: Managers' Fortunes Rise as Workers Get Bumpy Ride," *New York Times,* July 7, 1996, A7.

2. "Usual Weekly Earnings of Wage and Salary Workers," U.S Bureau of Labor Statistics, Current Population Survey, Table 1, http://www.bls.gov/cps/cpswktabs.htm.

3. Current Population Reports: Consumer Income Reports (P-60), U.S. Census Bureau, various issues, U.S. Department of Commerce, http://www.census.gov/prod /www/abs/p60.html.

4. *Economic Report of the President, 2010,* Table B-39, http://www.whitehouse.gov /sites/default/files/microsites/2011_erp_appendixB.pdf.

5. "America's Families and Living Arrangements: 2010," U.S. Census Bureau, Tables F1 and FG1, http://www.census.gov/population/www/socdemo/hh-fam/cps2010.html.

6. "Employed Persons by Class of Worker and Part-time Status," U.S Department of Labor, Bureau of Labor Statistics, Table A-8, http://www.bls.gov/news.release/empsit .t08.htm.

7. "Full-time and Part-time Workers: Mean Hourly Earnings for Major Occupational Groups," Table 2 in *National Compensation Survey, 2009,* U.S Department of Labor, Bureau of Labor Statistics, http://www.bls.gov/ncs/ocs/sp/nctb1345.pdf.

8. "Employee Benefits in the United States—March 2010," U.S Department of Labor, Bureau of Labor Statistics, news release, http://www.bls.gov/news.release/pdf/ebs2.pdf.

9. Calculated from "Consumer Credit," Board of Governors of the Federal Reserve System, Federal Reserve Statistical Release G.19, October 2010, http://www.federal reserve.gov/releases/g19/20101007; "Personal Income and Outlays: September 2010," U.S. Department of Commerce, Bureau of Economic Analysis, news release, http://www. bea.gov/newsreleases/national/pi/2010/pdf/pi0910.pdf; *Economic Report of the President, 1998,* Tables B-30, B-77, http://www.gpoaccess.gov/usbudget/fy99/pdf/erp.pdf.

10. Louis Uchitelle, *New York Times,* July 19, 1998, Section 4, 1.

11. Dean Baker, *The Productivity to Paycheck Gap: What the Data Show* (Washington, D.C.: Center for Economic and Policy Research, April 2007), Table 1.

12. Ibid., Table 5.

13. Jacob M. Schlesinger, "Low-Wage Workers Make Strong Gains," *Wall Street Journal,* February 5, 1999, A2.

14. Arloc Sherman and Chad Stone, "Income Gaps between Very Rich and Everyone Else More Than Tripled in Last Three Decades, New Data Show," Center on Budget and Policy Priorities, June 25, 2010, http://www.cbpp.org/files/6-25-10inc.pdf.

15. Jason deParle, "House Data on U.S. Income Sets Off Debate on Fairness," *New York Times,* May 22, 1992, A16, citing U.S. House of Representatives Committee on Ways and Means, *Green Book,* May 21, 1992.

16. *Income, Poverty, and Health Insurance Coverage in the United States, 2009,* U.S. Bureau of the Census, Series P-60, no. 238, September 2010, Table A2.

17. Emmanuel Saez, "Striking it Richer: The Evolution of Top Incomes in the United States (Update with 2007 estimates)," University of California, Berkeley, August 5, 2009, Fig.3, http://elsa.berkeley.edu/~saez/saez-UStopincomes-2007.pdf.

18. Barbara Ehrenreich, *Fear of Falling: The Inner Life of the Middle Class* (New York: Pantheon, 1989), 15 (emphasis in original).

19. "Executive Pay: Special Report," *Business Week,* April 19, 1999, 78.

20. Winerip, "Canton's Economic Seesaw."

21. Graef F. Crystal, *In Search of Excess: The Overcompensation of American Executives* (New York: W. W. Norton, 1991), chapter 13.

22. Keith Bradsher, "Widest Gap in Incomes? Research Points to U.S.," *New York Times,* October 27, 1995, D2, citing data from the Luxembourg Income Study.

23. Keith Bradsher, "Rich Control More of U.S. Wealth, Study Says, as Debts Grow for Poor," *New York Times,* June 22, 1996, 22, citing a new study of wealth from the University of Michigan's Panel Survey of Income Dynamics.

24. Edward N. Wolff, "Recent Trends in Household Wealth in the United States: Rising Debt and the Middle-Class Squeeze—an Update to 2007," Levy Economics Institute of Bard College, Working Paper 589, March 2010, Tables 2 and 4, http://www.levyinstitute.org/pubs/wp_589.pdf.

25. Ibid., 14.

26. Ibid., Table 9.

27. Ibid., Table 11. Further comparisons and analysis are available in Meizhu Lui et al., *The Color of Wealth: The Story Behind the U.S. Racial Wealth Divide* (New York: New Press, 2006); Sabrina Tavernise, "Recession Study Finds Hispanics Are Hit Hardest," *New York Times,* July 26, 2011, A1.

28. Arthur Kennickell, Douglas McManus, and R. Louise Woodburn, "Weighted Design for the 1992 *Survey of Consumer Finances,*" unpublished technical paper quoted in *Left Business Observer,* no. 72 (April 3, 1996), 5.

29. G. William Domhoff, "Power in America: Wealth, Income, Power." In *Who Rules America?* Department of Sociology, University of California, Santa Cruz, 2010, http://sociology.ucsc.edu/whorulesamerica/power/wealth.html.

30. David Barboza, "Amid Market Turmoil, Small Investor Is Steadfast," *New York Times,* August 13, 1998, D1.

31. Ron Suskind, "Ordinary People Show Extraordinary Faith, Reaping Rich Rewards," *Wall Street Journal,* March 30, 1999, A1.

32. James P. Smith, *Unequal Wealth and Incentives to Save* (Santa Monica, Calif.: RAND Corporation, 1995), 15.

CHAPTER 4

1. *Income, Poverty, and Health Insurance Coverage in the United States, 2009,* U.S. Bureau of the Census, Series P-60, no. 238, September 2010, Table B1, http://www.census.gov/prod/2010pubs/p60-238.pdf.

2. For discussion of the effects of the 1996 welfare reform, see Sharon Hayes, *Flat Broke with Children: Women in the Age of Welfare Reform* (New York: Oxford University Press, 2003); Jane Collins and Victoria Mayer, *Both Hands Tied: Welfare Reform and the Race to the Bottom of the Low-Wage Labor Market* (Chicago: University of Chicago Press, 2010); Katha Pollitt, "What Ever Happened to Welfare Mothers?" *Nation,* May 31, 2010, 8.

3. Calculations derived from *Income, Poverty and Health Insurance in the United States: 2009,* Table 6. Black population based on *The Black Population in the United States,* U.S. Census Bureau, 2008, http://www.census.gov/population/www/socdemo/race/Black-US.

4. Percentages calculated from *Indicators of Welfare Dependence Annual Report to Congress 2008,* U.S. Department of Health and Human Services, chapter 2, Indicator 5, http://aspe.hhs.gov/hsp/indicators08/ch2.shtml#ind5, and *National Population Projections,* U.S. Census Bureau, 2008, http://www.census.gov/population/www/projections/downloadablefiles.html.

5. *Indicators of Welfare Dependence Annual Report to Congress 2008,* chapter 2, Indicator 7a, U.S. Department of Health and Human Services, http://aspe.hhs.gov/hsp/indicators08/ch2.shtml#ind7.

6. A useful review of the data, methodology, and theories underlying the analysis of welfare dependence is in Mary Jo Bane and David T. Ellwood, *Welfare Realities* (Cambridge: Harvard University Press, 1994), especially chapters 2 and 3; and in *Overview of Entitlement Programs,* 440–447.

7. *Overview of Entitlement Programs,* 447–449.

8. Ibid., 447–448.

9. *Fiscal Year 2010 Budget in Brief: Administration for Children and Families: Entitlement Spending*, U.S. Department of Health and Human Services, http://dhhs.gov/asfr/ob/docbudget/2010budgetinbriefs.html. Federal Budget figure: *A New Era of Responsibility: Renewing America's Promise*, Office of Management and Budget, 2009, Table S-1, http://www.gpoaccess.gov/usbudget/fy10/pdf/fy10-newera.pdf.

10. Food stamp expenditures: *FY 2010 Budget Summary and Annual Performance Plan*, U.S. Department of Agriculture, Appendix, http://www.obpa.usda.gov/budsum/FY10budsum.pdf. Federal Budget figure: *A New Era of Responsibility*, Table S-1.

11. *Consumer Expenditure Survey, 2009*, U.S. Department of Labor, http://www.bls.gov/cex.

12. *Income, Poverty, and Health Insurance Coverage in the United States, 2009*, Table 6.

13. Motoko Rich, "Many Jobs Seen as Failing to Meet the Basics," *New York Times*, April 1, 2011, B1, reporting on "The Basic Economic Security Tables for the United States," released that day by Wider Opportunities for Women.

14. Mollie Orshansky, *The Measure of Poverty: Documentation and Background Information and Rationale for Current Poverty Matrix*, Technical Paper 1 (Washington, D.C.: U.S. Department of Health, Education, and Welfare, 1977), 234.

15. Randy Albelda et al., *The War on the Poor* (New York: New Press, 1996), 35, quoting Richard Saltus, "Bad Diets Hamper the Poor," *Boston Globe*, May 3, 1995, A3.

16. AFDC payments: *Annual Statistical Supplement, 2005*, U.S. Social Security Administration Office of Policy, Table 9.G1, http://www.ssa.gov/policy/docs/statcomps/supplement/2005/9g.html#table9.g1. Mississippi Department of Human Services, Division of Economic Assistance, http://www.mdhs.state.ms.us/ea_tanf.html. Dollar amounts from 2006 calculated by CPI Inflation Calculator, U.S. Bureau of Labor Statistics, http://data.bls.gov/cgi-bin/cpicalc.pl.

17. *Household Food Security in the United States, 2009*, U.S. Department of Agriculture, Economic Research Service, 2010, Economic Research Report No. 108, http://www.ers.usda.gov/Publications/ERR108/ERR108.pdf.

18. *Income, Poverty, and Health Insurance Coverage in the United States, 2009*, Table 4.

19. Sar A. Levitan, Frank Gallo, and Isaac Shapiro, *Working but Poor: America's Contradiction*, rev. ed. (Baltimore: Johns Hopkins University Press, 1993), 21, citing data from the U.S. Bureau of the Census.

20. *Poverty in the United States, 1992*, U.S. Bureau of the Census, Current Population Reports, Series P-60, No. 185, 4, Table 3.

21. *Indicators of Welfare Dependence Annual Report to Congress 2008*, chapter 2, Indicator 4.

22. Tim Padgett, "The 'Dangerous' Border: Actually One of America's Safest Places," *Time Magazine*, July 30, 2010, http://www.time.com/.

23. Ruben G. Rumbaut and Walter A. Ewing, *The Myth of Immigrant Criminality and the Paradox of Assimilation: Incarceration Rates among Native and Foreign-Born Men* (Washington, D.C.: Immigration Policy Center, 2007); Ramiro Martínez, Jr., and Matthew T. Lee, "On Immigration and Crime," in *The Nature of Crime: Continuity and Change* (Washington, D.C.: National Institute of Justice, 2000), 485–524.

24. Tim Wadsworth, "Is Immigration Responsible for the Crime Drop? An Assessment of the Influence of Immigration on Changes in Violent Crime between 1990 and 2000," *Social Sciences Quarterly* 91, no. 2 (June 2010): 546.

25. Richard Nadler, *Immigration and the Wealth of States* (Overland Park, Kans.: American Majority Foundation, 2008), cited in Devon Whitham, "Seven Immigration Myths and Facts," unpublished.

26. For details of state and local taxes paid by undocumented immigrants in various states in 2010, see "Unauthorized Immigrants Pay Taxes, Too," Immigration Policy Center,

April 11, 2011, http://www.immigrationpolicy.org/just-facts/unauthorized-immigrants-pay-taxes-too.

27. Eduardo Porter, "Illegal Immigrants Are Bolstering Social Security with Billions," *New York Times,* April 5, 2005, http://nytimes.com/.

28. "Summary of Immigrant Eligibility Restrictions Under Current Law," U.S. Department of Health and Human Services, 2009, http://aspe.hhs.gov/hsp/immigration/restrictions-sum.shtml.

29. Steven Raphael and Lucas Ronconi, "The Effects of Labor Market Competition with Immigrants on the Wages and Employment of Natives: What Does Existing Research Tell Us?" January 2007, Table 1, http://gsppi.berkeley.edu/faculty/sraphael/du-bois-review-january-2007.pdf.

30. "Statistical Portrait of the Foreign-Born Population in the United States, 2009," Pew Hispanic Center, Table 27, http://pewhispanic.org/files/factsheets/foreignborn2009/Table%2027.pdf. For wage rates: *Current Population Survey 2009,* U.S. Bureau of Labor Statistics, Table 39, "Median Weekly Earnings of Full-Time Wage and Salary Workers by Detailed Occupation and Sex," ftp://ftp.bls.gov/pub/special.requests/lf/aa2009/pdf/cpsaat39.pdf

31. Two papers are especially clear in laying out the basic findings and controversies in the field, with bibliographies leading to the major studies: Steven Raphael and Lucas Ronconi, "The Effects of Labor Market Competition with Immigrants," and Heidi Shierholz, "Immigration and Wages," *EPI Briefing Paper,* no. 255, February 4, 2010, http://epi.3cdn.net/81ac21ed8143664879_wvm6bakyu.pdf.

32. Steven Raphael and Eugene Smolensky, "Immigration and Poverty in the United States," *Focus* 26, no. 2 (Fall 2009), http://www.irp.wisc.edu/publications/focus/pdfs/foc262e.pdf.

33. Kim Bobo, *Wage Theft in America: Why Millions of Working Americans Are Not Getting Paid—and What We Can Do About It* (New York: New Press, 2008); Ruth Milkman, Ana Luz Gonzalez, and Victor Narro, *Wage Theft and Workplace Violations in Los Angeles* (University of California at Los Angeles Institute for Research on Labor and Employment, 2010), http://www.irle.ucla.edu/publications/pdf/LAwagetheft.pdf; "Wage Theft, Employment Law Violations Widespread in U.S. Cities," National Employment Law Project, September 2, 2009, http://nelp.3cdn.net/f29c51400cb0f0df9f_awm6bngun.pdf; Kirk Semple, "Study Finds Exploitation of Day Laborers," *New York Times,* January 9, 2011, http://www.nytimes.com/. For a comprehensive review of worker centers in the United States, see Janice Fine, *Worker Centers: Organizing Communities at the Edge of the Dream* (Ithaca: Cornell University/ILR Press, 2006).

34. For an excellent discussion of the psychological dimensions of the concept of the underclass, as well as the history of the idea and its consequences for public policy, see Herbert J. Gans, *The War against the Poor: The Underclass and Antipoverty Policy* (New York: Basic Books, 1995).

35. Robert Pear, "Fraud in Medicare Increasingly Tied to Claims Payers," *New York Times,* September 20, 1999, A1.

36. *Statistical Abstract 1997,* U.S. Census Bureau, Table 736.

37. Ann Huff Stevens, "The Dynamics of Poverty Spells: Updating Bane and Ellwood," *American Economic Review* 84, no. 2 (May 1994), 35–36.

38. *Income, Poverty, and Health Insurance Coverage in the United States, 2009,* 5.

39. Lee Rainwater, "Persistent and Transitory Poverty: A New Look," Working Paper No. 70, Joint Center for Urban Studies of MIT and Harvard University, June 1981, 14. Earlier findings are brought up to date and extended over a longer time period in Mark R. Rank and Thomas A. Hirschl, "The Likelihood of Poverty Across the American Adult Life Span," *Social Work* 43, no. 3 (May 1999).

40. We have seen that the working class is 63 percent of the labor force. Assuming that working class families are the same size on average as middle and capitalist class families,

63 percent of the population lives in working class families. It is safe to say that relatively few poor people have fallen into poverty from middle class and capitalist lives. The great majority of the poor cycle in and out of poverty from the bottom half of the population. If 40 percent of the population experiences poverty, and they are all from the working class, then those experiencing poverty at least once in ten years constitute two-thirds of the working class. Since some of the poor do come from families that are not working class, the fraction of working class families that experience poverty is less than two-thirds, but certainly more than half.

41. Bane and Ellwood, *Welfare Realities,* 41.

42. *Income, Poverty, and Health Insurance Coverage in the United States, 2009,* Table 4.

43. Ibid., Table B-2.

44. Ibid., Table 4.

45. Michael Zweig, "Six Points on Class," in *More Unequal: Essays on Class in the United States,* ed. Michael D. Yates (New York: Monthly Review Press, 2007).

46. William Julius Wilson, *When Work Disappears: The World of the New Urban Poor* (New York: Vintage Books, 1997).

47. Sylvia Nasar and Kirsten B. Mitchell, "Booming Job Market Draws Young Black Men into Fold: Surprisingly Big Gain by Low-Skill Workers Is Connected to Falling Crime Rates," *New York Times,* May 23, 1999, 1.

48. Data on rural/urban incidence of poverty in 1990 from Douglas S. Massey, "The Age of Extremes: Concentrated Affluence and Poverty in the 21st Century," *Demography* 33, no. 4 (November 1996), 395–412, Figure 2, compared with the fraction of people in the United States living in rural and urban areas (*Statistical Abstract of the United States: 1992,* Table 28). Of course, many more poor people live in U.S. cities than live in rural areas, but at least since 1970 the percentage of the U.S. population living in rural areas is less than the percentage of all poor people living there.

49. Gans, *War against the Poor,* 83–84.

CHAPTER 5

1. Adam Smith, *The Wealth of Nations* [1776] (New York: Modern Library, 1937), 14.

2. Ibid.

3. Leon Levy, interviewed by Jeff Madrick, in "Wall Street Blues," *New York Review of Books* 45, no. 15 (October 8, 1998): 10. Levy was partner and chairman of the board of trustees of the Oppenheimer Funds.

4. This basic idea has been elaborated by John Rawls, *A Theory of Social Justice* (Cambridge: Harvard University Press, 1971). Rawls, however, constructs his ethical principles outside of any particular society, before anyone knows his or her position in what will come. In reality, ethics are forged in the conflicts of interests among classes and other groups in actual societies. What is thought to be "right" and what "wrong" is complicated by the relative power of those who stand to win or lose according to the answer. This is why the debate over values and social ethics is not just a question of logic or the better argument. The debate over values is a contest of power.

5. Smith, *Wealth of Nations,* 48.

6. See, for example, T. Alterman et al., "Decision Latitude, Psychological Demand, Job Strain, and Coronary Heart Disease in the Western Electric Study," *American Journal of Epidemiology,* no. 139 (1994): 620–627; R. L. Repetti, "The Effects of Workload and the Social Environment at Work on Health," in *Handbook of Stress: Theoretical and Clinical Aspects,* 2nd ed., ed. L. Goldberger and S. Breznitz (New York: Free Press, 1993), 368–385; P. L. Schnall et al., "The Relationship Between Job Strain, Workplace, Diastolic Blood Pressure, and Left Ventricular Mass Index," *Journal of the American Medical Association,* no. 263 (1990): 1929–1935; Cary L. Cooper and Michael J. Smith, *Job Stress and Blue Collar*

Work (New York: John Wiley & Sons, 1985); Robert D. Caplan et al., *Job Demands and Worker Health* (Washington, D.C.: U.S. Department of Health, Education, and Welfare, 1975). Similar findings were reported in a nontechnical way in Erica Goode, "For Good Health, It Helps to Be Rich and Important," *New York Times,* June 1, 1999, F1.

7. Megan Murphy and Sharlene Goff, "Bank Chiefs' Pay Rises by 36%," *Financial Times,* June 14, 2011, http://www.ft.com/; Michael Powell and Andrew Martin, "Foreclosure Aid Fell Short, and Is Fading Away," *New York Times,* March 11, 2011, A1; Michael Mackenzie, "U.S. Regulator Warns over Delay in Funding Reforms," *Financial Times,* June 9, 2011, http://www.ft.com/; Louise Story, "Still Writing, Regulators Delay Rules," *New York Times,* June 15, 2011, http://www.nytimes.com/.

8. Charles V. Bagli, "Real Estate Developers Prosper Despite Defaults," *New York Times,* January 1, 2011, http://www.nytimes.com/.

9. Jennifer Steinbauer, "William F. Farah Dies at 78; Led Family Clothing Business," *New York Times,* March 12, 1998, D19.

10. Matthew Bishop, *Philanthrocapitalism: How the Rich Can Save the World* (New York: Bloomsbury Press, 2008). See also Paul Vitello, "In Catholic Schools, More Clout for Big Donors," *New York Times,* February 7, 2011, A1.

11. He Qinglian, *Zhongguo de xianjing* [China's pitfall], quoted in Liu Binyan and Perry Link, "A Great Leap Backward?" *New York Review of Books* 45, no. 15 (October 8, 1998): 19, 22.

12. Alex Kuczynski, "National Geographic Angers Its Photographers," *New York Times,* February 1, 1999, C1.

13. Jonathan Kozol, speaking to teachers at the American Federation of Teachers national convention, Boston, July 2006.

CHAPTER 6

1. For a pioneering and extremely influential statement of the principles, practices, promise, and pitfalls of labor-management cooperation, see Thomas A. Kochan, Harry C. Katz, and Robert B. McKersie, *The Transformation of American Industrial Relations* (New York: Basic Books, 1986). The general principles were also developed in an examination of the auto industry, and the GM Saturn facility in particular: Barry Bluestone and Irving Bluestone, *Negotiating the Future: A Labor Perspective on American Business* (New York: Basic Books, 1992). For a clear and thorough critique of labor-management cooperation, see Mike Parker and Jane Slaughter, *Working Smart: A Union Guide to Participation Programs and Reengineering* (Detroit: Labor Notes, 1994).

2. Nelson D. Schwartz, "Industries Find Surging Profits in Deeper Cuts," *New York Times,* July 25, 2010, http://www.nytimes.com/; Louis Uchitelle, "Unions Yield on Wage Scales to Preserve Jobs," *New York Times,* November 19, 2010, A1.

3. Analysis of the legislative history of the Wagner Act and its implications for the current labor movement is based on a fuller discussion in Michael Zweig, "Who Cares about Unions: Ethical Support for Labor as a Matter of Social Justice," in *Workplace Topics* 4, no. 1 (June 1994): 1–16.

4. See U.S. Senate Committee on Education and Labor, *National Labor Relations Board: Hearings* (Washington, D.C.: U.S. Government Printing Office, 1935).

5. David Brody, *Workers in Industrial America,* 2nd ed. (New York: Oxford University Press, 1993), 66.

6. Quoted in R. W. Fleming, "The Significance of the Wagner Act," in *Labor and the New Deal,* ed. Milton Derber and Edwin Young (New York: Da Capo Press, 1972), 135.

7. Two examples of this large literature are Richard B. Freeman and James L. Medoff, *What Do Unions Do?* (New York: Basic Books, 1984) and Lawrence Mishel and Paula Voos, eds., *Unions and Economic Competitiveness* (Armonk, N.Y.: M. E. Sharpe, 1992).

8. Brody, *Workers in Industrial America,* 124.

9. Quoted in Harry A. Millis and Emily Clark Brown, *From the Wagner Act to Taft-Hartley* (Chicago: University of Chicago Press, 1950), 3.

10. See, for example, Freeman and Medoff, *What Do Unions Do?*; Mishel and Voos, *Unions and Economic Competitiveness;* Michael D. Yates, *Why Unions Matter* (New York: Monthly Review Press, 1998).

11. *Statistical Abstract of the United States 1998,* U.S. Census Bureau, Table 713.

12. "Union Members Summary," January 21, 2011, U.S. Department of Labor, Bureau of Labor Statistics, http://www.bls.gov/news.release/union2.nr0.htm.

13. Samuel Gompers, *Labor and the Common Welfare* (New York: E. P. Dutton, 1919), 9.

14. Paul Buhle, *Taking Care of Business: Samuel Gompers, George Meany, Lane Kirkland, and the Tragedy of American Labor* (New York: Monthly Review Press, 1999).

15. Gompers, *Labor and the Common Welfare,* 22.

16. John Sweeney, *America Needs a Raise* (New York: Houghton Mifflin, 1997).

17. *Parade,* February 7, 1999, 6–15.

18. Diana Jean Schemo, "In Crowded GOP Field, Dole Was Hobbled by Her Stand on Issues, Not Her Sex," *New York Times,* October 21, 1999, A22.

19. Sheila D. Collins, *The Rainbow Challenge: The Jackson Campaign and the Future of U.S. Politics* (New York: Monthly Review Press, 1986).

20. For a compilation of statements through the 1980s, see Robert McAfee Brown and Sydney Thomson Brown, *A Cry For Justice* (New York: Paulist Press, 1989). For more recent information on religious understandings of labor issues, see *Faith Works* (monthly publication of the Chicago-based Interfaith Worker Justice).

21. United States Conference of Bishops, "Economic Justice for All: Catholic Social Teaching and the U.S. Economy," *Origins* 16, no. 24 (November 27, 1986): 423.

22. Pope John Paul II, *Laborem Exercens* [On human labor] (Washington, D.C.: United States Catholic Conference, 1981), 19.

23. P. T. Bauer, "Ecclesiastical Economics: Envy Legitimized," in *Is Capitalism Christian? Toward a Christian Perspective on Economics,* ed. Frank Schaeffer (Westchester, Ill.: Crossway Books, 1985).

24. Detailed information is available from Interfaith Worker Justice, http://www.iwj.org/.

25. Stephen Hart, *What Does the Lord Require? How American Christians Think about Economic Justice* (New York: Oxford University Press, 1992); William Saletan, "Gary Bauer's Moral Dilemma," *Mother Jones,* July/August 1998, 43–45.

26. *Statistical Abstract of the United States 1998,* Table 713.

27. "Union Members Summary," Table 1.

28. For a detailed argument on why rank-and-file control is necessary for a strong union, see Mike Parker and Martha Gruelle, *Democracy Is Power* (Detroit: Labor Notes, 1999).

29. Aldon Morris and Dan Clawson, "Lessons of the Civil Rights Movement for a Workers Rights Movement," *WorkingUSA: Journal of Labor and Society* 8, no. 6 (December 2005): 683–704.

CHAPTER 7

1. Katie Quan, "Global Strategies for Workers: How Class Analysis Clarifies Us and Them and What We Need to Do," in *What's Class Got To Do With It? American Society in the Twenty-First Century,* ed. Michael Zweig (Ithaca: Cornell ILR Press, 2004).

2. Patrick J. Buchanan, *The Great Betrayal* (Boston: Little, Brown, 1998).

3. Michael Vines, "The Free Trade Accord: A 'Bazaar' Way of Rounding Up Votes," *New York Times,* November 11, 1993, A23.

4. Sarah Anderson, Oscar Chacon, and Amy Shannon, "Alternatives to a Wall," Institute for Policy Studies, July 13, 2006, http://www.ips-dc.org/articles/alternatives_to_a_wall. For a broad historical treatment of the origins of the Hispanic population

in the United States, see Juan Gonzalez, *Harvest of Empire,* 2nd ed. (New York: Penguin, 2011).

5. Leslie Sklair, *The Transnational Capitalist Class* (London: Wiley-Blackwell, 2000)

6. Chrystia Freeland, "The Rise of the New Global Elite," *Atlantic,* January/February 2011, 49.

7. Ibid., 46, 51.

8. David Bacon, "Union Busting, Iraqi-Style," *Nation,* October 7, 2010; see also http://www.uslaboragainstwar.org.

9. Joe Alvarez, remarks to the Trade Union Section of the Industrial Relations Research Association, January 5, 1999, New York City.

10. U.S. Department of Labor and U.S. Department of Commerce, Commission on the Future of Worker-Management Relations (Dunlop Commission), *Fact Finding Report,* May 1994, especially chapter 3.

11. Kate Bronfenbrenner, "Final Report: The Effects of Plant Closing or Threat of Plant Closing on the Right of Workers to Organize," submitted to the Labor Secretariat of the North American Commission for Labor Cooperation, Washington, D.C., September 30, 1996.

12. Alan Howard, assistant to the president of UNITE, interview, June 7, 1999.

13. Kate Bronfenbrenner, ed., *Global Unions: Challenging Transnational Capital through Cross-Border Campaigns* (Ithaca: Cornell University Press, 2007).

14. Lance Compa, "The Multilateral Agreement on Investment and International Labor Rights: A Failed Connection," *Cornell International Law Journal* 31, no. 3 (1998): 683–712; R. C. Longworth, "Treaty Would Give Big Business More Influence," *Chicago Tribune,* December 4, 1997, http://articles.chicagotribune.com/; Paul Magnusson and Stephen Baker, "The Explosive Trade Deal You've Never Heard Of," *Business Week,* February 9, 1998, 51; Noam Chomsky, " 'Hordes of Vigilantes': Popular Elements Defeat MAI, for Now," *Z Magazine* 11, no. 7/8 (July/August 1998): 51–54.

15. *Statistical Abstract of the United States 1998,* U.S. Census Bureau, Table 1302.

16. Bank for International Settlement, *68th Annual Report,* 1998, 100.

17. "International Economic Accounts," Bureau of Economic Analysis, U.S. Department of Commerce, Table 2 (International Investment Position of the United States at Yearend, 1976–2009), http://www.bea.gov/international/index.htm#iip.

18. Bank for International Settlement data reported in *New York Times,* February 15, 1999, A11.

19. International Monetary Fund, *World Economic Outlook, 1998,* Table A22.

20. Derived from data in International Monetary Fund, *World Economic Outlook Report, 2010,* Table A9, and Lukanyo Mnyanda and Yoshiaki Nohara, "Currency Trading Reaches $4 Trillion a Day, Says BIS," *Bloomberg Businessweek,* September 1, 2010, http://www.bloomberg.com/.

21. Laurent L. Jacque, "The Currency Wars," *Le Monde Diplomatique* (English edition), December 2010, 1.

22. Jamil Anderlini and Chris Giles, "G20 Fails to Ease Tension over Monetary Reform," *Financial Times,* April 1, 2011, 6; Alan Cowell, "Scrutiny of German Leader Builds as Debt Crisis Rattles Europe," *New York Times,* June 19, 2011, http://www.nytimes.com/.

23. "Keeping the Hot Money Out," *Economist,* January 4, 1998, 69–70; Roger Cohen, "Redrawing the Free Market: Amid a Global Financial Crisis, Calls for Regulation Spread," *New York Times,* November 14, 1998, B9. Since the 2008 crisis, many business analysts and leaders have renewed these calls.

CHAPTER 8

1. See, for example, Sheldon Kamieniecki et al., eds., *Controversies in Environmental Policy* (Albany: SUNY Press, 1986), and Jeanne N. Clarke and Daniel McCool, *Staking Out the Terrain* (Albany: SUNY Press, 1985).

2. Lawrence Mishel et al., *The State of Working America: 1998–1999* (Ithaca: Cornell University Press, 1999), chapter 2.

3. Donald L. Barlett and James B. Steele, "Corporate Welfare," *Time,* November 9, 1998, 34–54; see also information posted on website for Citizens for Tax Justice, http://www.ctj.org.

4. Douglas Frantz, "Cruise Lines Reap Profit from Favors in Law," *New York Times,* February 19, 1999, A1.

5. Gretchen Morgenson, "House Cuts Could Force S.E.C. Layoffs: Agency Fears Increase in Internet Stock Fraud," *New York Times,* August 3, 1999, C1; David Cay Johnston, "I.R.S. Is Allowing More Delinquents to Avoid Tax Bills: Billions Could Be Lost," *New York Times,* October 10, 1999, A1.

6. "Bush and Gore Do New York," CBSNews.com, October 20, 2000, http://www .cbsnews.com/stories/2000/10/18/politics/main242210.shtml.

7. Ryan Lizza, "As the World Burns: Washington's Climate-Change Catastrophe," *New Yorker,* October 11, 2010, http://www.newyorker.com/.

8. Quoted in Elizabeth Kolbert, "The Nuclear Risk," *New Yorker,* March 28, 2011, 48.

9. Debra Dwyer, private communication, 1999.

10 Edward Wyatt, "Investors See Room for Profit in the Demand for Education," *New York Times,* November 4, 1999, A27.

11. Ibid.

12. For an evaluation of the issues in education, see Carol Ascher, Norm Fruchter, and Robert Berne, *Hard Lessons: Public Schools and Privatization* (New York: Twentieth Century Fund Press, 1996). For a thorough examination of the conceptual issues in the general privatization debate, and specific examples from different parts of the public sector, see Elliott Sclar, *You Don't Always Get What You Pay For: The Economics of Privatization* (Ithaca: Cornell University Press, 2000).

13. Doug Henwood, "Antisocial Insecurity," *Left Business Observer,* no. 87 (December 31, 1998): 7.

14. Steve Stecklow and Sara Calian, "Social Security Switch in U.K. Is Disastrous; A Caution to the U.S?" *Wall Street Journal,* August 10, 1998, A1.

15. Wyatt, "Investors See Room."

16. Ibid.

17. Since the first edition of this book appeared, the charter school debate has continued along much the same lines. Perhaps the most illuminating new resource is Diane Ravitch, *The Death and Life of the Great American School System: How Testing and Choice Are Undermining Education* (Boston: Basic Books, 2010).

18. Gregory Palast, "Free Market in Human Misery," *Observer* (London), September 26, 1999.

19. David Rohde, "District Attorney Reviewing Medical Care at City's Jails," *New York Times,* September 30, 1998, B7.

20. The London-based *Prison Privatisation Report International,* published monthly by the Prison Reform Trust, provides details of privatization effects worldwide.

21. Richard A. Oppel, Jr., "Private Prisons Found to Offer Little in Savings," *New York Times,* May 19, 2011, A1.

22. Amy Smith, "Strayhorn to Investigate Accenture," *Austin Chronicle,* May 19, 2006, http://www.austinchronicle.com. See also *Privatizing in the Dark: The Pitfalls of Privatization & Why Budget Disclosure is Needed, with a 50-State Comparison of Privatization Trends,* Progressive States Network, December 2007, http://www.progressivestates.org /files/privatization/PrivatizationReport.pdf.

23. Russell Mokhiber, "Crime Wave! The Top 100 Corporate Criminals of the 1990s," *Multinational Monitor,* July/August 1999, 9–32.

24. "Travel Scams," *Consumer Reports* 64, no. 1 (January 1999): 29.

25. John H. Cushman, Jr., "Some Bottled Water Is Called Unsafe," *New York Times,* March 31, 1999, A14.

26. Michael Lerner, "An Interview with Senator Paul Wellstone," *Tikkun* 16, no. 2 (March/April 2001): 9.

27. Jodi Wilgoren, "Nonvoters: Too Busy, Forgetful or Skeptical," *New York Times,* November 4, 1998, B14.

28. Michael Zweig, "Teaching to Student Values in the Early 1990s," *Review of Radical Political Economics* 24, no. 2 (Summer 1992): 109–114.

CHAPTER 9

1. Francis Fukuyama, *The End of History and the Last Man* (New York: Free Press, 1992).

2. See, for example, Ruy Teixiera, "New Progressive America: Twenty Years of Demographic, Geographic, and Attitudinal Changes Across the Country Herald a New Progressive Majority," March 2009, http://www.americanprogress.org/issues/2009/03/pdf /progressive_america.pdf; Jack Metzgar, "Two Cheers for the Decline of White Working-Class Voters," *Working-Class Perspectives,* March 30, 2009, http://workingclassstudies .wordpress.com/tag/race-and-class; and Jack Metzgar, "The Democrats and Social Classes," *Working-Class Perspectives,* November 10, 2010, http://workingclassstudies.wordpress .com/category/contributors/jack-metzgar.

3. Andrew Martin, "In Sign of Foreclosure Flaws, Suits Claim Break-ins by Banks," *New York Times,* December 21, 2010, A1; Gretchen Morgenson and Andrew Martin, "Battle Lines Forming in Clash Over Foreclosures," *New York Times,* October 20, 2010.

4. Dennis Jacobe, "Gallup Finds U.S. Unemployment Up Slightly in January to 9.8%, Underemployment at 18.9%, Compared with 19.0% at the End of December," February 3, 2011, http://www.gallup.com/poll/145922/gallup-finds-unemployment-up-slightly-january.aspx; U.S. Bureau of Labor Statistics, *Current Population Survey,* "Of Total Unemployed, Percent Unemployed 27 Weeks & Over, January 1948 to March 2011," http://data. bls.gov/timeseries/LNS13025703.

5. Andrew Fieldhouse, "Any Payroll Tax Cut Should Be Designed Not to Hurt Low-Income Workers," Economic Policy Institute, December 15, 2010, http://www.epi.org/, and author conversation with Fieldhouse, December 21, 2010. See also William G. Gale, "Five Myths about the Bush Tax Cuts," *Washington Post,* August 1, 2010, http://www.washingtonpost.org/.

6. Douglas Fraser, letter of resignation from the Labor-Management Group, July 17, 1978, http://www.historyisaweapon.com/defcon1/fraserresign.html. It is a sign of the collapse of labor resistance that this letter is not on the UAW website.

7. Noam Scheiber, "Loose Change: Inside a Shaken White House," *New Republic,* December 30, 2010, 8.

8. Lewis F. Powell, "Confidential Memorandum: Attack on American Free Enterprise System," August 23, 1971, in "The Powell Memo," April 3, 2004, ReclaimDemocracy.org, http://www.reclaimdemocracy.org/corporate_accountability/powell_memo_lewis.html.

9. See, for example, Mark A. Smith, *The Right Talk: How Conservatives Transformed the Great Society into the Economic Society* (Princeton: Princeton University Press, 2007), and John J. Miller, *A Gift of Freedom: How the John M. Olin Foundation Changed America* (San Francisco: Encounter, 2006).

10. *Citizens United v. Federal Election Commission,* 130 S. Ct. 876 (2010); Ronald Dworkin, "The Decision That Threatens Democracy," *New York Review of Books* 57, no. 8 (May 13, 2010), http://www.nybooks.com/.

11. Adam Liptak "Justices Offer Receptive Ear to Business Interests," *New York Times,* December 18, 2010, A1.

12. Kate Zernike and Megan Thee-Brenan, "Poll Finds Tea Party Backers Wealthier and More Educated," *New York Times,* April 14, 2010, A1.

13. See, for example, Ben McGrath, "The Movement: The Rise of Tea Party Activism," *New Yorker,* February 1, 2010, http://www.newyorker.com/; Kate Zernike, "Shaping Tea Party Passion into Campaign Force," *New York Times,* August 26, 2010, A1; and Jane Mayer, "Covert Operations: The Billionaire Brothers Who Are Waging a War against Obama," *New Yorker,* August 30, 2010, http://www.newyorker.com/.

14. Mark Lilla, "The Tea Party Jacobins," *New York Review of Books* 57, no. 9 (May 27, 2010), http://www.nybooks.com/.

15. Corey Robin, "Reclaiming the Politics of Freedom," *Nation,* April 25, 2011, 18.

16. Eric Lipton, "Business Background Defines Chief of Staff," *New York Times,* January 6, 2011, http://www.nytimes.com/.

17. Joe Scarborough, *Morning Joe,* MSNBC, January 4, 2010.

18. David A. Stockman, *The Triumph of Politics: Why the Reagan Revolution Failed* (New York: HarperCollins, 1986).

19. "Grover Norquist," SourceWatch, http://www.sourcewatch.org/index.php?title=Grover_Norquist.

20. Ryan Donmoyer, "Tax Incentives to Keep Jobs in U.S. Blocked in Senate." September 28, 2010, http://www.bloomberg.com/news/2010-09-28/senate-republicans-block-tax-incentives-to-move-foreign-based-jobs-to-u-s-.html; Ryan Donmoyer and William Selway, "Build Americas Left Out of Deal to Extend Bush-Era Tax Cuts, Officials Say," December 7, 2010, http://www.bloomberg.com/news/2010-12-07/build-americas-left-out-of-deal-to-extend-bush-era-tax-cuts-officials-say.html; David M. Herszenhorn, "Congress Sends $801 Billion Tax Cut Bill to Obama," *New York Times,* December 16, 2010, http://www.nytimes.com.

21. Carl Hulse, "Taking Control, G.O.P. Overhauls Rules in House," *New York Times,* January 5, 2011, http://www.nytimes.com/.

22. See, for example, Charles V. Bagli, "Cuomo Gains an Ally for a Looming Fight With the Public-Employee Unions," *New York Times,* December 10, 2010, http://www.nytimes.com/; and Mark J. Magyar, "Christie vs. the Public Employee Unions—Round 2," *NJ Spotlight,* September 7, 2010, http://www.njspotlight.com/stories/10/0907/0012.

23. Art Levine, speaking on *Democracy Now!* January 6, 2011, http://www.democracynow.org/2011/1/6/crackdown_on_organized_labor_states_call.

24. Steven Greenhouse, "Democrats Look to Clout of Unions as Vote Nears," *New York Times,* October 23, 2010, A12.

25. Rick Ungar, "Koch Brothers behind Wisconsin Effort to Kill Public Unions," *Policy Page,* February 18, 2011, http://blogs.forbes.com/rickungar/2011/02/18/koch-brothers-behind-wisconsin-effort-to-kill-public-unions.

26. A comparison for all states is in "Comparing the Costs of War with State Deficits," Center for Study of Working Class Life, http://www.stonybrook.edu/workingclass.

27. Michael Cooper, "Mayors See End to Wars as Fix for Struggling Cities," *New York Times,* June 17, 2011, http://www.nytimes.com/.

28. New Priorities Network, http://www.newprioritiesnetwork.org.

29. The Excluded Workers Congress, http://www.excludedworkerscongress.org.

30. Aldon Morris and Dan Clawson, "Lessons of the Civil Rights Movement for Building a Worker Rights Movement," *WorkingUSA* 8, no. 6 (December 2005): 683–704.

31. Kirk Semple, "A Boon for Nannies, if Only They Knew," *New York Times,* April 15, 2011, http://www.nytimes.com/; see also the Domestic Workers United website, http://www.domesticworkersunited.org.

32. Lewis Powell, "Confidential Memorandum."

33. Harry Bennett, *We Never Called Him Henry* (New York: Fawcett Publications, 1951).

34. From the rich literature on working class history, see, for example, Stanley Aronowitz, *False Promises: The Shaping of American Working Class Consciousness* (New York: McGraw-Hill, 1973); Richard O. Boyer and Herbert M. Morais, *Labor's Untold Story* (New York: United Electrical, Radio, and Machine Workers of America, 1955); Irving Bernstein, *The Lean Years: A History of the American Worker, 1920–1933* (Baltimore: Penguin Books, 1960); Irving Bernstein, *The Turbulent Years: A History of the American Worker, 1933–1941* (Boston: Houghton Mifflin, 1970).

35. John Stuart Mill, *Utilitarianism* [1861], ed. George Sher (Indianapolis: Hackett, 1979), 62.

Index

Teamsters union, 58, 126–27
Tea Party movement, 181–82
Television, 57–58
Temporary Assistance for Needy Families
(TANF), 77, 85. *See also* Welfare
"Temporary" jobs, 22, 38
Thatcher, Margaret, 118
"Third Way," 161–64, 168
Thomas, Clarence, 131, 133
Time magazine, 84
Trade, 143–45. *See also* International trade
"Traditional families," 63
Truck drivers, 29, 33, 126–27
Trumka, Richard, 35, 124, 189
Trump, Donald, 13
Turkey, 154

"Underclass," 2, 18, 36, 79, 87–89
Unemployment, 31, 63, 93, 159, 177, 186
Unemployment compensation, 177, 186
Union of Needletrades, Industrial, and Textile
Employees (UNITE), 151
Unions, 19, 24, 38–39, 52–54, 124–30, 192;
attacks on, 73, 95, 159, 165, 177–79,
186–87; declining power of, 53, 68, 124,
187, 189–90; and labor-management
cooperation, 11–12, 118–20; and media,
57–58, 137–38; membership in, 124, 138,
178; and "middle class" identification, 18,
56–58; obstacles faced by, 120, 150, 159;
and politics, 53, 138–40, 187; of professionals, 21–22, 23, 25–26, 28, 164, 196n28; and
race, 35, 53, 131, 133, 135; renewed vitality
within, 124, 188–89; and social protest
movements, 53–55, 131, 135, 168, 199n21;
transnational cooperation by, 150–52. *See
also* Strikes; *specific unions and federations*
United Airlines, 12
United Auto Workers (UAW), 11, 56, 135,
137–38, 145, 177–78, 192; concessions
accepted by, 126, 178; strikes by, 11, 50
United Electrical Workers, 135
United Nations, 149
United States Conference of Catholic Bishops,
136
United Steelworkers of America, 35, 151
Universal Declaration of Human Rights, 149–50
Universities. *See* Higher education
University of Phoenix, 27
Upward mobility, 41–48; and education,
46–48; and luck, 43–44, 45, 48; structural
limits on, 45–46, 47–48
U.S. Census Bureau, 90

U.S. Chamber of Commerce, 179–80, 181, 183,
186, 191
U.S. Department of Agriculture, 82–83
U.S. Department of Labor, 29–31, 45, 81, 85
U.S. Social Forum (2010), 189
U.S. Social Security Administration, 165
U.S. Supreme Court, 21–22, 130, 131, 161, 169,
179, 180

Vacations, paid, 63
Values. *See* "Family values"; Social ethics
Veblen, Thorstein, 48
Velazquez, Baldemar, 19–20
Vietnam Veterans Against the War, 54
Vietnam War, 53, 54, 199n21
Voucher plans, 165, 166, 168

Wackenhut Corporation, 166
Wadsworth, Tim, 84
Wages, 62, 65n, 126–27; executive compensa-
tion compared to, 68–69; effect of immi-
gration on, 85–87; falling real, 62, 64–65,
72, 129.–*See also* Minimum wage
Wagner, Robert, 120, 122
Wagner Act. *See* National Labor Relations Act
Walker, Scott, 95, 185, 187
"Wall Street," 74. *See also* "Wall Street and
Main Street"
"Wall Street and Main Street," 160, 175, 176, 188;
misleading rhetoric concerning, 175, 181
Wall Street Journal, 5, 71, 167
War on Poverty, 89, 93, 179
Watt, James, 159
Wealth, personal, 69–72; changing distribution
of, 69–70; defined, 69
Welfare, 79–83, 88, 90; corporate, 160; myths
concerning, 79–81, 93; "reform of," 77,
78, 79, 89
Welfare capitalism, 121
"Welfare queen" image, 79–80, 82
Wellstone, Paul, 169–70
Whites, 70, 72, 135; class composition of, 32,
33, 34; and identity politics, 54–55, 130;
political appeals to, 80, 136, 176; in pov-
erty, 80, 81, 90, 91–92, 93
Wilson, William Julius, 93
Wisconsin: attack on public workers in, 2, 95,
123, 150, 185, 187; labor uprising in, 188
Women, 18, 53, 63; class differences among, 34,
131–32, 133; discrimination against, 32,
52, 133; immigrant, 85; labor organizing
by, 107, 191; occupations of, 32–34, 38
Worker cooperatives, 12